TRAILS

AND

WIL...

TO...ARD SNOW COUNTRY
...RESTORATION

E.B.

ISBN: 978-1-4120-5817-9

*We at Trafford believe that it is the responsibility of us all, as both individuals
and corporations, to make choices that are environmentally and socially sound.
You, in turn, are supporting this responsible conduct each time you purchase a
Trafford book, or make use of our publishing services. To find out how you are
helping, please visit www.trafford.com/responsiblepublishing.html*

*Our mission is to efficiently provide the world's finest, most comprehensive
book publishing service, enabling every author to experience success.
To find out how to publish your book, your way, and have it available
worldwide, visit us online at www.trafford.com/10510*

www.trafford.com

North America & international
toll-free: 1 888 232 4444 (USA & Canada)
phone: 250 383 6864 ♦ fax: 250 383 6804
email: info@trafford.com

The United Kingdom & Europe
phone: +44 (0)1865 722 113 ♦ local rate: 0845 230 9601
facsimile: +44 (0)1865 722 868 ♦ email: info.uk@trafford.com

10 9 8 7 6 5 4 3 2 1

TO
All who treasure,
strive to conserve,
understand, and restore,
snow country wildlife

ACKNOWLEDGEMENTS

My forestry and wildlife professors at the Universities of Washington, and California, in Seattle and at Berkeley, first planted the idea for this book. Along the way ski instructors, patrollers, avalanche busters, and guides, National Park and Forest rangers, naturalists, wardens, and wildlife scientists, all contributed ideas. Doctor Ian McTaggart- Cowan, at the University of British Columbia, finally got me started writing, after explaining why the Craigheads really got kicked out of Yellowstone, and what I might do to improve that situation. Ranger Jack Hughes, at Olympic National Park, Axel Endresen in Norway, and Margrit Broennimann, my wife from Switzerland, were especially helpful, as were John Bonica, Sally and Don Portman, from the Methow Valley, and Dr. Susan Miller with Dr. Kenton Miller, from West Virginia, in reviewing chapters in preparation.

CONTENTS   Page Number

INTRODUCTION   13
1: SKIING – life styles and characters   19
2: AVALANCHES - safety and ecology   39
3: EDGES - ecological geography   53
4: FIRE: - thinning, forestry, and smoke   70
5: LIFTS - legal intrigue and precedents   85
6: TRAILS - as zoning tools   99
7: HUTS - dealing with impact   113
8: RANGERS - as wildlife managers   131
9: WILDERNESS – and the urban mind   147
10: MINERAL KING – vs. the Sierra Club   157
11: LYNX - and the keystone species   173
12: HURRICANE RIDGE - skiing in a Park   190
13: EARLY WINTERS - skiing in the Forests   213
BIBLIOGRAPHY   238

SPRUCE AND WEASEL (BOTH LIFE SIZE)

PREFACE

The Flying Squirrel appeared suddenly above us, in a graceful glide that exactly matched the angle of the slope we were skiing up. It glanced off the crests of snow drifts, sending showers of sparkling snow crystals into the spruce, fir, and larch trees it used like slalom gates on a ski racing course. Flying Squirrels don't normally come out in daylight, so we wondered if the helicopter that dropped us off had disturbed this one. Our flight path had been miles away however, so that seemed unlikely.

My client and I were on cross- country skis, and contrary to the popular image prevalent back then of nordic skiers as granola crunching cheapskates, this gentleman had paid for a helicopter lift and guide normally shared by four skiers. On his feet were the latest Telemarking skis with expensive plastic boots to match, but still we skied uphill in classic Scandinavian fashion, because he wasn't sure enough of his technique to be dropped off at the summit. Instead we were climbing up to his perceived comfort level for some cross-country downhill lessons, absorbed gradually over an idyllic day in the North Cascade Mountains of Washington State.

Just as the Flying Squirrel seemed about to pass us by, like some snobbish downhill skier or snowboarder, it swung up to a perfect tree landing over our heads and examined us with obvious curiosity. A few seconds of this rare intimacy were all we were privileged to get, as this cute little acrobat disappeared into the forest below.

We were on the north side of Goat Peak, a vertical mile above Mazama, at the head of the Methow Valley. During the fifteen years I guided helicopter skiers, probably more cross-country skiers were introduced to Telemark and parallel turns for backcountry skiing on this slope than any other in the North Cascades. Most of our time however was not spent on ski lessons. Most of my clients showed

far greater interest, in various areas of natural history, from geology to tracks in the snow.

These clients, in the 1980's and early 90's, were the vanguard of the steadily growing, but hard to count, constituency of cross-country skiers, often converts from downhill skiing and snowboarding. Their aversion to lift lines and any form of organized commercial activity drives the bean counters nuts, and unfortunately makes for under representation in recreational use statistics. They were, and still are, as much interested in nature as they are in skiing. For many of them skis are like hiking shoes, a means to an end, rather than ends in themselves.

Wildlife observation and a "wilderness experience" were their goals, and with enough money to helicopter ski, these people also had enough time and interest to be involved in the political processes that gave us the Endangered Species Act, the Wilderness Act, and so on. Their questions about winter wildlife and the boreal forests of ski country around the world, made me realize that even the new books on winter ecology were not really addressing all of their concerns.

They wanted to know why the Early Winters proposed ski lift resort failed to happen, and whether this was a good or bad thing, from a wildlife perspective. Would the Methow Valley be the first purely nordic ski area to trash a beautiful alpine landscape? Are proposed ski lifts the best way to shake an apathetic citizenry into action against ugly development? They were curious about helicopter skiing's future, ski huts, and the new ski lift resorts just north in Canada. Why were the Canadians able to successfully go ahead, while similar enterprises struggled or failed in the United States? Was Robert Redford's Sundance ski lift resort going to be able to survive without the over development so typical of most ski lift areas?

Travel to Norway and Switzerland was stimulated by questions like these, where friends living there suggested places where answers might be found. Canada however, with its similar wildlife and conservation culture, and where skiing is as natural as canoeing - in their vast boreal forests, was to provide the most useful information. Wildlife in the North Cascades is best described in Canadian literature, and what we saw, in the North East Cascades, is best understood by comparisons with Canadian wildlife and skiing experience.

Canada Jays, for example, were by far the most common wildlife we'd see, out heli-skiing. These camp robbers, gray jays, or "whiskey jacks" as they're variously called, typically joined us for lunch, along with the occasional Clark's Nutcracker, and of course Chickadees. Their activity patterns often provided clues about other animals. Canadian Lynx tracks produced the greatest interest in my skiers, and this was even before their Endangered Species Act listing, which later provoked popular attention. Lynx were just something these skiers were not used to. Moose, Cougar, and Coyote, were not nearly as common as Lynx, up high, and Bobcat were almost always down lower where the snow is less deep. We never did see Wolverine tracks in the helicopter ski touring areas, probably because they usually prefer denser forests to the west. I often saw their tracks, and even the animals themselves - on three occasions, up in the National Park, when I skied into my summer ranger patrol cabin to shovel off its fragile aging roof.

Mountain Goats and really deep snow also don't mix well, so although they're common in winter on south facing cliff terrain, my skiers (both nordic and alpine) usually didn't get to see them or their tracks. Our National Forest permit, in fact, put the majority of such sunny areas off limits to even fly over, for fear of disturbing the nursery bands of nannies and kids. Those goats we did rarely see would be lone billies, off on some scary cliff – like the south ribs of Mount Hardy.

Groomed ski trails make for easy travel if you're a predator needing to cover lots of territory. Cougar tracks sometime alarm cross-country skiers, and I often wondered why I saw Cougar tracks on groomed snowmobile trails up high, with only Snowshoe Hares to eat. After I realized that I saw Lynx tracks only off the groomed snow, it dawned on me that the Cougars were simply using the groomed trails to avoid having to "post hole" that is - struggle through deep snow, around cross-country skiers, on the valley trails below. Most surviving Cougars have learned that people are trouble, and that deer make the best meals with the least effort.

The common misconception that Cougars were after skiers, or Snowshoe Hares, or even Lynx, was dispelled by my own observations and by wildlife scientists who come to cross-country ski in the Methow. Lynx are deep snow specialists and if you've ever tried to travel in deep snow without snowshoes or skis, you know why they have the deepest snow territory almost entirely for themselves and their favorite food - Snowshoe Hare.

Coyotes do hunt along groomed ski trails down lower, where the snow isn't so deep and soft, but where Pocket Gophers and voles are forced out of their under-the-snow or "sub-nivian" tunnels, to cross the hard packed snow. Owls and hawks use the same tactic, but tiny rodents are only horsd'oeuvres for hungry Cougars, compared to the all-you-can-eat buffet provided by the Methow Valley's over abundant deer herds and wild west side drivers, in the form of lots of automobile collision road kills, and walking wounded, as easy pickings.

Explaining details like these to my heli-skiers and spring, summer, or fall nature hikers at the Freestone Inn, where I work as a naturalist, gradually convinced me that it was wildlife, more than wilderness, that really interested most visitors to the North Cascades, and probably many other snow country retreats. Thus it was that my 1965

Master of Forestry paper: *Roads Trails and Wilderness,* dealing with access management, evolved into *Ski Trails and Wildlife* for the 21'st century.

Native Americans had no word for wilderness, a foreign (to them) European concept born of the excesses of overpopulated western style civilization. Extinction rates have lately proved that our wilderness is only as functional biologically as the wildlife it contains, and that it needs lots of help from the surrounding landscapes, to accomplish this goal. Elk, Wolves, and Grizzlies, in Yellowstone are the current example most familiar to environmentalists, through the controversial best seller: *Playing God in Yellowstone,* by Alston Chase, which predated the Wolves. The vast matrix of semi-wild land surrounding wilderness is, by legal definition, subject to – or sometimes already developed with - roads, trails, ski lifts, lodges, huts, shelters, bridges, mining, logging, and grazing. All these developments influence wildlife over a greater range of habitat than any reserves.

Wilderness still matters, but biological scientists have proved that its context matters more, and so this book is primarily about the matrix of ski country surrounding Wilderness, Parks, and wildlife reserves of all sorts. This matrix is where the people needed to restore wildlife are found. Preaching to the choir, up in the Wilderness and out in the National Park or game range, doesn't reach the most critical broader constituency.

In 1971 the United States National Park Service told me I'd have to start wearing a gun, go to law enforcement school in Georgia, and give up my snow ranger job in Olympic National Park. I'd already resigned once before, when they sent me to the South West United States, so they weren't surprised when I resigned again to winter in the ski business, and summer as a seasonal ranger or naturalist in either the National Parks or Forests.

11

That led naturally enough to guiding helicopter skiers in the North East Cascades, but along the way there was also exposure to a wide variety of on-the-ground, and on-the-snow, field experience with wildlife and the human enterprises that interact with wildlife. In this way I was able to escape the office and patrol car that unfortunately insulate today's typical ranger from the wildlife and the people wildlife attracts. Of all these experiences, the most significant, for the health of wildlife, were those involving the ski trail and all that comes with it. Trail users of all sorts, like my helicopter ski tourers, are very often politically active people. If they could only somehow be provided with more accurate information, many of the disagreements dividing critical stakeholders like hunters and bird watchers, lift skiers and cross-country skiers, would disappear and, working together, they could be wildlife's best hope.

Restoration and skiing however are almost hopelessly mired in controversy. This book is intended to inspire readers into pursuing these topics in the depth provided by my extensive bibliography. What follows is almost guaranteed to offend both the political left and right. So read on if you dare, but be prepared for more questions than answers. Most of the answers are too complex for any one book, but there are some pretty good ones out there now, and hopefully more to follow.

CIRCA 1960

INTRODUCTION

Deep green forests, sparkling streams, lakes, and snowfields, on dramatic jagged peaks, surround a pastoral valley where vacationers cross-country ski near rustic lodges. High above, a single French helicopter deposits a load of alpine skiers and snowboarders into a wonderland of graceful corniced ridges, hanging over miles long natural ski runs which are formed by huge airborne powder avalanches - - safely away from any human habitation. By far the majority of helicopter skiers are the same kind that otherwise would be riding ski lifts. Cross-country skiers riding helicopters are the minority, but this valley has the unique terrain that makes such a seemingly impossible combination happen.

No other helicopter disturbs their adventure, and no chairlifts generate crowded ski trails, huge paved parking lots, or greaseburger feedlot style day lodges, complete with plastic signs, in the valley below. No ski patrol, in this valley, waits by toboggans at the top of lifts, ready to carry away the casualties. Instead the *nordic* ski patrol is out skiing with hundreds of cross-country skiers, very thinly spread over nearly 200 kilometers of groomed ski trails. Some are skiing to or from simple ski huts, but most are not far from those rustic lodges' hot tubs and cozy fireplaces, many of which still burn real wood.

Wood stoves even heat and cook for many residents courageous enough to buck the conventional wisdom that "woodsmoke is badsmoke", and thinning the forest for firewood is somehow upsetting "the balance of nature." Snowmobiles zoom over even longer, and much more spread out, groomed trails - far enough away from the skiers that conflicts are rare. Snowshoers follow their own marked trails, or the tracks of wildlife, in quiet pockets of woods too dense for comfortable skiing. Obviously this valley is doing things differently from much of the polarized and conflicted North American landscape. This is the Methow Valley, which includes the ghost of the once proposed, and bitterly fought over, almost ski lift resort called Early Winters.

Early Winters is also a historic place, just below the Canadian border, in Washington State, where native Americans pitched their summer camps to pick berries, gather roots, and hunt, before the notoriously deep and early snows made travel without snowshoes impossible. Culturally the Methow, pronounced Met-how, is part of Canadia. Like Scandinavia, and the European Alps, it has more in common with its immediate biogeographic surroundings, than with any nation state.

Wolves have been quietly returning to their former range, here in the North Cascades- a mountain mass hung with more glaciers than any other state except Alaska. Well, not always quietly, they do howl once in a while, but if anyone hears them – locals assure the listener that it must have just been a coyote that wasn't feeling good. The Methow Valley has enough trouble with endangered species, like the Lynx and Bull Trout, without adding another excuse for more legal action. Oh - yes, and Grizzlies have been confirmed here too, and the odd Moose, Elk, and Bighorn, wander through.

Mountain Goats play on the crags, while White Tailed Deer are increasing – as cattle are being fenced out of forests along the rivers. Washington State's largest Mule Deer herds kept an increasingly bold population of Cougars well fed, after hound hunting of these cats was outlawed in the 1990's. So bold were the Cougars, in fact, that hound hunting was reinstated by the state legislature in this and other counties where problems developed. Lynx range from the Spruce and True Fir boreal forest high country, down through transition zone Douglas-fir and even further down into Ponderosa and Aspen, when the Snowshoe Hares are numerous enough to tempt them into challenging their Bobcat cousins in the valleys.

14

Usually however, Lynx spend most of their time up in the Spruce-Fir boreal forest.

Early Winters, the second ever proposed ski lift area to have its case taken to the United States Supreme Court, was such an emotionally charged buzz word title, after thirty some years of litigation, that the name was dropped by nordic ski resort developers who bought the property after the ski lift ideas failed. Early Winters is still the creek, in its large watershed, a classic rock pinnacle, the old historic CCC (Civilian Conservation Corps) era ranger station and the campground, just a mile above Mazama. Arrowleaf, the lovely balsamroot sunflower, was chosen instead of "Early Winters," to identify the emergence of something called a "trails resort," which would have no ski lifts. Even this *Arrowleaf* resort however, was dramatically scaled down, from 1200 acres to about 200 acres and a Trust for Public Lands (TPL) conservancy. This process is something much bigger than the North Cascades, and partly why I chose Early Winters for the final chapter of this book.

Forest fires, wildlife, avalanches, and skiing are interdependent. Understanding their relationships is essential to boreal forest conservation biology. Obviously skiing occurs above, and north of, the boreal forest, and below, and south of, it too, but by far the majority of skiing takes place where snow dominates the biology, and trees allow the snow to drift in deep and soft enough for easy sliding. Misunderstanding these elements has led to the United States Supreme Court on two ski lift resort proposals: Mineral King and Early Winters. The first led to legal standing for trees, and the second marked the end of new ski lift resort development in the 20th Century, for the United States, while Canada and Europe enjoyed relatively steady growth.

Like Wolf and Grizzly reintroduction, drilling in the Arctic Wildlife Refuge, or abortion, ski development acquired symbolic significance far beyond its physical impact. The myths of this potent symbolism perpetuate repeated ski development controversies which only help to obscure and deny the perhaps too-scary-to-deal-with, overpopulation disaster.

Meanwhile the Wolf reintroduction in Yellowstone also benefited Grizzlies, Aspens, Beavers, water tables, birds, butterflies, tourist dollars, and the shoulder season occupancy slumps at adjacent ski resorts. The irony here is that legal standing for trees and nature marks the return of western society to respect for nature as something to which humans belong, rather than the other way around. This is an essential first step toward restoration biology, but only a very tentative first step.

Step number two is acceptance of the fact that first nation "Indian" cultures also modified nature, and in fact coevolved with it, from at least the time of the last ice age. Skiing ultimately forces its proponent participants, and their antagonists alike, to deal with nature's reality, whether to stay out of avalanches, save their ski cabin from forest fires, or prove snowmaking may adversely effect some endangered species.

Nature in the raw, including evolution - with Darwin and all that however, is obviously too much of a stretch for many. Coevolution is apparently an even tougher pill to swallow, and the lovely environmental myth of "pristine wilderness," where "the hand of man has never set foot" persists in the most liberal elements of society. Apparently only the hands and feet of European origin counted, in this rather racist view of nature. The newly evolving perceptions of how nature really works, year round and in the mostly remote boreal forests, is skiing's greatest impact on wildlife, and ski trails increasingly determine where and how nature's reality is finally perceived, in all seasons – but especially in winter. Skiing and ski trails of course also have direct physical impacts on wildlife.

Snow country populations are booming with new well heeled, politically influential, refugees, retirees, computer commuters, and the service industries needed to attend to these full and/or part time residents, in addition to the weekend guests and "snowbirds" that fly south in winter, to their condos in Mexico or Hawaii. Ski lifts are no longer the principle determinates of where these newcomers land. The Methow Valley, for instance, started booming when the ski lift ideas were finally abandoned. Many other snowy regions are seeing ski tracks in places completely removed from even the slightest possibility of ski lifts.

Ski trails are everything from old fashioned elongated clear cuts at the old downhill resorts, to more modern gladed runs with feathered edges, cross- country groomed tracks twelve feet wide or so, winding out hundreds of kilometers from posh nordic ski resorts, and even more "single tracks" set with a snowmobile or some hardy trail breaker on touring skis. Snowshoers too pack out trails followed by skiers and, while not nearly as extensive as ski or snowmobile trails, do impact wildlife in forests too brushy or thick to attract many skiers. Snowboards, and snowmobiles share snow country too, but skis remain the most influential to wildlife.

Snowmobiles are even more notorious and obvious, but remain predominately a working class social phenomenon, popular with people fond of, or at least tolerant of, loud noises and the conspicuous consumption of fossil fuel. Snowboards are restricted to lifts or very short distances from roads. They have yet to replace skis as the upper class snow toy of choice. Maybe that was part of Senator John Kerry's problem in the 2004 presidential election.

Wherever and however ski trails go, the most people go, winter, spring, summer, or fall. Skiing, in its many forms, is where the big money controversies are generated, and determine where big developments (such as the next Olympic venue), and highways go, where destination ski and summer resorts go, and therefore how wildlife is effected and perceived.

Snow country confrontations predictably revolve around the same topics.

CONTENTS (in a little more detail)

1: SKIING – life styles and the resulting cast of unique and highly diverse characters

2: AVALANCHE – risk management of skiers, snow-mobilers, dwellings, highways, and forest fire fuel breaks

3: EDGES – of Wilderness, buffers, late successional reserves, ski resort and heli-ski permit areas

4: FIRES – ecology and smoke, thinning and prescribed burning, foresters, smokejumpers and roadless areas

5: LIFTS – attracting impact, real estate, corporate developers, legal intrigue, and precedents

6: TRAILS – design and maintenance as zoning tools, versus "police state wilderness"

7: HUTS – attracting and dealing with impact, from shelters and cabins to helicopter and snowcat accessed lodges

8: RANGERS - wildlife and Wilderness managers, snow safety, and "analysis paralysis"

9: WILDERNESS and the urban mind - the pitfalls of environmental fundamentalism

10: MINERAL KING – vs. the Sierra Club, preventing ski lifts there, while allowing them at Kirkwood

11: LYNX – and the keystone wildlife

Two Pacific Northwest conflicts are classic:

12: HURRICANE RIDGE – in Olympic National Park where ski lifts and Wilderness coexist

13: EARLY WINTERS - on Okanogan National Forest where nordic skiing quietly eclipsed a thirty year saga of intense contention over a proposed ski lift resort.

18

Chapter 1: SKIING – life styles and the resulting cast of unique and highly diverse characters

Ski resorts are to skiing, what zoos, circuses, and game parks are to wildlife. Both skiing and wildlife could be, and sometimes are, wild and free. Reality now however, is that both are artifacts significantly different from their pre-industrial age origins, and both usually cost money. Skiing's cast of characters, in this context, is almost as diverse as the wildlife it influences.

Modern skiing, that is skiing for fun, as opposed to such serious business as hunting on skis, started in the Telemark district of Norway. This should not however, be confused with the new separate sport of Telemarking in the 21'st Century, which somewhat resembles this North Cascades version of a 1960's popular song.

THE TELEMARK DRAG
(to the tune of the Vatican Rag)
First you get down on one knee,
and fiddle with your binding – see
Stem your skis with great respect,
and Genuflect, Genuflect, Genuflect.
When in Stowe, do like the stoics,
flaunt your lycra, look heroic.
Stick some moleskin on your heels,
plastic boots – how secure they feels.
Fat skis are in, parallel's a sin,
knees down so low agin', dragin' the snow agin'
Doin' the Telemark drag

Snowshoe Thompson, the famous skiing mail carrier of the California gold rush, together with his downhill racing contemporaries, first brought skiing to popular attention in North America.

Thompson was Norwegian of course, and although archeologists are now tracing skiing back thousands of years earlier in remote Eurasian sites, it is Norway which gets credit for the birth of skiing as we know it in the 21st

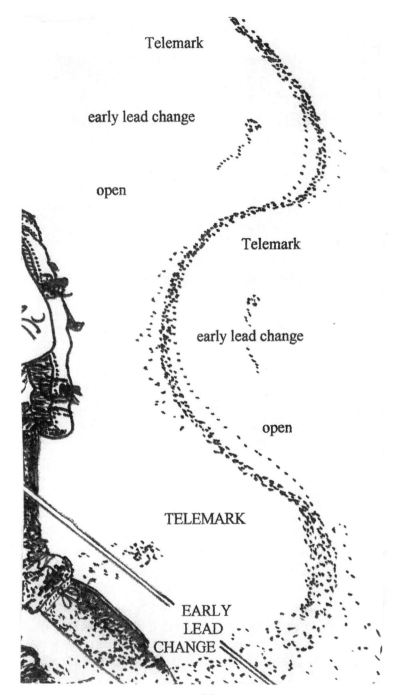

Telemark

early lead change

open

Telemark

early lead change

open

TELEMARK

EARLY
LEAD
CHANGE

Century. Sidecut, the curved sides, so obvious now on skis and snowboards, was first popularized by Sondre Norhiem, from Telemark - near Oslo, Norway, and also back in the 1800's. Up until then skis were primarily of utilitarian, rather than recreational, function. Turning on skis was, and still is, mainly for playing on skis in social situations, as opposed to the old business of literally skiing across the countryside.

My Norwegian friends told me a story of modern Telemarkers from America, visiting Lapland and hiring native Sami guides to show them the best Telemarking terrain. These guides showed up on wooden skis, with toe strap bindings, while the Yanks were outfitted in the latest plastic boots, fiberglass skis, lycra and Goretex. On top of the mountain these clients reassured their Sami guides that they would eat lunch and take some pictures at the bottom, so that their primitive wooden skis would have time to catch up. Thousands of vertical feet later the Americans arrived ecstatic and breathless, to find their guides calmly smoking their pipes around a lunch fire.

Another Norwegian, Jackrabbit Johansen, who supported his skiing habit with employment as an engineer, brought recreational skiing to eastern North America in the 1900's. He designed the first Canadian and American ski resorts, for both cross-country and ski lifts. He preferred cross-country, and was still doing it - at the age of 110. He died at 112, at the end of the 20'th century, and his biography, written by his daughter, is a fascinating account of both skiing and the industrial revolution which made its conversion from utility to sport possible.

Averill Harriman gets credit for the first chairlift, at his Sun Valley ski resort in 1936. Enclosed aerial lifts and surface lifts had already been pioneered by then in the Alps, but it was chairlifts which somehow hit a responsive note in the post World War Two recreation market. At that time the Marshal Plan had helped jump start the

standard
touring

OPEN

European ski resort industry into such a successful economic generator that American skiers dreamed of building similar resorts in the United States. Alpine, that is lift skiing, thus became "real or regular skiing" in the 1950's and 60's American mind set. Nordic, that is skiing "cross-country" without lifts, was thought of as "too much like work", and "only suited to flat country, because you can't turn those skinny skis." These life style prejudices and misconceptions persisted into the cardiac era of the 21'st century. Traditions die hard, but as aerobic exercise began to gain credibility as a healthy recreational goal, cross-country skiing had transformed itself into groomed trail skiing, and was thereby made accessible to the urban market.

Norwegians with relatives who died under the German occupation of World War Two, are understandably less than fond of Germanic cultures, including their skiing styles. This split between alpine and nordic skiing has carried over to the new world, where Republicans, in the United States, typically ski on lifts, if they ski at all, and Democrats can more often be found on cross-country trails. Even Senator John Kerry however, the 2004 Democratic presidential candidate, was a ski lift riding snowboarder – which may have cost him the election, after an over publicized on slope collision.

The image was one of over-privileged, materialistic indulgence. Certainly more Democrats ride lifts though, than cross-country ski, and this is a crucially important demographic fact for wildlife. Cross-country skiing, bird watching, Democratic Party, gung-ho environmentalists are probably wildlife's best friends because they're into wilderness, but they need lots of help from their lift riding cohorts and all those Republican hunters who may care less about skiing of any sort. All this is of course over simplification of gross proportions, but understanding political prejudices and alliances can make or break any given wildlife conservation or restoration effort. Part of this political problem goes back centuries, to political baggage of European origins.

More recently in North America, rural life styles have been severely changed when skiing settled into an area. Internationally famous resorts, such as Aspen Colorado, are the source of grim jokes about billionaires forcing the millionaires out. Once proud independent ranchers have been forced to sell their land, and take jobs in the service industries, catering to skiers. There is also a tremendous confusion about skiing among nonskiers.

Understanding enough of these old and new cultural clashes to assess their effect on wildlife, requires at least a peek into the innermost soul of skiing. Why was Canadian Sunset a popular hit tune about romancing on a ski trail ? Do stretch pants really figure into this? Sex and skiing are often compared among skiers, and a common joke states that "skiing may not be better than sex, but it sure lasts longer."

Ski trails come in three varieties: alpine, nordic, and the great ungroomed outback. Alpine trails connect the tops and bottoms of ski lifts, with wide enough swaths to accommodate great herds turning all together, like wind surfers on popular waterways. Nordic trails are typically only 12 feet wide, and likely to go anywhere. They too are socially oriented, as their patrons sexy outfits proclaim beyond all reasonable doubt. Ungroomed trails are usually summer trails that incidentally get skier traffic. They are the most extensive, but least populated - and your chances of romantic encounters in the Canadian Sunset style are slight. They are for "ski touring."

The separate sports of Telemarking and skating evolved at the close of the 1900's. The Telemark Drag includes inside jokes best appreciated by professional skiers and snow country innkeepers, who have lived and worked with the evolution of snow sports and their clientele.

Stowe, Vermont, is for cross-country skiers in America, what Mecca is for Muslims, or Bethlehem for Christians. It's where cross-country skiing first gained a commercial foothold in North America, in the mid-20'th century. And yes, their devotion is of religious intensity with extremely strong political consequences. Skin tight "Lycra" ski suits quickly followed, as did plastic boots and the resulting need for moleskin to take care of the inevitable blisters. Alpine skiers' stretch pants preceded Lycra, and although they also were sex symbols, they were not nearly as revealing as the one piece cross-country suits. The more active nature of cross-country skiing made these revealing garments both possible and practical, but the social need for cultural expression obviously was the overwhelming motivator.

My Norwegian mentors simply skied in shorts, equally practical, but not nearly as suggestively sexy. A few years later my employment as a cross-country ski instructor required that I too had to wear one of these silly suits. Years earlier I was required to wear stretch pants, to draw a pay check, for my first job on chairlifts. All that was in fashion dominated California, but it has spread inevitably to the ski industry world wide.

The awkward and tiring Telemark stance evolved quickly to reinvent downhill lift assisted skiing, while skating on skis requires frequently groomed tracks- similar to, but narrower than, lift serviced trails. Touring skis that are designed to ski ungroomed snow, as a means of travel rather than making fancy turns, became a relatively small share of the new ski market. They were replaced by these new skiing styles for the majority of cross-country skiers, but still survived among older skiers in North America, and in the birthplace of recreational skiing: Scandinavia.

Snowboarding excels at dealing with ungroomed snow of any consistency, as do the newer super wide and generously sidecut Telemarking skis. Like their alpine

POCKET GOPHER TUNNEL

skiing cousins however, the majority of these sliders spend most of their time on ski lifts and groomed slopes. This demand for groomed trails, combined with increased sidecut, and the stiff plastic boots needed to control that exaggerated sidecut, has led to an increase in speed, with a resulting increase in collision injuries, and the need for helmets. The knee pads of Telemarkers have been joined by elbow and hip pads, and thus has lift skiing evolved into a contact sport far removed from its graceful history of polite beautiful people in tailored stretch pants and Scandinavian sweaters.

Wildlife love all ski trails for their edges, except when tunneling under the snow - as Pocket Gophers and Voles (Meadow Mice) usually do. The forced exposure to predation, necessitated by crossing a packed trail, however has little effect on wildlife populations other than to make the drama of selective predation pressure more evident to skiers inclined to be interested in such matters as evolution. Wildlife mating activity is not associated with ski trails at all, in marked contrast to skiers.

Wedeln, the German word for tail wagging, was the curious dance performed by many skiers going downhill, in the 70's. "Itsy-bitsy turns" is surviving skier jargon that describes the same ritual. Jumping, in its many forms, is favored by all except the most serious cross-country racers and tourers. Students of wildlife mating rituals recognize these obvious primal physical movement patterns.

Sinuous arcing tracks in powder snow are no longer the exclusive domain of lift and helicopter skiers. Neither is obsession with them, or many of the other social problems, such as ski thefts, characteristic of alpine skiing and the waning industrial age that made ski lifts possible.

Telemarking, the new social sport of skiing downhill with free heels to please the crowds at alpine resorts, bears little resemblance to the centuries old Scandinavian turn which used the furrow effect to assist turning touring skis

27

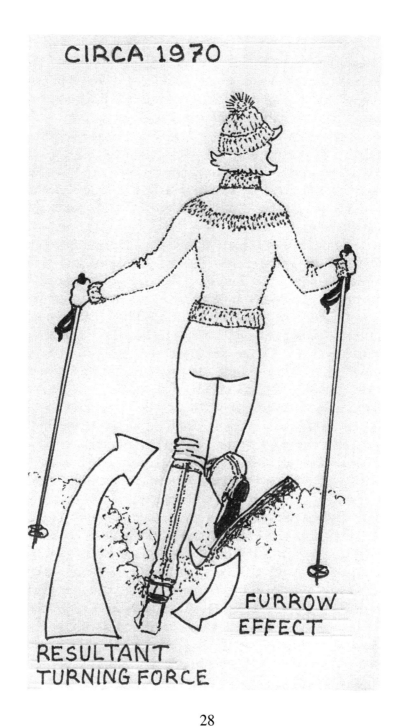

CIRCA 1970

FURROW
EFFECT

RESULTANT
TURNING FORCE

28

in ungroomed snow. Extreme sidecut, which makes modern skis and snowboards so easy to turn, only gets in the way when trying to cover as much distance as possible. Telemarking and "backcountry skiing" is, at the start of the 21'st century, in the same big boot stage of evolution that hiking was in the 1960's, when "waffle stompers" put their lug soled boot prints on American college campuses. It is as much a form of social protest, as a ski technique.

The Telemark turn is, for most skiers, a "snowplow" or wedge, or maybe a "stem Christie," done with the outside ski leading throughout the entire radius of the turn. This stilted modern form of the ancient tradition has become dogma, codified even in *Webster's Dictionary*. The fact that expert nordic skiers link turns without changing lead ("monomark") , or change lead at any point along the arc of a given turn, is still (as of 2007) viewed as heresy by some true believers.   More liberal skiers refer to this practice as "an early (or late) lead change." It still does however (again as of 2007) disqualify a racer who does it before the turning gates in a *Telemark* race.

Like most dogma this new age belief system does have some basis in fact. These facts however are long forgotten, or more frequently never were known, to the doctrine's most evangelical crusaders. These same true believers are often the political activists that force land managing agencies or ski developers into biologically destructive plans, and made environmentalism a dirty word for many voters and political writers after the evenly divided 2004 presidential election.   Their problem is ignorance of both skiing and wildlife, on top of the image of - especially for lift skiing - conspicuous consumption and its hypocrisy. Fundamentalist thinking is an obstacle to both better ski technique and better wildlife management.

Powder snow Telemarks, led with the outside ski, create a furrow effect turning force as the inside ski slides down the side of the outside ski's deep track. This only works if the inside ski is close enough to the outside ski to be included in its furrow, and only advanced skiers, who's style approaches parallel, ever feel this force. When they do, the sensation is as close to heaven as they're likely to get, and the mystique created is the source of both confusion and spiritual inspiration.

Otherwise nordic downhill skiing is like alpine skiing, and Lito Tejeda-Flores' book *Breakthrough on Skis* is the new testament of sidecut that has taken skiing far beyond his earlier book: *Backcountry Skiing*, or Steve Barnett's classic *Cross Country Downhill*, and Paul Parker's *Free Heel Skiing*. Bumper stickers proclaim "FREE THE HEEL AND YOUR MIND WILL FOLLOW." All this implies a spiritual side to this sport, widely regarded as grossly materialistic. Both extremes are true, and this breadth and variety are an essential part of understanding how skiing and wildlife interact.

Carving turns on one ski's, or a snowboard's, sidecut usually - as Lito describes, or on both skis usually – as Steve and Paul explain, are two valid approaches for opposite ends of the snow condition spectrum. None of this technique advancement however, changes the fact that most skiers, and snowboarders, alpine and nordic, never take advanced lessons, and are perfectly happy skidding their turns. Wide skis and big heavy boots are therefore preferred for downhill travel, as are groomed slopes and trails. The snowboard is the extreme of this infatuation with turning and jumping. Snowboards can turn easily, even in crusty and sticky snows, but are otherwise useless for oversnow travel. The split snowboard is evolution in reverse, attempting to get back some of the lost mobility. Snowboards and modern hourglass shaped alpine skis are in short, toys – in the purest sense of that word. They are for people watching people, not birds or any other kind of wildlife. Ironically however the most skilled of these snowboard riders often rediscover winter wildlife while snowshoeing up to some "sick" line, inaccessible by any other means. Snowshoeing, like ski touring, is ideal for reconnecting with nature in winter.

Snowboards, alpine and Telemark or "backcountry" skis, share a dependence on auto or ski lift transport. This confines and concentrates their impact on wildlife along mountain highways. Nordic skiers too are concentrated by roads, even though nordic skiing predates the petroleum age by thousands of years. Groomed snow makes skiing easy and very attractive to the 21'st century's predominately urban market. Grooming is therefore essential for the survival of commercial skiing, which is in turn essential for the survival of wildlife.

Winter wildlife is only as safe as enough people, knowing about it, choose to protect it through the political process, to paraphrase David Brower. Even chairlift riders are exposed to the outdoors in winter. Although this may seem like an inconsequentially small step to the dedicated naturalist, it is still an essential first move for many urbanites, otherwise isolated from the natural world in winter. David Brower, the "archdruid" made famous by John McFee's best selling book, and Dave's controversial love-hate relationship with the Sierra Club, was referring to wilderness with this statement of inescapable political reality. Simply *knowing* is too often the missing link.

21'st century wilderness is being "loved to death" by recreationists who would be more than happy (especially in winter) to play outside wilderness, if only there were more opportunities to do so. Such trail opportunities can concentrate people, away from critical wildlife habitat, by inspiration as opposed to regulation. This is the carrot, rather than the currently predominate stick approach to wildlife and wilderness management.

Small numbers of nordic skiers, on light touring gear spread their impact over vast areas of the world's boreal forests. If other ski regions follow Scandinavia's example,

32

ski impact could change as dramatically as backpacking's has. The late 1900's growth of groomed snow nordic trail skiing has the potential to kick off an even greater change, if skiers rediscover how to ski natural ungroomed snow on light touring skis. Wildlife management might be easier if they don't, but backpacking's precedent looks ominous. Skating on skis, with its nearly absolute dependence on sophisticated grooming, may be our best hope to keep future nordic skiers out of wilderness and away from critical wildlife habitat.

This diversionary tactic works best if applied within sight of wilderness. Some watchable wildlife nearby is also extremely helpful. In short, nature education works best, and reaches the most heathens, at the edges of our wildlife preserves.

Sophisticated green politics followed the backpacking revolution, as the 1960's generation of activists discovered the summer half of the earth's life support system. The winter half may be next, and in evolutionary terms could prove more significant. Evolution is the philosophical, and often theological basis for active green politics, and thus are ski trails destined toward the mainstream of human events. Humanity is an evolutionary product of ice age stress, as Loren Eiseley's writings eloquently explain, and so are snow country forests.

Boreal forests cover more of the earth's surface than any other forest type. Skiing spread from Scandinavia to other northern forests, in its original nordic form, until the industrial revolution. Then fossil fuel based cultures adopted skiing's alpine style with mechanical lifts. Their recent flat growth curve, only kept from actual decline by snowboarding, has seen a corresponding increase in cross-country, or nordic skiing, as it is variously referred to.

The required juxtaposition of highway, airport, or railroad, together with favorable snow covered hills, and materialistic affluence, so necessary for alpine skiing, doesn't restrict natural snow nordic skiing. Impact from our exploding post industrial populations could therefore be much different, and more widespread. Meanwhile however, and most probably forever, the major and most significant impact on wildlife is, and will be, determined by ski trails. This is true even for summer use because ski trails provide the short loop trail, or lift assisted, experiences most vacationers prefer.

Alpine skiing's ecologically unsavory reputation taints all skiing, and plastic ("Lycra") fashions skied along machine groomed cross-country trails don't help this image problem. These highly visible groomed track skiers however, may be just the tip of an iceberg nordic population ("God's frozen people" – ala Garrison Keillor) happily breaking their own trails, while wearing surplus woolens, or other establishment defying fashions, much like the snowboarders. They blend in so well that they are impossible to count, and extremely difficult to sell new skis to, or categorize. Their impact is therefore much harder to see or assess, unless maybe you're one of them. Check the line up at the opening of the Methow Valley's annual fall ski swap, for instance. Are they a still quiet majority, or an - as yet, negligible minority? And how do they interact with the more visible and accountable ski world, other than frustrating nordic ski suppliers ?

The popular illusion of nordic purity has a germ of truth in it, just like the stem Telemark turn does. Nordic ski impact is different, but it is certainly not pure, and the hypocrisy of that illusion tends to irritate alpine skiers and the ski lift industry.

Ecologically literate skiers have learned to distrust the environmental fundamentalists' knee jerk reaction against all ski development. Ski huts for instance, obviously concentrate backcountry impact, and can therefore be a wildlife management tool second only to trails in their effectiveness. Destination ski and summer resorts are the most concentrated impact centers in the boreal forest bioregion. Hal Clifford's book *Downhill Slide*, published by the Sierra Club, downplays this potentially positive impact, and partly as a consequence has been written off and mostly ignored by alpine skiers. This is unfortunate because his book is a carefully researched critique of the corporate ski world. It's well worth reading by anyone interested in helping the downhill ski lift industry be a more responsible contributor to our environment, especially our skiing environment.

The key is to design, and renovate as necessary, ski trails and their related huts, lifts, villages, and resorts, into landscapes that are good neighbors to adjacent National Park and Forest Wilderness wildlife habitat. If skiers can be enticed to sleep at ski areas instead of commuting to snow as day skiers, or hauling huge recreational vehicles for overnight accommodations, society may be ahead in terms of net energy savings. More energy still could be saved if cross-country skiers would allow lifts to transport them up to the most skiable snow, as is the case at Silver Star and Sun Peaks resorts in British Columbia, Canada. Snow removal on high altitude parking lots together with their approach roads is a major consumer of energy.

Whistler-Blackcomb's obvious success is partly due to this factor. Their 5000 foot vertical elevation differential is not so much an asset for allowing long ski trails, as it is to provide for less snow removal costs at the often rainy base village. Unfortunately, for many cross- country ski areas, lifts are not an option, because they're viewed as instruments of the devil, and the agents of unacceptable life style changes brought in by alpine skiing. Ski trails, huts, lifts, and resorts built away from ecologically sensitive areas however, can be much more effective than Wilderness permits and attendant cop rangers.

Fire management is the biological frontier of wildlife management; not campfires, forest fires. The late 1900's "stoves only" fetish was displacement activity by the bureaucracy in denial, trying to ignore the principle agent of biological change. The heretical concept of managing, instead of fighting, fire is finally starting to be accepted. Rangers are essential players in this regard, and their influence effects wildlife habitat through both fire and ski area management.

Avalanche paths are one of nature's fire breaks. Telemarkers, snowboarders, backcountry and heli-skiers use them as ski trails, thereby compacting avalanche path snow, and altering fire as well as avalanche cycles. Avalanche path vegetation is both pruned and watered by the resulting artificially structured snowpack. Any trails cleared wide and high enough for skiers are firebreaks too.

Cross-country trails have by definition the widest spread influence, directly on wildfire and wildlife. Alpine ski lift trails, by contrast, concentrate their impact on forest fire fuels threatening the relatively high value real estate and substantial infrastructure involved with lift skiing. Their extra width makes them better fire breaks than cross-country trails. Their other impacts are concentrated also, from concerts to mountain biking, and conferences, to employee ghettos - down valley in the lower rent district. Their indirect impact on wildlife is much greater than their direct impact, because of the large numbers of people they attract, and thereby keep away from the consequently less populated surrounding country.

Wildlife management requires both dispersion and concentration of human impact. Designated campsites are required, even in legally established Wilderness Areas, when the limits of acceptable biological change have been breached. They are to wildlife, on a small scale, what huts, lifts, and resorts, are on the landscape and regional scales.

One of the environmental establishment's most popular illusions is that dispersion alone can solve all the problems of skier impact. Cross-country skiing, in this conventional wisdom, is "good," and alpine lift skiing is "bad." Nordic skiers actually can often be just as socially oriented as alpine skiers. Their races can draw crowds in the thousands, and Telemarkers spend much more time on lifts than in the real backcountry. Even relatively uncrowded groomed track skiing supports some major operations, most notably Royal Gorge - in California's Sierra Nevada, Mont-Sainte-Ann and Gatineau Park – in Quebec, the Engadine in Switzerland, the Gunflint Trail in Minnesota, and the Methow Valley, in Washington's North Cascades. Most groomed track nordic skiing however occurs adjacent to alpine lift areas. Even Royal Gorge, the Engadine, and Mont-Sainte-Ann fall into this category, with their handy proximity to major ski lift resort complexes. The "loneliness of the cross-country skier" is as much a myth as is the one about it being "too much like work."

Still these illusions persist as dogma in many environmentalist circles. Dogma and hypocrisy need each other as amply demonstrated in the arena of social ethics, religious warfare being its most blatant example. Environmental fundamentalists have fallen into a similar quagmire, and skiing's greatest contribution may be to lead the way out. The exit strategy is to honestly face human influences on wildlife, in all seasons, and all habitats, but especially the huge boreal forest – with its unavoidable and intimate relationships to snow and the sport of skiing.

Ski area management has become as complex as wildlife and wilderness management, and all three professional specialties are far removed from most skiers, wildlife and wilderness advocates. Ski trail planning and management however, transcend all three, and are too important to be left to specialists - especially rangers that don't even ski.

Chapter 2: AVALANCHE - risk management of skiers, dwellings, highways, and forest fire fuel breaks

"FIRE IN THE HOLE" echoed off cliffs above pregnant snow slopes. Two pounds of explosive lay softly on about twenty tons of fresh snow curled out in an overhanging cornice. Winds during the preceding night's storm formed both this obvious cornice, and the more subtle, but even more massive, soft "pillow" of wind modified snow below, on the lee side of Kirkwood ski area's steep ridge line. Most snow flakes made it over the ridge and settled gently between and below those lee side cliffs. In the process however, they lost some of their delicate symmetry. Virgin snow they are not ! Life is tough in the mountains, and these wind battered snowflakes are only the start of events with more social implications.

Fuse sputtered along the sparkling powder snow. Time to place gloves securely over ears, open mouths, and wiggle jaws to insure that eustachian tubes are clear. That sparkle was surface hoar frost, the equivalent of dew, on cold clear and humid winter nights. It meant that the storm had broken before dawn, and that the "pillow" had time to "ripen." Time that is, for "virgin" snow to settle out from under the multi-ton shell, or "slab," of wind compacted, just a bit more worldly perhaps, but somewhat damaged snow immediately above. The "wind slab" itself however, being stiffer, had not had enough time to settle down onto, and bond securely with, the more respectable snow below. These kind of thoughts are a peek into the minds of the professional ski patrollers that had just tossed the two pounds of dynamite out onto the cornice. Exactly where and how it was tossed were a result of an analytical process that was both scientific - the product of formal avalanche schools, and seat-of-the-pants intuition - the product of the school of hard knocks.

Nature probably would have taken care of this avalanche hazard eventually, but skiers are impatient. They wanted that bowl's powder snow by early morning lift opening, before California's intense spring sun turned it into the glop known as "Sierra cement."

Sputtering stopped as the fuse disappeared into the snow, and out of site. "Hmm, it penetrating better than expected, ought to give it a good kick." But that also meant humidity probably built up only toward the end of the storm, and therefore an extra top heavy snow profile. "Could be a big one" was going through these patrollers minds, more than any rigorous scientific analysis, as they eased out for a better view, taking care to stay back of any possible ridge top fracture. "Want to watch this baby go! Such a beautiful slope to mess up, all the way down to where those tracks come across. - - TRACKS!? ----- FRESH TRACKS! Holy (bleep), there they are, two pinheads on skinnies !"

Eyes shut involuntarily as the blast imploded off surrounding cliffs, and by the time they opened, and focused, the cornice had dropped and the pillow ripped open a four foot deep fracture, 200 yards across the crown of the slope. A split second later, snow buckled 100 yards below the crown fracture, as it curved down at each end, then sheared off in two sidewall cracks straight toward the valley, and those "skinny" cross-country skiers, below.

These fractures, at the top and sides, freed an undulating mass of snow to force itself over the compressed - then buckling - then ripping, bottom fracture. Everything in its path was soon ripping too, but the center flowed faster than the sides and bottom, so the slab rolled over itself, with the top continuously overtaking the toe and sides, sucking in more snow from the sides, and deeper down into the snowpack - than the initial slab release. Air too was both sucked in from behind and pushed out in front, creating an "airborne powder avalanche," that makes a whooshing noise, while echoes of the dynamite blast faded out across the valley. Next the whoosh turned into a roar, and what looked like a huge cloud accelerating like (and sounding like) a jet plane taking off, shot toward the skiers below, much faster than it's taken you to read this, or even think about it.

The out-of–bounds skiers, wisely, did not try to outrun the avalanche. Instead they poled themselves into a descending traverse, leading to the edge of the slide path, (created by previous large avalanches) and the relative safety of the deep forest. Clouds of snow raised higher than even the tallest trees, and the patrol on top couldn't see the outcome until they slowly settled and cleared.

Base was notified by radio, to standby for possible rescue, and a patroller immediately checked boundary closure signs to insure they hadn't been tampered with. A few more blasts echoed off other "snow safety" routes around the valley, then all fell quiet as the entire ski resort waited for the snow cloud to settle. Radio silence was automatic because everyone working that early in the morning knew that seconds can mean the difference between life and death for a skier suffocating under an avalanche. Minutes later, the cloud settled, revealing tracks safely into the forest, and run out debris of lumpy snow that did not. They were lucky to be alive, but unlucky to be local cross-country skiers from the resort's night shift taking a short cut home. Their season passes, and whole reason for working nights at this fancy resort, were soon hanging idle in the ski area manager's office.

In the 1970's "Pinheads" were cross-country skiers using the preferred binding of that era, which consisted of a light metal toe piece with three pins designed to fit into three holes in the toe of light leather, and extremely comfortable (by modern standards) European made ski shoes. These soft "ski boots" were clamped down onto the pins by light metal wire, spring loaded, bales. "Skinnies" referred to their nordic skis, which back then were much thinner than alpine skis, but their tendency to be "skinny" people also contributed to this nickname. These slender bodies were also famous for their skinny dipping, a hold over from the 1960's, and so the term "skinnies" stuck, as shorthand for nordic skis, and skiers - well into the 1980's and beyond. The Telemark revolution in ski technique however, increasingly found nordic skiers riding lifts, especially after fresh snowfalls. Modern Telemarking skis, with exaggerated sidecuts, full steel edges, and big plastic boots, no longer require soft new snow to enjoy lift serviced skiing, which means even more counter culture types working at ski lift resorts. This cultural melting pot at ski and summer resorts is central to the influence of skiing on wildlife.

Telemarking, in the 21'st century, has become the sport of using very specialized nordic ski equipment to enjoy alpine, and usually lift serviced, terrain. Poorly paid ski lift area workers are prime Telemarking candidates for at least two reasons. The first is cost, because even old wooden touring skis can be used to enjoy powder snow, and the planned obsolescense of modern skis means that last season's fancy skis and boots can be picked up quite cheaply at ski swaps and ski area bulletin boards.

The second reason is aesthetic and political preference. A person inclined to drop out, for a year or two - and work at a ski resort, is likely to have counter culture values, although the adjective *skinny* may no longer apply to either their skis or body type. Ski lifts to them are probably viewed as a means of small temporary financial assistance, and more importantly - access to the "locals" ski world, and the chance to more thoroughly learn this very hip new sport. The next logical step in this cultural progression, even for snowboarders and alpine skiers, is out-of-bounds, "off piste," and into the "backcountry." A few may aspire to access "wilderness" on skis, preferably with a group of like minded skiers. Thus it was, that the short-cut going home seemed perfectly logical, until they discovered the hard way, that avalanches occasionally go airborne and sometimes descend much farther than usual. "No wonder there aren't many big trees at the bottom of that avalanche." Ignorance of avalanches, their ecological effects, and how they are modified by human activity is inevitably widespread.

Frequent skiing and explosive use on avalanche paths means more, but smaller slides. At well run resorts especially, slides seldom travel far down their historic routes. Chain saws must be used to keep slopes open, that were originally chosen for their avalanche maintained natural clearings. Still there is nothing to stop the odd storm from setting up a big one occasionally, and woe to anything in its way.

Avalanche safety suffers when the need for social protest cannot be satisfied with just Telemark posturing - literally, and closures are violated. "Yeah, the patrol is just keepin' all that powder for themselves." Telemarkers often wear their own unique fashions to get their social protest message across, but genuflecting is their primary tribal identification. This very exaggerated fore and aft displacement of their skis is only possible with free heel bindings, and some of this displacement is necessary for stability – without alpine heel bindings to lean against. My hardest task, usually - when teaching Telemark turns, is to keep this fore and aft spread within safe limits. Overextension is tiring, and leaves the knees particularly vulnerable. Lateral stability also suffers, leading to repeated stabbing with ski poles. Signature knee pads help mitigate collision injuries, but do nothing to prevent connective tissue damage. These are minor safety problems however , compared to ducking under the ski lift area's boundary ropes, or skiing past the CLOSED AVALANCHE DANGER signs.

Avalanches are only the most dramatic natural force associated directly with skiing. Their real significance is twofold. The first is that their hazard to human safety absolutely dictates where and what is possible, in steep snow covered mountains. The second is that everything else on avalanche prone slopes is also dominated by this irresistible force, even forest fires. Avalanche paths are natural fire breaks, and fires in turn often clear slopes enough to increase their avalanche activity.

The complex intertwining of avalanche risk and ecology was first realized in the European Alps, with "protection forests." No, these were not run by the mafia. Foresters in Europe discovered the soil impoverization results of clearcutting about three generations of trees ago, and not being particularly historically oriented, North American foresters seem to be taking about two generations of trees to make the same discovery. Patches of sacred woods now rise above most alpine hamlets, often after a history of tragedy, followed by expensive reforestation. Trees often had to be planted behind mechanical snow stabilizing structures, and as they matured they were, and are, carefully and continuously thinned to guard against insect or disease outbreaks common to the over stocked forests of North America.

This sophistication did not come easily. Avalanches were attributed to witches, rather than deforestation in centuries past. Superstition plagues us still, but more in America than in Europe. The school of hard knocks has simply been in session longer "over there." Wilderness is our modern equivalent of witches, and misconceptions regarding the natural forces we try to shelter there, are the biggest obstacles to its conservation, management, and restoration.

Avalanche professionals eventually learn that even the biggest explosive charges they can deliver do not always guarantee safety. They learn that what the ocean is to the shore, the river is to the valley, and the fire to the forest, the avalanche is to the mountain. They learn to manage avalanche risk, and hope for snow safety.

Every other year, in North America, avalanche professionals get together for International Snow Science Workshops. In 1976 I presented a paper, titled *Avalanches in National Park Planning*, to such a gathering in Banff, Alberta, Canada. My first task was to explain the different approach National Parks have been trying to take toward catastrophic natural phenomena since the 1963 Leopold Report. Disturbance ecology was a relatively new concept back then, and even the academics attending this meeting had been schooled in the old Clementsian climax theories about forest ecology. Clements was famous for promoting the idea that natural forest succession, after disturbance, proceeded in orderly fashion to a predictable assemblage of self perpetuating species. His detractors argue that disturbances such as fire, flood, insects, hurricanes, or avalanches, seldom permit this kind of predictability.

Dying Sequoia trees, thousands of years old, and overpopulated Elk herds also dying off in embarrassingly unnatural numbers, forced the National Park Service to commission Dr. Starker Leopold, and a "blue ribbon" committee of distinguished academics to investigate. Starker was the son of Aldo Leopold, the famous author of the environmental movement's old (1948) testament: *Sand County Almanac*. This procedure is necessary, in the American political system, whenever counter cultural results are anticipated.

Any forester or wildlife manager, worth his or her salt, knew not only what the *Leopold Report* was going to say, but also that it was necessary for these academics, and not the Park Service, to say it. Congressional appropriations required to run the Parks depend on votes from both sides of the aisle, so matters not explicitly covered in the *King James Version* of the *Bible* need to be handled with extreme delicacy. Sure enough, Leopold's committee released findings that Smokey the Bear and predator control had both run afoul of mother nature. Fire was going to have to be returned to the Sequoia groves, and something was going to have to reduce Elk numbers, or more than just Sequoias and Elk would be dying. Predator and fire "control" persisted into the 21'st century, in spite of successful wolf restoration at Yellowstone in 1995, and fire "management" finally starting in more than just Sequoia National Park.

Back in 1976 however this was still new stuff, and few ski industry people had any faith that the National Parks and Forests would be changing much in the near future. They were right of course, but tolerated this idealistic young ranger from Olympic National Park, because he seemed to be anticipating the kind of thinking that might hopefully someday change the institutions skiers have to contend with. Rumors were going around the room too, that he actually was a skier himself.

Even underpaid seasonal ranger-naturalists like I was, in the mid-1970's on Olympic's Hurricane Ridge, can figure out that interfering with any natural process usually has myriad side effects. I also had been fortunate to study for my Master of Forestry degree under Dr. Starker Leopold, in the mid- 60's, and was spending my winters on Kirkwood Ski Resort's professional ski patrol. One of the reasons I'd chosen to work at Olympic was that during a previous tour there as a year round sub-district ranger, the Mountain Goat population had exploded. As an ex-smokejumper, and now avalanche technician, I was ready to help investigate the effects of this introduced herbivore on the uniquely isolated flora of the Olympic Mountains. Surrounded on three sides by salt water, and lowlands on the fourth, Olympic's situation fit nicely into the then emerging theories of "island biogeography."

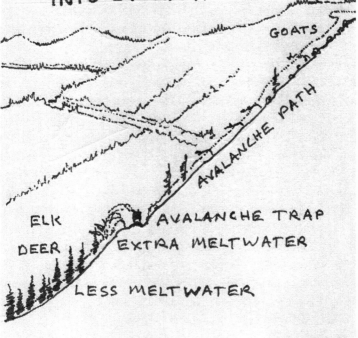

HURRICANE RIDGE ROAD
OLYMPIC NATIONAL PARK

LOOKING SOUTHWEST
INTO STORM WINDS

GOATS

AVALANCHE PATH

ELK
DEER
AVALANCHE TRAP
EXTRA MELTWATER
LESS MELTWATER

Avalanches kill both goats and skiers. They also clear goat pastures and natural ski runs. My challenge was to explain all this conservation biology theory to my fellow bomb tossing avalanche hunters, without coming off like the "posy sniffers" of Yellowstone's Elk farming political joke. Our rocky mountain private enterprise professionals have a contemptuous familiarity with both bureaucratic fumbling, and starry eyed young rangers.

What I hoped for from this international gathering of academics and pirotechnitions, were their opinions on how plowing the Hurricane Ridge road through ten major avalanche paths was going to effect avalanche ecology, and indirectly fire ecology too, along with exotic goat influences and consequences.

Plowed roads across avalanche paths catch sliding snow. Plow crews sometimes knock off the downhill berm, to let as much snow as possible slide across, and on down the slide path. However there's more overtime to be made if they don't, and the road might be closed on more weekend ski days that way, meaning fewer of those obnoxious skiers, parading around in their tight pants. Sometimes avalanches even get diverted down the roadway itself, filling the plowed slot with even more snow to be removed at taxpayers' expense, and provide extra snowmelt on the roadside. In isolated situations such as National Parks, with bureaucratic bosses not inclined to get out of the office much, especially during snow storms, there can be a lot of "work for the working man" on the line.

The net effect of all these physical, sociological, and ecological factors, is for the plowing itself to outweigh everything else – even the impact differential of snow slides crossing a road, which may speed up, slow down, or stop the snow, depending on its state of plowing. More snow melt water just down from the road, and less avalanche impact below the road were expected. But the odd slide kicking off airborne from the roadway's "ski

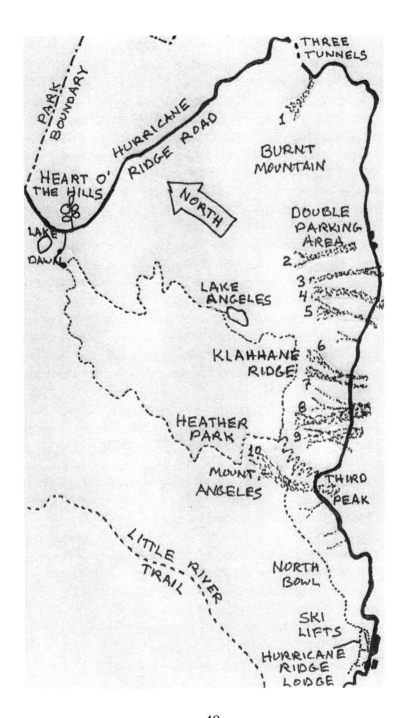

jump," and clearing more than the natural amount of trees, was also predicted as a likely result. More vegetation right below the road means more chance for a roadside fire to get away. Fewer avalanches running all the way down the natural slide path means more standing vegetation there, even if plowing has robbed it of snowmelt water formerly available. When it does get knocked down eventually, by that odd big slide, there'll be more fuel for a fire there too. All this sounded like forces tending to work in the direction of artificially enlarged, and widely distributed, disturbance ecology.

Norwegians, Canadians, Austrians, Americans, and Swiss all agreed that if Olympic National Park was actually serious about restoring and sustaining natural conditions, the *Hurricane Ridge road should not be plowed,* when there are significant amounts of snow on the roadway. The Canadians, Austrians, and Swiss, from Rogers Pass in British Columbia, Canada, also warned that if explosive control of avalanches ever became established, so would an artificial forest. The skiing would be ruined that way, along with the natural disturbance ecology and wildlife habitat. That at least had been their experience at Rogers Pass. Even the most dedicated road safety experts appreciate the finer things in life, such as skiing and the opportunity to maintain and observe native wildlife. Their mandate at Rogers Pass however, on the trans-Canada highway, simply did not allow such refinements.

Since I gave that paper, the state of Washington's Department of transportation has been able to forecast snow removal budgets from ecological surveys of vegetation in avalanche paths crossing their roads. The pioneering studies were from the University of Washington's botany department.

Helicopter ski guides also use vegetational clues, to both find optimal skiing conditions and avoid avalanche hazards. Ski area designers can and do employ these same methods, but obviously they have not always done so.

Avalanches and fires (bounded typically by avalanche paths) are the principle vista clearers of high mountain forests. They not only create lovely meadows and berry patches, they also let travelers see the spectacular high starting zones of other avalanches: the summer snowfields and glaciers that make alpine scenery so appealing. Climbers however, know that avalanches also create escape cover for wildlife, in the form of practically impenetrable brush fields. Depending on soil type, weather patterns, terrain, and resulting avalanches, a vast array of habitat types are created and maintained or changed. This lush variety, including the edges between different plant communities, is why avalanche country tends to be especially rich in both quantity and variety of its native wildlife.

Roads and trails are both the principle viewing platforms and means of backcountry access. Therefore it is a significant geometric coincidence that avalanches and roads, or trails, usually cross at right angles. Road impact especially can therefore spread for miles below the roadway itself, by its influence on avalanches alone. When fire eventually hits this altered state of fuel affairs, the road can effect the entire watershed, and beyond - should the resulting, artificially intense, fire jump ridgelines. Ski lifts, or sightseeing trams and gondolas, by contrast, tend to line up parallel to avalanche tracks, and their impact therefore is potentially less significant. Service or access roads - to cable lifts, however, can negate this biological advantage all too easily, without careful design.

Roads, trails, ski lifts, tramways, and wilderness, interact with wildlife in such basic ways that we tend to not think about them, and thereby neglect the most significant influences on wildlife. Plowing roads, for instance, is taken for granted, and yet no single activity uses more

51

fossil fuel, kills more wildlife directly - through road kills, or alters wildlife indirectly - through avalanches and fire. Before the more widespread influence of fire alone can be factored in, the edges of roads, trails, and land use designations, such as Wilderness, wildlife reserves, parks, scenic areas, grazing permits, ski lift, snowmobile, and helicopter skiing areas must be accounted for. They, like avalanches, act as firebreaks or significant influences on fire behavior and subsequent ecological effects.

Chapter 3: EDGES – of Wilderness, buffers, late successional reserves, heli-ski permit areas, and fire breaks

This subject is on edge, even a little edgy, because edges define the different wildland classifications left to us by an imperfect political process. These realities, geographical, topographical, ecological, sociological, political, and even psychological - - all surrounding edges, influence how wildlife and their sanctuaries are managed. The more or less civilized matrix, in which wildlife attempts to survive, is most definitely of increasing concern, but it is the edges themselves where some of the most important action takes place. That action is as varied as out-of-bounds skiing or hunting (i.e. poaching powder or wildlife), rationing Wilderness visitation, saving endangered species, and saving ecological processes - such as evolution itself.

Transitions between the various aspects of these realities, can be a little disconcerting. It's a little like stepping over the edge of, and into, a National Park - by mistake, with your trusty dog and the pistol you carry for grouse, which are in season out in the National Forest surrounding this particular Park. The ranger, writing you the violation notice, points out the boundary signs nailed to trees, but you observe that they are widely enough spaced that they're easy to miss, and don't contain any regulations - just "NATIONAL PARK BOUNDARY."

Welcome to the complex maize of wildland regulations and designations, which you may not always be aware of, or agree with, even if you are able to keep up with them. Ignorance is no excuse they say, so you sign the ticket, but harbor resentments which may forever influence how you feel about rangers, National Parks, environmentalists, and the wildlife they are supposedly protecting. This is how psychology and sociology get mixed up with geography, ecology, topography, and inescapably – politics. So hang in there, as I try to smooth out this necessarily somewhat bumpy ski trail.

Most wildlife prefers edges, and ski trails provide them in abundance. In any forest with enough snow to allow skiing, and enough moisture to support trees, there is shelter on one side, and food or easy travel possibilities on the other. Predators and their prey, like edges for slightly different reasons, but reality for both is that the essentials of life are found where forests provide variety. Fires, floods, avalanches, wind storms, and different soil types, provide natural edges, as do the animals themselves. Ski trails often follow game trails, and this has been going on for probably at least 10,000 years, since the big glaciers retreated, and wildlife followed the plants, that followed the melting ice, and humans followed both. Skiing is at least 8000 years old, and archeological finds keep pushing that date back

Because skis are potentially faster than snowshoes, frequently used ski trails tend to be wider. Downhill ski trails are correspondingly wider than cross-country ski trails. The Sierra Club book: *Downhill Slide*, documents abuses by the corporate ski industry primarily involved with ski trails wide enough to look like clearcuts. Even clearcuts, however ugly they may look, and however badly they may deplete the soil's long term productivity, still provide edges favored by some kinds of wildlife: Elk and Moose for instance. So different kinds of edges, and different kinds of ski trails, provide for different kinds of wildlife.

Nickel Plate cross-country ski area, next to the Apex Alpine ski lift area – above Penticton, in south central British Columbia, Canada, has avoided the icy snow bomb "death cookie" problem, common to narrow ski trails, by simply opting for slightly wider ski trails. Trees, with branches hanging over narrow ski trails, intercept snow, which often hardens - with multiple freeze-thaw cycles, before it falls onto the trail. Nickel Plate's trails aren't so wide that a Lynx wouldn't cross, but they are wide enough, to allow loggers clearing the trails to make a little profit, and incidentally let in a little more sunshine. Sierra Club policy against "commercial logging on public lands" would perhaps like to prevent these sorts of ski trails, or maybe that bit of policy wasn't thought out so well. It certainly was intensely debated, and put up to a vote of their entire membership. Ski trails aren't the only problem with that policy, and it's adoption caused many of us to drop our Sierra Club memberships.

Ski trails provide access for wildlife and summer trail users. This access occurs both along the trails themselves, and through a mosaic of both natural and artificial edges. "Trails are for tourists, vee ski da voods" is a rallying call for expert skiers to quit showing off to the crowds, and seek instead a more natural and, by implication, more worthy challenge. These brave souls will cross over the ski trail's edge briefly, shorten the lift lines briefly, brag about their "off piste" adventures extensively, and probably induce others to eventually take this same bold move, briefly. These are small individual actions, but collectively they add up to more interaction with a more natural environment, and all this was made possible for this specific population, by the existence of a ski trail with edges that allowed, and maybe even encouraged this lift line reducing activity, in an area made safe for it by skillful edge design, and management. The ski school might even supply an instructor, with a colorful European accent and manner, to lead the class. These edges of "da voods" are usually the result of chainsaws, guided by ski area planners and managers, even on those narrow, natural looking, and perhaps overly shaded, cross-country trails.

When snow melts in the Spring, ski trails' edges can continue to entice off trail adventures, not in the same volume as when the lifts and/or grooming machines are facilitating access to this temptation, but still with enough to require thoughtful management of that use, by resorts that have a real bottom line stake in their off-season occupancy rates. Management of groomed ski trails is pretty obvious, but other edge management is more subtle, and it involves trails on wider playing fields.

Even edges produced by natural processes, like fire, are increasingly influenced by human activity. A century of artificial fuel build-up impacts Wilderness and roadless areas especially, because of limited edge access (both physical and political) for fuel reduction. Repeated fire disasters on the wildland/suburban interface tragically illustrate how politics alone can prevent fuel reduction. Back-to-nature sentimentality replaces common sense most frequently near the edges of Wilderness, exactly where road edge access for fire fighting equipment is most limited. Wilderness with a capitol "W," is legally roadless land, which also prohibits all wheels and motors. Foresters and wildlife managers have long recognized that wildlife seldom respects political boundaries, and that if species requiring remote habitats are to be preserved and restored, more than the Wilderness itself will have to be kept roadless and motorless. This is the buffer concept.

Political and administrative boundaries, like those around Wilderness, Parks, or ski areas, too often are drawn with insufficient regard for natural edges, and the processes creating, maintaining, or changing edges. Many boundaries were located before the current crop of wildlife legislation was enacted. Now however, endangered species may legally require the maintenance of habitat edges, that cross political and administrative boundaries. Many of these edges involve bureaucrats and resort managers who are not used to talking to each other, and because of their often divergent legal mandates, different constituencies, and ownerships, aren't necessarily inclined to initiate dialog, unless forced to by legal action.

PINE MARTEN

Meanwhile, back on the ski trail, the rules are pretty straight forward. Signs and posters advise that reckless skiers and snow boarders may loose lift privileges, but experienced skiers know that's no guarantee of safety. So skiers feeling endangered by a snowboarder or reckless skier may seek the edge of ski trails for cover too. While waiting for that "schussboomer" to go by, they may notice tracks of weasels and Martens checking discarded lunch sacks, and fast food packaging, for edibles, or for mice doing likewise. Carefully designed ski trails sometimes provide such refuge areas with easy access for less skilled skiers, and good sight distance - for when they feel brave enough to join the traffic again. A nice view is also very desirable, and maybe also a bench, picnic table, or shelter. Such trail edge amenities also shorten lift lines, decrease accidents, and supply loyal repeat customers. At their best, there are opportunities for romantic encounters "on that ski trail," which the 1950's popular song, *Canadian Sunset*, popularized.

Soft edges on ski trails are nice too, especially on the downhill side where an out of control skier is most likely to windmill into the trees. Christmas style trees, with branches all the way to the ground, make the softest edges, and incidentally the best wildlife cover.

Acrophobia is "an abnormal fear of being in high places," according to *Webster's Dictionary*. Ski patrollers usually notice that this condition is often stimulated by looking over the edge of something, like a double black diamond - experts only - ski trail or steep mountain road. Severely steep terrain's basic incompatibility with normal human security needs is probably the biggest barrier to better understanding of edge impacts in the mountains. Most people lack sufficient experience with how snow avalanches or rock slides, and alpine torrents of mud and debris flows, can obliterate or significantly change landscapes. Even the simple act of falling down a steep

58

hill, rolling with that fall and recovering safely, as smokejumpers, cowboys, and skilled skiers, do routinely, is completely foreign to most modern urbanites. How to get back up after falling down on skis is often the most challenging part of a beginning ski lesson. Fire behavior in very steep topography, with explosions uphill, or rolling fire brands - spreading fire downhill, are witnessed by few people who live to pass along their knowledge. Objective judgments about edges in steep terrain are therefore usually made on the basis of theoretical observations from consultants hired by land managing agencies, or private developers. Retired former smokejumpers or avalanche technicians often lack the urban credentials to break into the consulting game. Happily there are enough exceptions to this unfortunate situation, particularly in ski resort area planning and management, to provide a few positive examples. Unhappily, the ski industry generally has low credibility with the environmental community.

The edge of a road or trail in steep terrain, or at the edge of a cliff, is only the obvious beginning of its influence, yet boundaries of Wilderness have to fall where it is politically expedient to keep roads, ski trails, or sightseeing trams, for instance, out of lands valued more for their pristine scenic quality or wildlife. If such a boundary is drawn close enough to the unwanted feature to exclude it, then the buffer function will have to be provided by the preserve itself, thus compromising the edge of that preserve - to the extent the sights, sounds, smells, or other influences pervade their surroundings. This slightly ungainly situation is necessitated by our distrust of bureaucrats to competently administer any legally designated buffer zone. The roadless controversy of the Clinton and Bush administrations in the United States, is the quintessential example of this dilemma.

Biological corridors, linking the edge of one reserve with another, are about genetic interchange. Political resistance to this concept is the result of an underlying societal problem that effects reserves over a much wider geographic area than acrophobia does. Most of the boreal forest is after all, quite flat. Fear of death generally, and the resultant resistance to the evolutionary facts of life and death, sex, natural selection, and genetics, ranks a close second to acrophobia, even in the mountains, in obstructing public understanding of edge impacts.

Edges are basic to evolution because it is the changing of environments that selects those fittest individuals who will pass on their genes to the generations which may, or may not, succeed in new places. Global warming for instance, is driving species like Red Squirrels to evolve at an accelerated pace, as they are forced farther north, or up to higher elevations. These ecological processes effect all life: from Grizzly bears to squirrels, and on down to the micro-flora and fauna that form soil on land, and plankton in water, and are the basis of our food chains, clean air and water, and organically compatible environments that sustain us, including the aesthetics of natural landscapes.

Evolution is a long way from universal acceptance, and the Wilderness advocating left is pitted against the religious right, in an ongoing battle for political supremacy. This holy war between biologists and "wise users", Darwin and "intelligent design", has placed ski areas in the crossfire. "The Bambi Syndrome" was the title of a 1993 article in *Natural History Magazine* exploring the Freudian roots of our collective inability to recognize our own mortality and sexuality, and how "the Disney version" myths increasingly rule the political world, the way biblical myths used to (and in some cases still do, as in the George W. Bush administration) and to much the same disastrous effect. Richard Schickel's 1968 book, titled: *The Disney Version*, explores this modern mythological phenomenon in fascinating historical detail. It is recommended reading before tackling heavier later works such as Jerry Mander's *Four Arguments For The Elimination Of Television*, published in 1977, or his *In The Absence Of The Sacred – the failure of technology and the survival of Indian nations*, 1991. All three books cover the progressive alienation of our human perceptions from biological reality.

Edges are so basic to everything, from evolution to firebreaks, that they too often get overlooked in the political scuffles over ski lifts, trails, huts, Wilderness, and wildlife. Humans evolved at the forest edge. Sex and violence, those staples of our customs and superstitions (and Hollywood plot lines), almost all relate to flirting or fighting near edges. Robin Hood wisely ventured only briefly from the relative safety of Sherwood Forest.

Highly visible raw edges are usually what make many downhill ski trails and clearcuts offensive to most eyes. The biologically negative implications of these abrupt edges take second place to the emotional perception of ugliness. The Spotted Owl – clearcut showdown has hurt alpine skiing's public image particularly hard, because of its similar visual impact. Biologically most alpine ski trails are narrow enough to benefit a wide range of wildlife. They just look ugly, because they are so obviously unnatural. Ski trail planners are consequently feathering their edges more now, and even designing "gladed" ski trails, where grooming machines and skiers both, have to pay attention to the trees purposely left, or even planted in the trail itself.

Huts are relegated to the edges of Wilderness, and resisted even there, for fear that the crowds they attract will detract from "wilderness values," like solitude. Buffer and roadless, or "backcountry" legislation have been introduced, without success, in an attempt to provide a place for huts and other user friendly structures and regulations, such as allowing mountain bikes or larger group sizes. What we are left with are defacto buffers.

61

These are lands on either side of Wilderness, or other reserve, boundaries that serve to mitigate the impacts of civilization on nature, and vice versa. The best are so topographically inhospitable to roads, or snowmobiles, that they don't need Wilderness designation to stay wild. Mountain bikes, helicopter skiers, outdoor education and Girl Scouts, Boy Scouts, or horse packing groups with more than twelve sets of eyes are OK here.

Roadless areas and "late successional reserves" are second best because they exist only at the tender mercy of our political process. Still they too can be safety valves for otherwise politically explosive edge conflicts. To work, however, the bureaucrats in charge of them have to either be knowledgeable about wildlife management and forest ecology, or be willing to take advice from those that are. That potential willingness, in turn, is often dependent on how brave they are to take on appeals and lawsuits by well meaning, and sincere, but sadly ignorant environmental pressure groups.

This problem is why some retired foresters and wildlife managers, such as myself, try to stay involved with as many environmental groups as we can be effective in educating. Not all are receptive obviously, and we would be foolish to waste our time, efforts, or money, on them. Being retired helps immensely, because we are perceived as being out from under the influence of corrupt corporations and politicians. Four of the most effective and receptive organizations, at this turn of the century are: the *Rocky Mountain Elk Foundation, International Wolf Center, The Nature Conservancy,* and the *Winter Wild Lands Alliance.* Of course there are many more, but I only mention these here, because of their effectiveness at dealing specifically with edge issues.

Ski lifts become mass transit extensions of road and rail systems, increasingly used for sightseeing in summer, and therefore acting as buffers, in this case diversions - to keep people occupied outside of - the more wild territory, just beyond. Like methadone for the heroin addict, cable lifts get folks out of their cars and SUVs. They are also the most energy efficient way to move people vertically in steep mountain terrain.

Roads, especially dirt roads in steep ground, are notoriously destructive of wildlife habitat. This is a problem for aquatic and terrestrial species alike, and includes the effects of erosion, and the fragmentation of habitat. Major highways in the Canadian Rockies, and the Washington Cascades, are starting to mitigate both their edge impacts and road kill problems, with over and under passes which allow both avalanches and wildlife safe passage. These concrete structures however are extremely expensive, which is partly why there are more cable lifts in the European Alps. The other principle reason is that most of these lifts were built without American influence. Ski lifts press up against Wilderness at White Pass and Crystal Mountain in Washington State, Jackson Hole in Wyoming, Whistler-Blackcomb in British Columbia, and Banff in Alberta, just for starters.

"You have to draw the line somewhere" expresses the edge dilemma in familiar human terms, but our newly found wildlife friends, such as Spotted Owls, Grizzly Bears, Bull Trout, and Wolves, have edge requirements ski area managers, and highway engineers, are increasingly forced to become familiar with. Boundaries drawn, or roads, lifts, and trails, designed with the aid of competent biologists, are less likely to inspire future lawsuits, adverse publicity, and expensive changes later on.

Biological corridors between Wilderness areas, or other reserves, increasingly mandated as a means of facilitating genetic exchange between these extremely limited wildlife sanctuaries, will impact ski areas especially. This is where evolution comes into the edge picture, because it is an ongoing process, both itself and the public's gradual acceptance of it. Lands wild enough to serve this corridor function tend to be found along rivers and mountains, which puts cross-country trails and ski lifts, respectively, in a potentially delicate situation. The proposed Jumbo Glacier Resort, just west of Panorama Ski Resort, in southeast British Columbia, Canada, was (as of 2007) exactly in this position. The north–south wildlife corridor in the Purcell Mountains was cited, by this proposal's opponents, as being potentially blocked by a large scale ski lift resort.

Ski trails however, can actually facilitate wildlife mobility because of their extensive edges, providing that activity related to those trails is managed to insure that it is also wildlife friendly. Some such restrictions occur quite naturally, like the tendency for ski areas to limit hunting for safety and aesthetic concerns. The potential problem is much more political than biological, because of skiing's anti-environmental reputation, resulting from many past development conflicts. Robert Redford's Sundance ski lift resort in Utah for instance, has a far more wildlife friendly landscape than Park City or Vail. Jumbo Glacier's proposed resort, will likely be defeated, even though it could be a better edge caretaker than the alternatives, depending on just how each is planned.

Trail edge impacts are greatest within one day's travel from the trailhead, which is usually at the Wilderness edge. This is the range of the typical weekend overnight backpacking trip. Without huts the only feasible solution to sanitary problems is limiting use, typically with permits and reservation systems. Day hiking and skiing impacts are even greater, along the first mile of trail edge. Trailheads without sanitary facilities compound this problem. Ski areas serve as ideal trailheads in this regard, and the edges of their trails are more sanitary, and safer for, and less disturbing to, wildlife as a result. This is especially true in winter, because the fecal contents of the entire season's "cat holes," in the snow, flush out within the very short spring run off period. Third world slum conditions can take over a legally designated Wilderness all too easily, without skillful edge management. Precision edge location, together with skillful design and maintenance of edge related facilities are the best means of minimizing hassles, and actual negative impacts on wildlife. Huts or lifts, illegal in Wilderness, can be the most user friendly way to attract people away from wildlife sensitive areas. Negative impacts can then be absorbed in places legally and practically designed to take care of them. Where defacto buffers, in the form of roadless areas outside Wilderness, are lacking – the edge itself is all we have left to deal with impact. That makes it more challenging, but not hopeless, and ski areas can be ideal edge caretakers in this situation.

Snow provides a unique seasonal buffer opportunity. This happens when unplowed roads convert structures at the ends of those snowed in roads, into potential ski huts. It could be a trailhead surveillance ranger station, which incidentally is the best way to prevent "car clouting," the common criminal practice of burglarizing unattended vehicles. Or it might be a previously summer only resort, which - if guaranteed freedom from snowmobiles, could be a destination for skiers. Longer snowed in roads, too long to be attractive for skiers, are perfect for snowmobiles - or snow coaches, where snowmobiles are unacceptable, such as in Yellowstone National Park

Snowplowing money saved by not plowing such roads, could instead be spent winterizing that ranger station, campground restroom, or resort, and thus provide ideal backcountry recreation opportunities that can be managed unobtrusively to guide people where wildlife is disturbed the least, during the most critical winter survival months. Such ski hut style, that is snowed in and oversnow accessed, overnight facilities cannot do the job alone. They in turn need to be buffered from overuse, and reservation style restrictions, by adjacent country inns, hostels, ski lodges, and resorts, catering to the plowed road crowd. In other words, the recreation opportunity spectrum has to provide enough different strokes, for different folks, in all seasons now, to avoid conflicts.

Mountain Home Lodge near the resort town of Leavenworth, in the North Cascades of Washington State, provides the opportunity to witness these theories in operation. In winter their guests ride in on snowcats over a snowed in summer only road. Their terrain allows both cross-country skiers and snowmobilers to base out of the same lodge, while also accommodating snowshoers, and snowplayers – with a super long sledding and tubing hill. Spectacular scenery in an exclusively isolated setting, makes Mountain Home Lodge a showcase example of private enterprise doing it *right, on* the winter wilderness edge. The pun is intended !

Doing all this right, *right on* the edge, isn't easy, because there's too much we don't yet know about how nature's edges work. We do know that what happens along edges in winter is just as, or even more important, than in summer, because wildlife is under greater stress then. We also know that public perceptions of edge phenomena, such as evolution and fire ecology are themselves evolving at an increasing rate. "Sex and the Pope" has already been the cover story for *Newsweek Magazine*. Darwin's place in the Kansas public schools makes the national news, and the first books exploring fire ecology are out in the popular press. Previously forbidden topics, "too hot to handle," are up for discussion and debate, in an increasingly free information network.

The newly legitimate topic of most immediate concern for ski country is forest fire fuel build up. The edge of the last, and the next, forest fire will probably not coincide unless they happen to be up against a fuel break the size of an airborne powder avalanche path, major lake, or river. We know that snow, is a major factor in how fire shapes the boreal forest, and that this influence extents far beyond avalanches.

Good examples of this influence, at work through the skiing culture, are the Late Successional Reserves, set up by former president, Bill Clinton, back in the 1990's, for the Pacific Northwest National Forests. The edges of these reserves happen to butt up against, and even include ski trails, in places like the upper Methow Valley, in north central Washington State. Within these reserves the preservation, management, and restoration of old growth forest conditions for the endangered Spotted Owl, Canadian Lynx, and other wildlife, is mandated under the Endangered Species Act. Realistically this requires sophisticated fuels management to prevent unnatural catastrophic, stand replacing, fires from wiping out owl habitat especially. Backcountry skiing, ski touring, snowboarding, snowmobiling, and helicopter skiing all take place, as legitimate existing recreational uses, within these reserves. Far from being a detriment to wildlife there however, they actually hold the keys to more sophisticated management, especially near the edges.

Fuel breaks are essential near these edges, because they are the suburban/wild land interface. Homes and resorts will burn up, along with the owls' habitat, unless fuel reduction is somehow accomplished. The logical way to do this is by thinning strips of forest adjacent to lodges and homes, and up ridge lines from these valley based fuel breaks. Paying for this work requires only surmounting political obstacles, because these fuel breaks can simultaneously serve as ski trails for the slowly, but steadily expanding (Methow Valley) groomed trail system. The small trees cut, can be utilized for firewood and rustic furniture construction. The few sawlog size trees that will need removal for skier/tree collision safety, snowmobile or grooming snowcat accident prevention, can be milled onsite, and sold locally by resident, portable band-saw, mill operators.

A few (but only a few) of the ridge line fuel breaks should be groomed, mainly for efficiency – so a loop pattern can be followed, rather than having to double back on the longer trail just groomed uphill. This saves fuel, in addition to machine maintenance and labor costs. Most of the ridge line, gladed - fuel break, trails can be for ungroomed powder skiing, as is increasingly popular for both Telemark and touring skiers. Helicopter skiers already demand ungroomed snow, and the new wider skis and snowboards give them the means to fulfill their fantasies. New snowmobile designs, together with increasingly skilled riders, allow them access to the ridgelines also. Wildlife concerns however, mean that machine access to ridgelines may not always be desirable, and so fire safety will have to be weighed against the needs of Lynx, for instance.

Just to make things more interesting in a Late Successional Reserve, the Lynx happens to do best in early, rather than late successional forests. Old growth forest management may have to decide which endangered species to favor in some cases. Who makes these decisions, whether it is about Cougars and Big Horn Sheep in California's Sierra Nevada, or Spotted Owls and Lynx in the North Cascades, involves everyone from wildlife reserve managers to whoever chooses to contribute to public participation outreach programs, appeals, or law suits over decisions once made. Fuel breaks, along forest edges and ridgelines, thinned enough to stop crown fires, are also open enough to supply the early successional plant stages that favor Snowshoe Hare and therefore Lynx. Escaped fires, such as the 2003 Needles fire in the Methow headwaters, may supply plenty of early successional forest, even in "late successional reserves." The ideal

68

proportion of early and late, or intermediate successional stages can best be worked out, if wildlife managers are aware of the physical possibilities ski trails provide.

This fuel reduction at the edges of reserves is only a small start in the direction of realistic old growth and wildlife preservation and restoration. The bulk of these reserves are roadless and therefore the province of smokejumpers and helicopters. This takes us beyond the edges and into what is, and hopefully will continue to be, a middle ground between legal Wilderness and the roadside playgrounds where the majority of recreationists would rather be, if only we can somehow take advantage of the opportunities edges supply. Unless the edges of such reserves are well managed, skiers will get to ski the "big burns," and Spotted Owls will have to find new homes.

The edge examples cited so far have been from the North American Northwest, where avalanches compete with fire for the attention of wildlife biologists and most especially skiers. The boreal forests of snow country however, cover vast areas too flat to provide avalanche action. The natural edges predominating in this domain, are lakes and rivers. This is the land of cross-country skiing, snowmobiling, canoeing, motor boats, and float planes. Water is as important as snow for ski trails and wildlife here, and fire is the primary sculptor of the forest.

Chapter 4: FIRE ecology and smoke, thinning and prescribed burning, smokejumpers and roadless areas

Snow drifts lasting into summer, or even just late spring, can prevent tree growth from getting started, if those drifts persist year after year. This is exactly what happens on the lee side of ridge tops in timberline boreal forests. A long narrow meadow results, between the ridge top and the other side of where the drift peters out. Skiers take advantage of such natural ski trails, often without realizing how they are maintained. Arno and Hammerly, in their beautifully illustrated book: *Timberline*, call these alternating lines of meadows and trees – ribbon forests and snow glades. Yes, that is plural, because the dense trees resulting from their extra snowdrift melt water, form a second drift in their lee, another snow glade, and so on.

Smokejumpers are the fire personnel that typically get to deal with fires in the often remote areas where these ribbon forests occur. These are the best trained and most experienced fire technicians the boreal forest has ever seen. They not only know a lot about fires, because they get to work more of them, they also are motivated in this learning process because they get the most challenging terrain, in the most remote areas. That's why they parachute in. When it's too far to send in ground crews, for the initial attack, or even a helicopter rappelling crew cannot arrive soon enough either, then the faster, longer range, fixed wing aircraft, carry in the jumpers.

They learn fire behavior primarily as a survival and safety skill, but along the way they also learn how fire effects the forest. Forestry college student often work as smokejumpers, like I did. This allows them to experience a wide range of forest types, and to get first hand experience with the most wide ranging natural disturbance they'll probably be dealing with in their upcoming careers. Consequently they often are pretty good fire ecologists

71

already, but there is an even greater motivator for most of them: they love to jump. The sooner they can put out each fire and get back to their base, the better their chances for another jump. Their supervisors encourage this tendency because it increases their available personnel.

Natural fire breaks, such as snow glades can be used to greatly speed up the time it takes to dig a control line around a fire. Avalanche paths and rockslides work just as well, but any break in the forest canopy will do. Any line of trees in snow country can produce this same effect, and rock outcrops or changes in soil types, often do. Each tree line produces another drift and so on, until the combined effect of multiple natural snow fences dissipates, or is deflected by some other wind modifying feature in the landscape.

Snow drift patterns and their resulting forest mosaics are at least as complex as the topography they cover, and fire plus fire suppression, adds another layer of complexity. If for instance jumpers get rained on, and the boss radios that it rained even harder on other fire crews, there's no longer a rush to get back to the jump base. Should their fire still be burning there is the opportunity to apply more sophisticated fire management. This situation is a natural start, probably in unnaturally dense fuels, and has already been partially contained by the time they get word to change tactics. "The spotter thinks it's safe to let it burn out the dog hair on the east side of the lake. How's it look down on the ground? "

Fire management plans for many National Parks and Wilderness areas now call for letting fires burn more naturally, so these folks might stay with their fire, maybe get some more food dropped in, or get permission to fish in that nearby lake, since overtime is no longer needed. I quickly learned to always carry a few fish hooks and leader, when I was a jumper. A fire line might be dug on the side toward the edge of the Wilderness, but not on the part of the fire headed up to some safely remote alpine area, or out between lakes big enough to also be safe.

The Endangered Species Act resulted in Court decisions requiring maintenance of conditions, especially fire conditions, which restore the natural forest mosaics that endangered species evolved with. Fire fighters therefore often become fire managers, minimizing any adverse impacts their efforts may produce, and where feasible trying to maximize any positive effects. Such biological refinements are not always possible however, because real world restraints, such as budgets and threats to life and property, also compete for fire crew time.

Fifty plus years of smoke jumping, and other modern techniques, have built up such artificially high amounts of fuel, that minimum acreage burned is not necessarily an objective. If conditions are safe to let a fire burn, it may be desirable to use the opportunity to reduce the fuel loading, and start restoring the natural fire ecology. This will be weighed against the immediate needs on other fires, the potential for needing fast response times on anticipated fires, and the potential for threats to life and property. So the biological ideal is seldom achieved. Budgetary and political restraints intertwine as complexly as snowdrifts, terrain, and fire behavior.

Career smokejumping scientists would make the optimum fire crews, but whatever degree of scientific guidance we can get out to the fire line is an improvement. Computer software that provides ecological as well as short term fire behavior outputs is increasingly available in ever more portable hardware. The all too common misconception, that fires are not being managed beyond the reach of roads, stems from the mental disconnect that most people have with smokejumping. Jumping out of a perfectly good airplane into a burning forest is not within the cognitive reach of many folks, who are not intimately involved with forest fires.

"Let burn" fire management comes under political constraints. The term itself is a product of media hype, and persists in spite of continuing effort by fire professionals to educate reporters. Political boundaries and concerns about smoke during tourist season, or for communities near forests where elderly people, or anyone with respiratory conditions lives, are part of the decision framework. Only those fires safely surrounded by natural firebreaks, and deep inside legal Wilderness, or other reserves with documented fire management plans, can ever be allowed to "let burn," completely uncontrolled, with no personnel on site.

Usually any fire is closely monitored, at least from the air. Clouds can get in the way of safe flying however, so often it's best to have skilled observers on the ground. In Olympic National Park one summer I was hired to provide mountaineering safety advice and supervision, for a wide variety of crews, cleaning up a military aircraft crash site. When lightning started fires in the nearby timberline forests, I was in the best position to observe. This was back in the mid-1970's, so my former district ranger and the fire management officers were concerned that this old smokejumper would revert to old habits and simply put out their fires. Consequently I received repeated radio instructions to just observe and report, "we repeat, DO NOT suppress the fires Eric." They were burning in subalpine fir clumps surrounded by wet meadows, in foggy, unflyable weather conditions, so "let burn" worked well in that case, but an on-the-ground knowledgeable observer was essential.

Just one of the many lessons taught by Yellowstone's 1988 fires, was that the availability of fire personnel has to be part of the decision tree. This is especially true during "lightning busts." These highly sporadic episodes of exceptionally intense thunderstorm activity are when most natural fires get started. It's also when smokejumpers especially, but all fire crews, get stretched to their limits. Safety dictates that sleep deprivation does not become an additional hazard. Letting a few fires, inside Wilderness, burn unattended may be part of the strategy, at least until more threatening fires are controlled. However it's just as likely that a fire ideally fitting the biologists' prescription for fuel reduction, or fire dependent plant stimulation, may have to be controlled early, to free crews for more critical fires elsewhere. Fires on the edges of Wilderness areas are the toughest judgment calls, and fire managers know they're bound to get in trouble sometimes, no matter what they do. It's the kind of trouble that can cost you your job, because of the intense political pressure.

Fire budgets do best right after severe fire damage. Good fire managers, who are able to avoid disasters, (like good avalanche technicians) have to work harder to maintain adequate budgets, than their less fire savvy peers. The as yet uneducated public winds up pressuring their representatives in government about the wrong things to maintain optimum fire management. This means that those wishing to work smarter, as opposed to harder, may resort to letting PR considerations dictate some of their decisions. Monty Atwater – in his classic book: *Avalanche Hunters* – tells how, in his years as the Forest Service's first snow ranger, he needed a headline quality avalanche accident , or near miss, about every three years to keep his budget.

Smokejumpers are one of the very few wildfire programs to maintain anything like adequate training, and not surprisingly they also pioneered more ecologically aware fire management. Norman MacLean's 1993 best selling book *Young Men and Fire* is the first to introduce smokejumping to a mass audience. There have been adventure books, and memoirs of sorts, but they never caught much readership. MacLean's book put readers face to face with an out-of-control fire, as close as most are ever likely to get. It was criticized by ecologists for not taking advantage of the audience it reached to educate them more, either about fire ecology generally, or smoke jumping specifically, as it is routinely carried out. My opinion is that a book like his was a necessary first step, and that hopefully later books will catch on too, providing a more complete portrait. Even most environmentalists have not grasped the magnitude of smokejumping's ecological impact on Wilderness and roadless areas.

Margaret Fuller's 1991 book *Forest Fires*, was the first reasonably priced popular book to explore a balanced approach to fire management. Steve Arno, the coauthor of *Timberline*, cited at this chapter's beginning, has published the best book on fire so far (2007) . *Flames in Our Forest* (2002), was coauthored by Steven Allison-Bunnell, a self confessed former tree hugger. This confession introduces its readers to the first book to adequately address how environmental misconceptions have figuratively tied the hands of fire managers. Arno is a retired Forest Service Research scientist, and private forest owner and manager.

Since the publication of these two books, many excellent articles have appeared in mainstream conservation journals. Some of the best have been, and probably will continue to be, published by the Rocky Mountain Elk Foundation, in their magazine *Bugle*, and The Nature Conservancy in their magazine. Both of these organizations actually own lands on which they, like Steve Arno, actually manage fire for wildlife. They are the leaders, in fire ecology and restoration biology generally.

Better fire management generally means more open forests, more berries, more - and more varied - wildlife, and incidentally better skiing. Fire ecologists have learned not to mention the skiing benefit however, because it could severely lessen a fire management plan's chances of passing muster with environmentalists. The former fire management officer (FMO) for North Cascades National

Park told me that she'd gotten all my recommendations into the Stehekin fire plan except the one about using ski trails for thinning the forest prior to prescribed burning. Thinning – yes, skiing – no, too controversial, and we're talking cross-country skiing in the Lake Chelan *Recreation* Area, which is run by North Cascades National Park.

Stehekin is a cross-country skier's touring paradise. It could have excellent groomed trail skiing too, but for its past history of controversy. The National Park Service manages this Recreation Area, because it's adjacent to the Park, and was at one time considered for inclusion within the Park itself. Stehekin has no road access, and lies at the upper end of 55 mile long Lake Chelan, a spectacularly scenic fjord penetrating into the North Cascades' eastern flank. You get there by boat, float plane, or trails. I used to ski in during the years I was a seasonal backcountry ranger there, 1983 – 1987.

Stehekin's citizens are a very independent and unique group. They are the reason it is a *Recreation* Area, as opposed to the National Park, and they are not particularly fond of the National Park Service or the environmentalists who wanted to put them into the Park, and still force the Park Service to often manage it as if it were in the Park. Before the current fire management plan was adopted, environmentalists proposed barging fire wood up lake to Stehekin, which was a typical eastern Cascades jungle of "dog hair" Douglas fir thickets. Rather than thin this obvious fire hazard the Park had designated a fire wood clearcutting area, which didn't sit very well with anyone, except some bureaucrats, I guess. Anyway that nonsense is behind us, and the ski touring there is still great, some of the best in the northwest.

Alston Chase's best selling book *Playing God In Yellowstone – The Destruction of America's First National Park* (1986), was quite popular in Stehekin. The Park's superintendent even recommended it to the seasonal staff,

with the warning that they might not agree with everything that's in it. Chase documents both ignorant preservationists, and the bureaucrats that give in to their political pressure, with the resulting destruction. Starting with Beaver and Elk competition, and the resulting lowered water tables, Alston proceeds through forest fire fuel build-up and predator control, completing the circle back to Elk overpopulation. His closing chapters attempt to analyze how preservationists lost touch with the natural world they hoped to save.

Wolves, reintroduced in 1995, have begun to help remedy many of the problems outlined in Chase's classic critique. Many more problems remain, but it is likely that his book helped convince America that it was indeed high time that we put the Wolves back where they belonged.

The superintendent was right. We seasonals didn't agree with Chase on everything, and opinions were far from unanimous. Many summer seasonals belong to the environmental fundamentalist way of thinking that Chase so eloquently described. I thought he misrepresented the *Leopold Report*, mistakenly linking it to the then prevalent National Park policy of "natural regulation." This is a bureaucratic fantasy based on John Lennon's song: *Let It Be*. It's a relatively new offshoot of preservationism which holds that Parks, such as Yellowstone, will take care of themselves if we just "leave them alone." Another way this is sometimes stated is: "no management is good management," or alternatively: "Wilderness management is an oxymoron." Some might call this the *spiritual* side of Wilderness and wildlife, and at least a few scientists sympathize with this outlook, while also realizing that it doesn't work well in practice.

Dr. John Craighead's much more pragmatic ideas are expressed in the 1991 Yale University published book *The Greater Yellowstone Ecosystem*, edited by Kieter and Boyce. Chase, John Craighead and his twin brother Frank, together with Leopold, all agreed that hands on management is needed, if anything like natural wildlife populations are to be maintained in our overpopulated real world. The 1989 *Gordon Report*, sponsored by the National Parks and Conservation Association to update the *Leopold Report*, came to the same conclusion. The Craighead brothers spent most of their lives studying the Yellowstone ecosystem. Dr. Frank Craighead's earlier book: *Track of the Grizzly* documents their pioneering bear research, and the Park's attempt to suppress it. His final Chapter - in the book, #11: Bureaucracy and the Bear is a classic account of tax dollars in action. Restoration of wildlife diversity subsequent to the reintroduction wolves in 1995, has verified the conclusions of all four studies.

Yellowstone's and North Cascades' problems are just two samples of similar situations throughout North America, and I suspect other countries with boreal forests, judging by what I read in journals like *International Wolf*. The key point for skiers to take from this is that healthy, wildlife supporting and good natural skiing providing, boreal forests evolved with, and depend on fire. "Leave it alone" mythology persists into the 2000's in spite of all this, and has inspired a 2005 book *Gardeners of Eden* by Dan Dagget. In it he focuses entirely on this difficult social/ecological problem, which is much broader than fire ecology, and interacts with all aspects of wildlife management. Readers interested in pursuing the ideas I've applied here in snow country, to warmer regions, couldn't do better than to start with *Gardeners of Eden*.

Pacific Northwest concerns in this regard are examined in *Keeping It Living: Traditions of Plant Use and Cultivation on the Northwest Coast of North America*. This 2005 book, edited by Douglas Deur and Nancy J. Turner, refutes the Eurocentric ideas about both fire and other aspects of vegetation management. It calls into question the popular industrial age concept of "natural landscapes," and opens the way for wilderness (gasp!) management.

Obviously this bears on credibility, and is explored further in chapter 9. Dagget, Deur, and Turner are not the only voices in the wilderness, as the books Arno has coauthored strongly suggest. *1491: New Revelations of the Americas Before Columbus* by Charles Mann looks at fire from a prehistorical perspective. Why Native American ecological influences and their coevolution with wildlife have been suppressed is explored by Alston Chase, with historical references to the American National Parks.

Ski trails themselves, as fuel breaks and access for thinning the forest, together with the desire of ecologically sophisticated skiers for more open forests, are the principal physical impacts of skiing on wildlife. This is true for both alpine and cross-country skiing, and it is overwhelmingly positive. Ski resorts, and adjacent residential areas, can have either positive or negative physical effects, depending on how they are planned and managed. Fuel reduction around structures, and wetland retention, are usually the key points to watch for.

Far greater than either of these factors however, is the ability of skiing, and all snow sports, together with their resorts, to expose their urban and sun-belt clientele to the winter half of the life support system. Skiing is an all consuming and total immersion experience, where the overpowering sensations of flight capture the soul. It consecrates much of snow country into holy ground, psychologically on par with Wilderness. So far so good, but unfortunately many ski areas are adjacent to Wilderness and roadless areas, and not all skiers are familiar with fire ecology. Worse yet nonskiers often know even less about it. The stage is therefore set for the legal equivalent of religious warfare, when new ski resorts are proposed, or old ones seek to expand. The issue of air quality, born of urban smog, has come to be almost as volatile as lifts, and tends to center around them.

This holy war mentality, as exemplified by the arson attack at Vail, Colorado, although usually started with existing lifts, or a lift proposal, persists even when there are no longer any ski lifts involved, as demonstrated at Early Winters. Smoke may turn out to be a 21 st century surrogate for ski lifts, since lift skiing itself is often no longer, or maybe never was, an issue for a specific site. Stehekin is an example of the latter, and smoke is often the primary stumbling block in the way of realistic fire management for restoration ecology, in either case. Ski areas just happen to be where the forest meets the largest concentrations of people, their potential for air pollution, and highly valuable infrastructure.

Woodsmoke, pronounced as I've spelled it, as a single word, has obviously been around for a while. Some old timers still prefer it, to what comes out of the tailpipes of all those SUVS. Smog from overdeveloped ski areas, such as California's Lake Tahoe or Colorado's Vail, often gets physically mixed up with, and politically confused with, woodsmoke. Wood stoves are easier to restrict than tailpipes, and so the resulting inability to burn the forest fuels as firewood often compounds the already dangerous fuel build-ups. The "stoves only" wilderness management policies also further confuse the urban mind. Even if our past century of artificial fuel build-up hadn't occurred, there would still be smoke over the boreal forest. There just wouldn't be as much.

The campfires of native americans helped reduce the chance of unwanted fires, by stripping the ladder fuels from the lower parts of trees. Backcountry campfires still serve this function where they are allowed. Bureaucratic simple mindedness has extended the "stoves only" policy, which is valid in heavily used timberline areas, to thickly wooded forests, and brainwashed a whole generation of urban backpackers into thinking fuel choked tinderbox forests are the "natural" ideal. This misconception still survives, as a corollary to the "leave it alone" dogma, in spite of all the articles in main stream environmental magazines, and many books dealing specifically with the widespread use of fire as a management tool by native Americans, such as *Fire Native Peoples and The Natural Landscape*, edited by Thomas Vale, 2002.

Logging is usually cited by political conservatives as the logical alternative to smoke, and the European Alps demonstrate that it is a possible solution. Cable systems there haul logs as well as skiers, and some of the best managed forests can be found in Switzerland. Wild fires are not a problem there, because they have managed their forests with adequate fuel breaks. They have also obviously abused and eliminated forests from much of the alpine landscape. Monocultured forest plantations have taught the Swiss, and should teach Americans, that there are better ways to manage forests.

Wildlife survives in the Alps, but hunting and fishing opportunities are far fewer than in North America, and wilderness doesn't exist. We can't have it both ways. Either we domesticate our forests entirely and sacrifice most of the wildlife we traditionally have enjoyed, or we put up with some smoke. Overpopulation dictates at least some of the former, but wildlife and wilderness will also have strong political backing for the foreseeable future.

Smoke can be, and is being, managed with ever increasing sophistication. I burn my thinning slash during the spring and fall, never on weekends or holidays, and ideally on foggy snowstorm days with enough wind to dissipate the smoke. Some of my neighbors use chippers, instead of burning. The United States Forest Service, which surrounds the thin sliver of private land where I live, manages their smoke much the same way I do, only they are constrained by bureaucratic formalities, and trying to maximize the areas burned, with still inadequate budgets, for both proactive fuel reduction and recreation.

They have done almost no burning in my immediate neighborhood for two reasons. The first is the Late Successional Reserve which means potential appeals and lawsuits from environmentalists, that they have no legal budget to deal with. The second is that I live right next to ground zero for the Early Winters saga, making the likelihood of legal challenges, to whatever they might propose, almost a certainty.

What makes this incendiary puzzle of smoke, old growth, Spotted Owls, ski trails, and Lynx, into the political impasse known as "analysis paralysis"? Other Forests have other mixes, of wildlife and fire ecology, but for mountainous regions of the boreal forest the most potent element is the ski lift. Just the suggestion of ski lifts is all it takes.

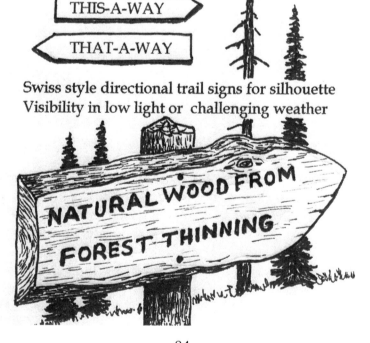

THIS-A-WAY

THAT-A-WAY

Swiss style directional trail signs for silhouette Visibility in low light or challenging weather

NATURAL WOOD FROM FOREST THINNING

Chapter 5: LIFTS attracting impact, real estate, corporate developers, legal intrigue, and precedents

Ski lifts are often cited as the destroyers of pristine alpine areas. They are claimed to be as destructive as logging, over grazing, or forest fires. This "conventional (environmental) wisdom" is just as simple minded and erroneous as those myths about forestry and cows. Thinning and selective cutting, producing wood products certified to be harvested from sustainably managed forests, have begun to dispel the first myth. Dan Dagget's book: *Beyond Rangeland Conflict – Toward a West that Works*, has barely made a dent in the second. Still, it's into its fourth printing, and his second book: *Gardener's of Eden*, (2005) promises to appeal to broader audiences than the ranchers he wrote for in the first. Finally, and at long last, accepted by informed environmentalists is the truth about Smokey the Bear. Fire was, and still is, a hard one to sell, but it looks like we've at least reached a tipping point in public opinion there. Lifts will be just as challenging for many of the same reasons forestry, grazing, and fire were.

What Enron did to accounting, and clearcutting to forestry, overgrazing still does to ranching. Ugly ski areas do the same for ski lifts. It wasn't just long lift lines, or escalating lift ticket prices, painfully uncomfortable boots, out of control – foul mouthed snowboarders, or greasy plastic food service. It was the all of the above, plus employee ghettos and the litany of abuses Hal Clifford details in *Downhill Slide*. The point is that it doesn't have to be that way now, anymore than forestry still has to be destructive clearcutting.

Directing impact from skiers is easy, when they are attracted to groomed trails and lifts. American teenagers especially gravitate toward lifts, while their elders often prefer quieter snow sports. "The family that skis together, fights together." is an old ski patrol saying, which cautions watchfulness toward any group of two or more with evidence of emotional ties. Sometimes I felt like a marriage counselor back when I was a professional ski patroller. Cross-country trails near lifts do well, because they allow family members to pursue individual interests, and still regroup easily afterwards. Lift areas that encourage a variety of nordic and "off piste" sliding activity, even off snow activities, also enjoy steadier cash flow and fewer backside search and rescue missions.

Decreasing demand for lifts in the 1980's and '90's made litigation against lift proposals an intolerable additional development expense. New lift areas in the United States were stopped for 22 years, until 2004 when Tamarack started up in central Idaho. Vail and Mammoth, the two giants in the U.S., survived only after restructuring under Chapter 11. Norway's largest lift complex, at Voss – east of Bergen, had to be taken over by the town at its base. Oppdal Norway had to convert chair lifts to surface lifts. Mount Ashland, in southern Oregon, was also purchased by the town of Ashland, to keep their economic generator going. Little Loup Loup, between the Okanogan and Methow Valleys in Washington State had to be bought out by a non-profit institute, to keep its two lifts operating. Only central Europe and Canada seem to be able to consistently support lifts, and it is European vacation patronage of, and immigration to, Canada's ideal snow and terrain that has helped lifts do better there, than down in the States.

The style of lift development, or lack of it, seems to be critical. Big resorts generally do better than the little ones. Liftless areas, like the Methow, are increasingly successful, but some nordic areas are using lifts to help disperse crowds, as well as to teach Telemarking. High speed detachable lifts were especially good at drawing business in the 1990's. Success or failure financially, and impact on

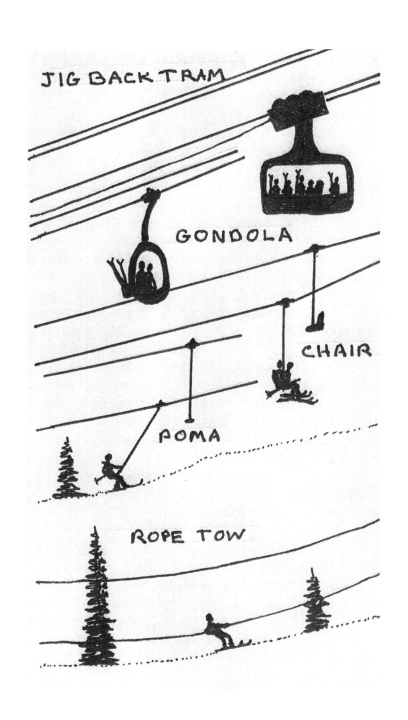

JIG BACK TRAM

GONDOLA

CHAIR

POMA

ROPE TOW

the surrounding wild lands, is critically determined by lift type and layout, together with the ski trails they service.

Rope tows were the first lifts invented. They survive only in a few areas now, because of the extremely limited terrain they can service and the inordinate hand grip strength needed by their patrons. Surface lifts of all sorts share the rope tow's terrain handicap, but given the appropriate slopes – are the most efficient, because snow bears the skiers' weight, instead of a sagging cable bumping over sheave wheels at every lift tower. The *Poma,* surface lift, is a detachable - which allows higher line speeds. It has been the most successful, with lengths up to a mile, and the capability of accommodating angles in the tower line. Surface lifts require maintenance of the up-ski track, adjustment of the cable height - if snow becomes too deep, and they inhibit, or prevent, skiers from crossing the up-ski track.

Aerial cableways, or so called "tramways" in the engineering jargon, eliminate these three labor intensive drawbacks. Chairlifts are the industry standard, and are preferred, especially by Americans. Double chairs were most common initially, but the trend has been to replace them with triples and quads, or even six seaters, for higher capacity and operating efficiency. Fixed grip chairs were the older design. They space carriers evenly all along the cable loop, so that loading speed and line speed are identical.

Detachable chairs load slowly, on a separate track, then reattach to the main cable. They travel at speeds typically twice as fast as fixed grip chairs. Enclosed gondola carriers can be put on the same line, as can semi-enclosed "bubble" chairs, which allow loading with skis on the feet. Nordic skiers, snowboarders, and sightseers can all use detachables with much less anxiety than fixed grips. Summer use too, especially mountain biking, works better with detachables.

BUBBLE CHAIRS

Trail capacities need to be over twice that for fixed grips, and this restricts some terrain to lifts with less capacity. This together with customer preference for the slower, more user friendly, loading and unloading speeds of detachables, led to invention of the light detachable. These can use lighter tower configurations, and put fewer carriers out on the cable, at greater spacing. This convenience of high speed and easy loading, and then unloading onto less crowded trails, might seem the best of both worlds until economics figures in. Top and bottom, acceleration and deceleration equipment is complex and expensive, and this combined with fewer ticket sales, pushes the industry toward the crowded assembly line ambiance that skiers are increasingly voting against with their feet. A few areas are retaining their old fixed grip chairs as a result, and light detachables may have a higher ticket price.

Skiers tire more quickly on detachables. Bars do more, and earlier, afternoon business, and so does the ski patrol. Single ride, half day, or their modern computerized equivalents are replacing the all day ticket.

Gondolas are sometimes confused with jigback trams, because the term "tramway" is also applied to gondolas and even chairlifts. Jigbacks have just two large carriers, in which the passengers stand. These two carriers are counter balanced against each other, so that one is going up, as the other is going down – passing each other in the middle. Jigbacks and gondolas are both totally enclosed which makes them more suitable for long cable spans, high above the snow. Spectacular accidents have damaged the reputation of such high configurations, like the Italian tragedy when a low flying jet fighter plane cut the cable. Any aerial cable way shares this vulnerability to falling accidents, and ski patrols have to train for evacuating passengers with ropes, in the event of mechanical failure. Such evacuations however, have become increasingly rare as both lift manufacturers and ski area management have matured to become a highly professional industry.

Helicopters are big business only in British Columbia, Canada. Elsewhere they are frosting on the ski cake, restricted by price and environmental concerns. National Parks that allow even a little flight-seeing face increasing complaints about noise, and legal Wilderness areas prohibit any type of aircraft below minimum altitudes. Anywhere that self propelled backcountry skiers become more numerous than heli-skiers, the majority seems to rule. Utah's Wasatch Mountains have already restricted heli-skiing, and legal challenges elsewhere have been attempted by an increasingly vocal opposition. Oppdal in Norway, lost their helicopter in the 1980's, and France outlawed heli-skiing about the same time. Ironically there is actually little impact on wildlife. Heli-ski operators can't afford the expensive air time it would take to harass wildlife the way mass audience T.V. filmmakers do. The deep snow demanded by heli-skiing is incompatible with almost all large animals.

Mountain Caribou in British Columbia are the only possible exception to this, but even here it is the clearcuts sometimes used as bottom landings, not the helicopters, that are the real problem. Away from clearcuts, trees are cut for bottom landings, on only a very few of the majority of heli-ski landings. Such clearings take very little space, and usually avalanches do all the clearing required.

One time our fuel truck had a mechanical problem, which delayed the helicopter's return flight, so we guides pulled our folding saws out and trimmed some small trees. Our clients helped too, tossing the cuttings far enough away so as not to get caught up in rotor turbulence and be a safety hazard. It kept us warm while we waited, and it made the bottom landing more obvious, from the air, amidst the scruffy, beat up, little trees at the bottom of the avalanche. Keeping warm turned out to be the most lasting benefit however, because the next week's storm, and resulting avalanche, swept all our hard work away, and allowed the helicopter an even bigger bottom landing.

The only lasting impact of heli-skiing is the huts made possible by aerial access, and they warrant a chapter all their own. Landing stakes, stuck in the snow to guide pilots in poor light and/or blowing snow conditions, melt out in the spring and summer, and are typically retrieved by guides and clients for reuse. Revisiting the sites of winter adventures, with flowers all about, is a pleasant summer pastime, which also helps keep your legs in shape for the next winter. So when you see hikers headed down the trail with wistful smiles and peculiar looking stakes sticking out of their packs, that's what's going on.

Snowcats are subject to all the restrictions of helicopters except weather. Terrain is their biggest limitation, and it confines them to mountains they can climb up, which still provide steep enough terrain for enjoyable powder skiing. Although such situations are extremely rare, when they do occur, they can be very successful. Recent technical innovations for less noisy operation, and less toxic emissions, promise to insure a continuing place for this kind of lift. Even cross-country skiers, not requiring any vertical lift, can use "snow coaches" to replace even more obnoxious snowmobiles, in places like Yellowstone.

Snow cats can roll off the sides of steep roadways, although such accidents are extremely rare. It's more likely for them to simply slide off, without tipping over, but at least they can't fall out of the sky, or off the cable. If manufacturers are able to make further improvements, this may be the ski lift of the future. Even global warming which is forcing European areas to extend their cable lifts to higher elevations, at great expense, doesn't hurt snow cat operations nearly as much. Like the helicopters, they can simply move to wherever the snow survives.

Well designed lifts of whatever type, on the right terrain, with attractive base facilities, have the potential to provide relief for overcrowded wilderness. Done wrong however they also have the potential to overcrowd both the ski trails they serve directly and the surrounding backcountry. Groomed cross-country trails adjacent to lifts serve as refuges for skiers tired of the downhill scene. They also act as filters through which more backcountry oriented skiers may find enough solace, so that they don't need a wilderness fix.

Cable lifts are the most capitol intensive focus for impact , because they are the hardest of all ski facilities to get past environmental laws and aesthetic opposition. They are the hardest to stay in business with, once built, and the hardest to move, or sell, if things don't work out. Summer business is an increasing factor for both economic survival and impact on wildlife. Certain trails off the lifts may have to be closed to mountain bikes or hiking, if Grizzlies are in the area, for instance. Deer drop their fawns typically in June, and the edge habitat supplied by ski trails is often ideal for them, if they're not disturbed. Summer trail traffic is substantially less than in winter, so these wildlife closures still leave plenty of trails for whatever summer use a resort is able to attract. Typically summer activity is oriented more towards water, even in the mountains. This leaves more than enough options for lift maintenance, and wildlife, closures.

Net energy costs per persons transported vertically, in steep mountains are less with cable lifts, in the long run, than any other means. The greater the vertical difference in elevation, the greater the savings. Snow removal costs, alone, on the alternative road way, and parking lots at the top, account for much of this. Greater efficiency, with less traffic, pavement, road kills, and habitat destruction, however, should be all too obvious. Automobile oriented Americans, used to deep snow in their ski area parking lots, at first ridiculed Whistler-Blackcomb's soggy base area snow, caused by their low elevation. By the turn of the century however, its obvious success dramatically demonstrated that lifts serving the (then) tallest vertical in North America are good for more than just the rare occasions when the skiing is good from top to bottom.

If National Parks in the United States had incentives to save, rather than waste taxpayer's money, plowed roads in Sequoia, Yosemite, Lassen, Crater Lake, Rainier, and Olympic, would be replaced with lifts or oversnow shuttle buses - "snow coaches," Yellowstone style. Mount Shasta is a National Forest ski touring area that could also use its snow plowing money to provide a more wildlife and skier friendly environment. The new political acceptability established for these "snow coaches" by the snowmobile controversy in Yellowstone, may turn out to have been its most significant blessing, in the long run. Meanwhile in Canada, lifts for their National Parks bear less political baggage, and have allowed resorts like Sunshine and Lake Louise, near Banff, to provide a much nicer experience than could have been done with roads alone.

Over-snow shuttle buses may prove most useful as the political ice breaker, pun intended, to show how much quieter and user friendly it is - to not plow roads. Then maybe the conceptual leap for environmentalists to accept aerial cable ski lifts will be possible. The mobility and versatility of the snowcat is its greatest asset, either as a forerunner to cable lifts, or as a supplement to them, or to a helicopter - when it can't fly because of weather. They can haul freight for hut skiers, while simultaneously grooming their ski trails, and hauling passengers.

If enough snowcat operations can be scattered about a region's snowed in roads, they may prove more desirable for many situations than aerial lifts, even in the long term. The key factor is how concentrated the use either already is, or is anticipated - or is desired, to be. Proactive planning is still a possibility for a few areas. An established use however, like say Badger Pass ski lift area in Yosemite National Park, California, has too many skiers to service with snow coaches from down below at Chinkapin. It would take too big a fleet, making too much noise, guzzling too much fuel, and polluting too much air; almost as bad as the cars, busses, and snowplows. The only alternatives in a fuel scarce future are either phasing out some (or all?!) of the existing lifts, or run a gondola up from Chinkapin. Every area's terrain, market, politics, and biological needs are unique. Aerial lifts are simply the most efficient and most visible people movers. They aren't necessarily the best for every situation, and the growing popularity of cross-country skiing, together with the cultural incentives to produce more fuel efficient vehicles, of all sorts, are the trends to watch.

Different kinds of lifts attract and hold different kinds of people. Nature preserves in Japan, Australia, and the Caribbean, use cable lifts to let visitors enjoy jungle wildlife without being able to feed it, be eaten by it, or otherwise interact in negative ways. High speed lifts attract high speed skiers, and snowboarders. Old slow double chairs, or surface lifts, cater to more laid back sliders. Fall line lifts attract the tower line show-offs, bombing down recklessly to impress their captive audience. Tower pads are standard in America. Lifts off the fall line, enough to make following their tower line into a tedious traverse, will allow more wildlife viewing opportunities. The carnival ride quality to any aerial lift attracts more and different people than liftless resort areas, such as the Methow. Double chairs are more romantic than triples and quads, or six packs.

As nordic skiing and the fuel problem grow together, the challenge may be to transport cross-country skiers on lift systems that are designed very deliberately to be as unattractive to alpine skiers and snowboarders as possible.

Certainly the worst fears of the industry came true when the romantic double chairs were replaced with quads. Talking to a ski school director, my age in Switzerland, about changes in our profession with the change in lifts and clientele they attract, he quietly broke into tears. Could the return of the double chair bring back the "good old days"?

Recycling old double chairs to areas that purposely run them slowly for easy loading of cross-country skiers and sightseers, makes sense from a conservation viewpoint. Off fall line tower placements also makes them easier to blend unobtrusively into the landscape. Ski trails then cross at an angle sharp enough to not tempt the tower line exhibitionists, and the trees thinned down gladed trails break up the necessarily straight tower line. Ski trails for this concept would also have to traverse off the top, before the fall line sections could be accessed. This would force a slower pace for all, and restrict snowboarders to the few trails remaining closer to the fall line.

Telemarkers and ski tourers could be sorted out by still longer traverses, which incidentally would reward them with correspondingly longer fall line trail segments, once they had "earned their turns," and coincidentally shortened the lift lines. And yes, also saved the ski lift owners something on their electric bill. Freedom from snowboarders, without resorting to outright prohibition, gets back to the carrot, versus stick approach; inspiration instead of regulation.

Lifts are development generators for real estate, and have attracted distant corporations into the ski business. Hal Clifford's *Downhill Slide* paints us a grim picture of the results. Maybe that was partly what brought tears to the Swiss ski school director's eyes. Switzerland and Austria have lots of lift areas that prove it doesn't have to be that way. Robert Redford's Sundance and Nancy Greene's Sun Peaks are leading the way toward more aesthetic developments in North America. Even Vail is remodeling their base areas to bring them back to human scale and Whistler village brags about their pedestrian core. It's definitely a significant, and long overdue, trend.

Ski Area Management Magazine discusses the details of these cultural shifts, and is required reading even for those of us in the cross-country end of the ski business. There really isn't that much difference in the two branches. We both deal with giving people the opportunity for fun in the snow. Some people are just more interested in people things, while others prefer nature, and most like a little of both. The name of the game, in either extreme, is still taking care of people. Wildlife has no chance if we don't first take care of that. This is a lesson that applies to all conservation efforts. Popular political support is essential.

The legal intrigues and precedents swirling around skiing primarily involve lifts, either actual or proposed. The most famous of these, at least among students of environmental law, is Mineral King. I earned the wrath of many downhill skiers with my 1978 editorial in *Powder Magazine* which explained that avalanches were the reason Disney's proposed lift resort was as much a fantasy as Mickey Mouse. The intrigue there was that Mineral King had become bigger than its physical reality. Like Mickey himself, Mineral King had, and for some people still has, a spiritual life as a martyr to environmentalism, who's memory will never die. Conversely, it established the precedent for the right of natural objects to have standing before the law, as do corporations and ships at sea. Two books deal specifically with Mineral King: John Harper's *Mineral King – Public Concern With Government Policy*, with the site specific historical record, but much less notoriety than the second.

Christopher Stone's book : *Should Trees Have Standing*, examined the dissenting opinion of Supreme Court Justice William O. Douglas, that has become as much a classic, in its own realm, as Stanley Kubrick's use of the Mickey Mouse anthem as a requiem for the ending to his Vietnam War film: *Full Metal Jacket*. With it, Kubrick mourned both the deaths of soldiers and civilians, and the death of establishment ideas about America's role in the world. The Mickey Mouse song could just as well have been the requiem for the dreams of downhill skiing that died as a result of America's inability to comprehend nature in winter, avalanches in this case.

Early Winters also made it to the Supreme Court, with a proposed lift development. Its controversy extends, at this 2007 writing, into the neoconservative saga of George W. Bush and his attempts to overturn much of the environmental laws and precedents of the previous four decades, including Mineral King. Like former Secretary of the Interior James Watt, and his obedient president: Hollywood's Ronald Reagan, George Bush's embarrassing incompetence has only stiffened the resolve of nordic skiers who migrated to the Methow, knowing it was finally, after 30 some years of bitter litigation, safe from lifts - and all that used to come with them. Ski lifts, in effect - ironically and indirectly, may have saved the Methow from over development. But there's much more to skiing than lifts, and as nordic skiing matures, lifts may no longer be the critical catalyst they were, once upon a time, but not so long ago. Ski trails however show no such signs of impending obsolescence.

Chapter 6: TRAILS - design and maintenance as zoning tools, versus "police state wilderness"

Big game trails were improved first, and are hard to distinguish from the engineered versions in many landscapes. Elk trails in Olympic National Park can be pounded into the soil by the passing of just one herd, going around one timber blow-down. Olympic is famous for its record size big trees, so such Elk detours can wind up far enough away from the original trail to make things confusing for hikers. Skiers following Elk trails may have no more impact than busting off a few tree limbs, to allow passage over deep snow. I look for those high broken branch ends when the avalanche path or fire scar, I've just skied down, ends in heavy forest. That just may be the best way out. It may also be where the antlers of some monster size bull Elk or Moose broke off the branches to break me a ski trail, to another opening in the forest

Native American moccasin traffic, on trade routes, pounded in well established treads going to many of the same places we go today. These trails were thousands of years old before the relatively recent European invasions. Most of their trails however, were exactly the same ones the big game animals made, because their interest was focused on the animals for meat.

Horse trails came next, but they weren't engineered, in the way we think of it today, until European settlers caught up with Coronado's accidental gift to the Native Americans. Mustangs made trails too, on their own, but not many up in snow country forests. High country Native American horse trails roughly followed the same old trade routes, over the high mountain passes. Horses do better on gentler, more consistent trail grades however, so their trails started to resemble our present day switchbacked serpentines. Trail grades obviously weren't laid out with survey instruments, as was the officially anal

U.S. Forest Service custom, but the easiest routes were found nevertheless. Lacking saws these early riders went around blow-downs, much as the Elk do, only they knew that fire could open the forest for easier travel by horse or foot. Consequently these sorts of detours were not as common as you might guess, and fire - we are now finally documenting - was used much more commonly, and at higher elevations, than previously assumed. Fire also improved grass, which they used on site, instead of bailing it, and hauling it around in trucks.

Horse trails and ski touring through ungroomed snow go together nicely, because they require similar brushing clearance and turning radius lengths, on the switchbacks. Later Forest Service horse trails to fire lookouts, or mining trails, often had uniform grades ideal for skiing up with climbing wax, in the old traditional Scandinavian style. Switchbacks wide enough for pack trains even allow good skiers to navigate them without having to stop for kick turns, when descending.

Seasonally integrated trails, managed for minimum impact, allow wildlife and their habitats to adjust, as vegetation, shelter, and reproductive needs change. A trail which allows troops of whooping, yee-hawing skiers, or stinky roaring snowmobiles, through a previously quiet winter woods, may not be optimum for wildlife. If however, such impacts are concentrated away from critical wintering areas, by both the trail design and seasonal closures, combined with corresponding winter trail grooming, parking, shelters, sanitation, and signage, we have the potential for obtaining more political support for wildlife. If wildlife viewing opportunities can also be provided, along with adequate interpretive information to explain the necessity for seasonal closures, so much the better. Winter is only the most likely seasonal closure time. Spring usually comes second, with fawns and bears needing some extra privacy. Revegetation projects on previously abused areas may involve summer and fall too.

Many cross-country ski trails follow snowed in, or abandoned, logging roads. There are usually plenty of them near where lodges are gearing up for this, gradually but increasingly popular, sport. Old logging roads also often have the more consistent and gentler grades that appeal to nordic skiers, and they are wide enough to accommodate the two track grooming equipment demanded by skating skiers. Snowmobiles can groom narrower trails, but these trails can be harder to ski, so most cross-country resorts keep at least one two-track snowcat around to groom with. Snowmobiles work out best for touch up grooming between major storms, to save gas and maintenance time.

Logging roads are a mixed blessing, because their grades are often *too* consistent for enjoyable skiing. This can be both boring, on the climb up, and too fast for comfort, on the way down. The ideal nordic ski trail has variety built in, with the ascents in long steps to get the pulse rate back down periodically, and on the descents offering something besides the necessity to hold a snowplow for long stretches. Skid trails usually found adjacent to logging roads lend themselves nicely to provide this kind of relief. They also often facilitate loop connections.

Skiers far from nordic ski areas sometimes join snowmobile clubs for the privilege of skiing trails groomed for, as well as by, machines. Snowmobile trails are also groomed with two-track cats equipped with attachments to smooth out the washboard created by heavy traffic. The wider machines are needed for efficiency at grooming a user friendly surface. Following the track of one snowmobile, in deep snow, with another snowmobile is not easy, and can be extremely frustrating. The old track "age hardens," typically in only 20 minutes, like any disturbed snow. The adjacent undisturbed snow tends to become steadily softer under most winter weather conditions. Consequently any snowmobile attempting to follow, hours or days later, usually gets stuck repeatedly – and its driver learns that it's easier to make a fresh track.

Skiers often experience the same problem attempting to balance on a narrow "platform" of age hardened snow. If you've ever had to get a snowmobile unstuck repeatedly, you understand why most nordic ski trails follow old logging roads and skid trails, and why two-track snowcats are used to groom ski and snowmobile trails. The groomed surface is similar enough in both cases that skiers looking for more distance or fresh scenery, will use snowmobile trails after they have been freshly groomed. Sometimes a friendly sled jockey will stop and offer you a ride, or a tow, to the top. Be advised that thermal conditions in such circumstances can be dangerous to the skier's health, because of the wind chill experienced wearing only light cross-country clothing. I've had to pull my stocking cap down over my face to avoid frostbite, on such occasions.

Alpine ski trails are usually dozens, or even hundreds, of feet wide. This creates a very different forest habitat from a nordic ski area's trails. The feathered trail edges increasingly favored to avoid that "clearcut look," also provide a buffer zone for skiers in trouble. There are more places to stop and adjust bindings, goggles, or clothing, or get out of the way of faster skiers. Natural forest openings from blowdowns, fire, or avalanche, often can supply the soft trail edges that otherwise would take many years to grow. Coniferous trees exposed to full sunlight in such openings keep their branches all the way down to ground level, like Christmas trees. Once assured of continued full sunlight by a ski trail, these soft trees will maintain there branches rather than self pruning as they would if the forest canopy is allowed to close in. Bare tree trunks, exposed when a closed canopy is clearcut, are an invitation to injuries on either alpine, or the downhill portions of nordic, ski trails. Skating on nordic trails has increased this trail design and maintenance consideration because of the greater speeds involved, even on the flats.

A careless or sleepy snowcat grooming driver, or logging contractor, can tear off many years growth of this natural trail edge padding. Sidehill situations are the most prone to these equipment damage problems, but every trail layout and forest condition is unique. Terrain, trees, wind, sun, and snow work together in a complex mix that requires years of professional forestry training, together with local trail maintenance experience, to understand fully. The forestry challenge is to not just create trails, but to create them in ways that allow their economically efficient maintenance over the long term as the forest inevitably grows and changes from a variety of influences.

A tree hit by enough skiers, or grooming implements, to put a cluster of colored pins on the ski patrol's trail map, probably will not survive next summer's chain saw work. Steel edged skis can add their cuts to young trees, and the cumulative effects of all this tend to widen trails, some times beyond what may be ideal for shade, wind protection, wildlife, and aesthetics. As Telemarking and skating increase in popularity these considerations will increasingly apply to all ski trails.

Nordic ski trails must also consider how the forest will burn. Narrow trails, widely spaced, are far less effective firebreaks than wide and clustered alpine trails. The nordic ski area operator who doesn't want a crown fire to destroy the shade and snow fence provide by trees, had better give fuel reduction some serious thought. Tossing the trees and branches cut, off to the trail edge, can make nice temporary wildlife cover, but is not usually a good long term solution. Stacking firewood beside the trail for fall pick up by either truck or snowcat is better, while branches may have to be either piled and burned or chipped and spread along the trail surface. Labor costs can be clustered conveniently this way too because mowing is also a fall requirement at most nordic areas. If some of this work is done with a snowcat, there is the advantage of packing the early preseason snow into a firm base, and being able to discover and fix potentially hazardous trail obstacles. Spring is usually the best time to drag logs out of the woods alongside trails, because the deeper, more consolidated, snow minimizes soil disturbance. Ideally such logging opens up the forest on either side of the trail enough to stop a crown fire.

Sunshine, vista clearing, and wildlife viewing are just a start at guest pleasing trail details. Native plants will probably be favored by broadcast burning, as opposed to the piles of slash burned or chipped, usually required for fire safety after the initial trail cut. Wildlife and flowers for summer trail users may also require sophisticated grazing management of whatever livestock is in your area. The state Game Department may be able to modify hunting seasons, bag limits, and other details effecting the resort's bottom line. In turn they may be appreciative of the intimate local knowledge, of both flora and fauna, obtained by the process of caring for trails and the guests who use them. Coordinating all this often requires the services of a good forester. If he or she is really good, they'll also be able to accomplish all these aesthetic guest pleasers, while simultaneously returning some profit directly from the timber removed initially, and the subsequent and ongoing thinning required to maintain optimum trail conditions.

Hunting survives as a destination sport in a few areas, which may influence how trails and their adjacent forests are managed. Upland birds or big game animals all have different habitat requirements. Most lodge operators however are finding that catering to hunters drives away the more lucrative bird watching, new age, customers. In some cases a judge's decision in an endangered species legal action will leave little choice as to how the forest is managed. The Spotted Owl is only our most famous of these situations. Bull trout and Salmon have frustrated trail expansion efforts in the Methow, for instance, even though the trails proposed would actually improve wildlife conditions. Convincing a judge, an advocacy group, or a young bureaucratic biologist, with limited forestry training or experience, can be a daunting task. It can even help motivate old timers to write books.

National Park or Forest areas subject to irrational and ignorant political pressure may be forced to gear some or all of their trail design and maintenance to PR considerations. Stehekin in the North Cascades is the prime example of this. Off season fuel reduction has obvious advantages in these cases. Over-the-snow logging also can be easier on the budget, do less soil disturbance, keep key personnel on the pay role during the otherwise slow spring season, while simultaneously sparing those sensitive urban eyes and ears from the trauma of witnessing "commercial cutting on public land."

Sophisticated loggers can do a wonderful job in this regard. By contrast however, a sloppy operator dragging logs against the trees not cut, can leave some ugly obvious scars, even on the most carefully laid out thinning shows. Here also is where a good forester can save both money and bad publicity, by laying out the sale to make it easier for the skidders to get the logs out without making a mess. Ski trails designed to do double duty as skid roads for over-the-snow or other minimum impact logging systems, can be a great asset.

In Olympic National Park , where I worked on trail crews, we had really big trees that had to be cleared off trails and campgrounds that received intense public

105

scrutiny. Anyone familiar with the history of this Park knows how extremely intense this political surveillance was. So how did the trail crew handle it ? No problem, in the off season when no one's around, a little dynamite could make those cut log ends look very natural. Under less pressure here in the Methow, 40 years later, I instead counted the annual growth rings on a big old growth down log we had to cut for a new ski trail, marked them with a permanent black pen, and inscribed 300+, since we don't know when the tree fell .

Trail design and maintenance as a zoning tool for back country and Wilderness management may follow these practical fundamentals only, if first the basics of economic and political survival are assured. Seasonally integrated trail systems provide ideal opportunities for unobtrusively sorting out potentially conflicting recreation styles. Snowmobiles and nordic skiers or snowshoers, plus the lodges where quiet winter people stay, are the most widespread examples of this urgent need.

Trailhead parking is the first order of business in this regard. Physical barriers to keep machines off the nordic trails are essential, but do little good if the parking situation forces these incompatible uses together where the first impressions are made. Separate parking is therefore the first priority. The nature of physical barriers is the second. A locked gate with attractive terrain behind it , is an invitation for trouble.

Grooming machine access should ideally be hidden from the eyes of snowmobilers. Skier access from their parking area should be narrow and wooded enough that it does not act as a visual temptation for snowmobiles. Better yet are trailheads at the nordic lodges themselves. This arrangement frees guests from the necessity of getting back in their cars to access the skiing. No windshield to scrape beforehand, and no snow melting inside the car afterwards. Snowmobiles can have this same situation at

SNOWMOBILE PROOF BRIDGE

their lodges also, and both types of users have the added peace of mind that comes with knowing that your vehicles and belongings have less chance of being stolen or vandalized when under the surveillance of lodge personnel and your fellow guests.

Ski school teaching areas similarly separated from the distraction and safety hazard of faster skiers by trees do better than those requiring signs or fencing. Trail merging situations can be designed so that big obnoxious SLOW signs, and speed control fences are not needed. These apply equally to nordic and alpine ski areas. Ski school students are very often extremely self conscious and embarrassed to be seen flailing and falling in front of the public's eyes. Slow skiers likewise can be uncomfortable when subjected to fast skier traffic. It's much more than safety that's at stake here. Skiing is ideally a positive aesthetic experience, and anything that detracts from that hoped for good time will tend to have skiers thinking about another resort for their next vacation.

Bridges safe for horses, work for skiers too. Foot logs do not. Snow country usually has enough water crossings that bridges become very useful management tools. Sorting out horses from hikers, or mountain bikers from bird watchers can often be done unobtrusively with bridges. The summer horse bridge that needs, in winter, to keep snowmobiles from crossing however, may require an entrance passable to horses but not to snowmobiles. This may be less than ideal, because if there's an obviously discriminatory structure it may invite vandalism at worst, and lingering resentment at best.

Bridge design, perhaps with seasonally removable handrails on one or both sides - to shape the snow into a formidable enough side slope, might be the best solution. Skiers can easily traverse side slopes impassable for snowmobiles. Every mix of seasonal uses and terrain is unique. Some may be difficult, awkward, or physically impossible without well thought out combinations of parking, plowing schedules, road closures, bridges, trail locations, huts, and grooming patterns. For instance the foot log crossing of a raging torrent, originally designed to keep horses out of a fragile meadow early in the summer, may also prevent skiers from going there in winter. That meadow might be a desirable place for skiers, perhaps to avoid avalanches or snowmobiles. A cable suspension bridge passable to only hikers, snowshoers, and ski tourers might fit that situation.

Such complexity serves as a buffer itself, because it obscures the fact that recreationists are being manipulated. The Wilderness edge, whether abrupt or including some roadless buffering backcountry, can serve ideally, to filter out conflicting uses from each other, and the wildlife in and around the Refuge, Park, or Wilderness Area. "Friction factor" management is a term used by some, but this implies negatives. Positive features, "carrots," need to predominate if management is to be successful. Permits and cop rangers may still be necessary, but their numbers can be reduced, and their very presence should be a red flag indication of design and management problem areas. These are places to avoid if you're on vacation, and areas to get knowledgeable, professionally skillful, corrective action if you're a wildland or resort manager.

Education is often cited as a solution to wildland management problems, and in the long run that approach is valid. In the short run however, design solutions are needed that make it easy to take the safe and wildlife friendly actions, and difficult to take the unsafe options. Education may follow if the initial experience is positive. Education will likely fail if trail design leads to negative interactions.

Ski trails can provide dilution solutions to many wildland pollution problems. Nordic trail complexes around resorts, such as Sun Mountain - in the Methow Valley, have more than enough summer trail possibilities to keep large numbers of recreationists happy outside the Wilderness. Horses, bikers, hikers, and bird watchers can all also be conveniently and unobtrusively sorted out. The maize of old logging roads and skid trails inherited typically by ski resorts allows loop trail configurations with very little need for expensive, and initially unsightly, earth moving. Where National Forest logging roads are adjacent to the resort's private roads, they too can be eventually incorporated into the trail system.

Eventually is unfortunately the key word, because the "leave it alone" mythology has penetrated the ranks of even the U.S. Forest Service, particularly among the "ologists." These new specialist, scientifically trained and environmentally inclined, newcomers to the management matrix, have proved as damaging as the old "timber beasts." Unable to see the forest for the salmon, or Lynx, or Spotted Owls, or Grizzlies, or Timber Wolves, they blunder on, backed up by equally narrowly focused "ologists" in other federal and state agencies, and citizen pressure groups.

Some NGO's (non government organizations) have unfortunately become self serving and self perpetuating bureaucracies. There may be financial turf to defend, office complexes and staffs to support, and all this infrastructure usually off in some city, far removed from the wildlife they're supposedly trying to save. The result can be an inbred culture of socially reinforced ignorance and arrogance. It has become known, among wildlife and forestry professionals, as "the controversy industry."

"Eventually" as a result, can take very discouraging amounts of time, money, and effort. "Analysis paralysis" can be overcome, but it may take an NGO with pockets as deep, and with political savvy to match, as possessed by Trust for Public Land. It took even TPL almost ten years to bail the Methow Valley out of the mess Early Winters had produced. They were able finally to get the Forest Service on board, but not until after they had to watch fire suppression money wasted blocking off the old Pacific Crest Trail, and a historic connecting bridge demolished, to appease their internal "ologists" and backers in high and far off places.

The owners of the Wilson Ranch, at the base of the infamous Sandy Butte-Early Winters Ski Lift saga, had to pay out thousands of dollars to finance the environmental paperwork required for just 100 feet of nordic ski trail. Wilson Ranch is right adjacent to the TPL Arrowleaf Conservancy, and their ski trails are interconnected. The 100 feet of new trail was needed to connect their privately owned trails to the old Forest Service logging road, open to the public, immediately behind their small Country Inn and cabins resort. Wilson Ranch serves both cross-country and heli-skiers, so maybe the helicopter, with its alpine skiers, was the problem here. Prejudice against skiing sometimes works in mysterious ways.

TPL's expertise was greatly enhanced by the fact that some of their key personnel were cross-country skiers who skied Early Winters just for the fun of it. Getting out of the office environment is key to making good decisions. Skiing home at night after a day at work heli-ski guiding or teaching cross-country skiing, I'd sometimes meet TPL people, or their counter parts with Nature Conservancy. They knew the 1100 acres at Arrowleaf intimately, and the results show that.

Trans-boundary situations often need unique solutions, as was the case at Arrowleaf – part of the larger Early Winters Complex. Sometimes even the best efforts of NGO's, like TPL, are not enough to break up the political log jams that occasionally get in the way of sound wildlife management. Legislation may be required in such cases. NGO's specific to trails are increasingly part of this scene. The Pacific Crest, Washington State, and Methow Valley trail Associations are examples of some of those involved in the Northeast Cascades. These organizations, and the legislation that sometimes is required, bridge the gaps that occur when trails cross interagency and private land boundaries. Bureaucracy often has built in institutional limitations, where job security gets in the way of sound decision making. Well informed citizen involvement with trails is therefore essential. The challenge is to integrate recreational and biological wildlife needs into a workable management plan. "Leave it alone" doesn't cut it.

Huts bring these two, often antagonistic and separate, concerns into sometimes confrontational situations, not unlike those involving lifts. The scale is smaller at each hut site , but the geographic spread is far greater. Like fire, huts effect the entire boreal forest, not just the mountains. Trails are the web connecting them all together.

Chapter 7: HUTS – attracting and dealing with impact, from shelters and cabins, to helicopter and snowcat accessed lodges

Concentrating impact is the principle effect of huts. Absorbing impact can then be accomplished efficiently, by using the right technology. Shelters of nearly any sort, including the ruins of old ones, draw curious people. Like trails and bridges, huts mark the locations chosen by previous travelers. Even ugly, dirty, stinky, structures, full of mice, graffiti, freeze-dried leftovers, ants, flies, spiders, and Pack Rats, will still inevitably attract, and that is their value for ecological restoration. The choice of design, location, and technology all effect the degree to which impact is mitigated. They don't have to be neglected third world style hovels.

Ostrander ski hut, in Yosemite National Park, was the first ski hut I stayed in. It was handsome looking, built in the sturdy stone masonry and log beams construction manner, that is often referred to as classic "Parkitecture." It's hut keepers, a young couple, kept it spotless – and knew all the good ski routes. That was March 1960. The previous summer I'd cleaned up three sided shelters in Olympic National Park, as part of my trail crew job. Most of them were in filthy condition and we only had instructions to make minimal repairs. We were the TRAIL crew, not the HUT crew! But there was no hut crew.

Many of those old shelters and cabins, off in roadless areas, have since been burned down by misguided rangers, who perhaps thought such action would enhance the "wilderness quality." Many were eyesores, and Pack Rat perfumed, and there may have been no money in their budgets for huts, but now the impact at those sites is more spread out, and as a result greater in terms of wildlife habitat. The sites may look more natural to the untrained eye, but behind every bush within walking distance of the good campsites is a smell not particularly natural, and the rodent population there is probably spreading human specific pathogens to the local water supply.

The term *ski hut* has evolved to include any permanent, or semi-permanent, structure – yurts for instance, that require or encourage ski access. Its origins are European, where the impact of generations of backcountry travelers naturally evolved into functional structures that maintained the surrounding landscapes in a condition acceptable to the local cultures. Canada's culture is much more closely tied to the European, and their "huts" reflect this tradition.

Later (1962) hiking through the Canadian Rockies, I encountered huts even nicer than Ostrander, such as Assiniboine Lodge south of Banff. By 1968, with my own Hurricane Ridge sub-district to look after, in Olympic National Park , I still had lots of stinky little three sided backcountry shelters, but I also had a vision of something better. So when a local group of cross-country skiers asked to put in a ski hut at the old Waterhole campsite, out by the Obstruction Point road, I was cautiously optimistic.

I told them it sounded like an excellent idea to me, but that I'd have to clear it through Park channels. When permission finally arrived, winter was nearly upon us. The ski club's boat trailer carried in both halves of the 16 by 8 by 8 foot, "A frame" hut, just before snow fell.

Then SURPRISE, permission was denied, and the hut must be removed. Why? "No reason you" (lowly field rangers, or local skiers) "need to know about" – so it was obviously political. "But sir, the road won't be drivable until sometime next July. Should we order a helicopter ?"
"Oh ? - humph - well then, no one can use the hut, unless it's an emergency." We rangers did our best to explain this bureaucratic mystery to the skiers, but they were much more politically savvy than our bosses apparently realized. An official notice of non-use was posted at the hut, along

114

KLAHANE RIDGE

TO PORT ANGELES

HURRICANE RIDGE ROAD SKIER ACCESS AND SNOWPLAY FREE

COX VALLEY MOSTLY SNOW FREE

SKI TOURING SNOW GOOD TO DEER PARK 12 MILES BEYOND WATERHOLE

PT LAKE O

MOUNT ANGELES

X SKI ROUTE 3 MILES

OBSTRUCTION POINT ROAD HURRICANE RIDGE NOT PLOWED

HURRICANE POINT ROAD

WATERHOLE 3½ MILES

LITTLE RIVER VALLEY SNOW MOSTLY FREE

POMA LIFT

ENDING PLOWING

HURRICANE RIDGE LODGE

HURRICANE HILL

XC SKI ROUTE 1½ MILES

OLD ACCESS ROAD (CLOSED)

ELWHA RIVER VALLEY USUALLY SNOW FREE

with a sign out sheet for passing skiers for use in case of an emergency.

By spring the register of "non-use" was so long, and contained so many influential names, that the word from on high changed again, and the hut could stay. During the next decade the hut was so popular that pre-season drawings had to be held for each weekend, and at least one safety incident, involving an unusual (for nordic skiers) broken femur occurred. Luckily the hut was there for this real emergency.

The Obstruction Point road is one of only three directions skiers can usually go from Hurricane Ridge. The other two are short day trips. Obstruction then is the obvious route of choice for skiers out to really stretch their legs. Skiing is already concentrated along this, and the other narrow ridge tops, and Waterhole has the only forest thick enough to provide shelter from a storm. It has been used as a campsite since long before Olympic National Park was established, in 1938.

In 1991 a new district, or maybe he was chief, ranger announced that Waterhole's hut was closed, - except for emergency use. *Signpost Magazine*, then a hikers' periodical for Washington State, published his official press release along side a reader's letter pleading for the hut's survival. The ranger's text included a statement that the hut had never been approved. Those not inclined to study history are likely to repeat it, so I wrote in a letter to *Signpost*, setting the record straight. The tiny hut was still there in 2006, but lightly used compared to its earlier years, when ski touring hadn't yet been eclipsed by the fascination with turning provided by Telemarking.

Political pressure against huts in the United States is a curious phenomenon. It might have something to do with Boy Scouts and "tenting tonight" as some sort of heroic sport. But more likely it is the uniquely American quest for a nostalgic make-believe "wilderness experience" free of "development." Whatever the reasons may be, anti-hut sentiment is a serious political force to be reckoned with.

When Liberty Bell Alpine Tours proposed a hut at the headwaters of Cedar Creek, between Silver Star Mountain and Kangaroo Ridge - here in the Northeast Cascades, I got to read the Forest Service's "public scoping" letter file. We might as well have suggested another road across the North Cascades! The inability of many Americans to honestly face up to their impact on wildlife, and the world, is somehow focused into the hut controversy too. Liberty Bell decided not to build that hut even though permission from the Forest Service was obtained. Public controversy, however, was not the deciding factor. A soft heli-ski market, and an insecure liability insurance situation, perhaps both related to Canadian heli-skiing accidents, simply made it a bottom line business decision.

All this was back in the 1980's when the North Cascades' Early Winters ski lift resort looked inevitable, and the Forest Service was partnering with ski developers to actively promote ski lifts and all that comes with them: heli-skiing, huts, and the big boys such as Aspen and Disney. Remember Mineral King. Thus it was that I got to guide the then district ranger to the proposed hut site by helicopter. My forestry education and background made me the logical choice for this duty, while our other guides got to take care of our regular, and much more fun, heli-ski yo-yo operations not far away. We'd get picked up after sampling one of the ski runs that the hut might access, but most of our time was spent looking over the proposed hut site in detail.

Two foresters far away from their bosses, possible microphones or eavesdropping by anyone, tend to talk a bit more frankly, and with the whole forest in mind, not just what happens to be bureaucratically in line at the time, or promising for a business possibility. We were looking beyond helicopter access which can literally fly away at

117

the whim of the market, or popular opinion. What we saw was a much better hut location. It was lower down in the same remote watershed, and would be accessible by future ski tourers, should Scandinavian style skiing ever become popular in America. There were indications, back in the 1980's, that this was a possibility. The resulting Forest Service paperwork reflected this by allowing a range of hut locations, including the one two foresters preferred. Who knows, some day when we're both gone, that document may surface, and result in a better decision for both future recreation and resource management.

The fortunes of huts and heli-ski access in Canada effect the whole ski industry. They are second only to Europe in the number of ski huts, and first in the world for heli-skiing. They certainly influenced our proposed ski hut in Cedar Creek, and my own personal place within the ski industry and the National Forest and Park bureaucracy.

Understanding what comes next requires a preview of the ranger situation and events as far away as North Carolina, where Duke University has been a center for research into alpine and subalpine ecology. The resistance to huts has been primarily an American cultural anomaly. It is complex and involves the ability of rangers, and/or their wildland and wildlife manager administrators, to comprehend and deal with backcountry impact. Rangers too often live in the same fantasy world as their urban constituents. They too grew up with TV and computers as their primary cultural influences, and their "escape" to a career in the Forest, Park, or Wildlife Refuge often still has them tied to these modern cultural icons. This is especially true of those that are promoted to office jobs.

My curiosity about naturalism, or whatever we should call this phenomenon of irrational resistance to anything, including huts, that reminds people that overpopulation is impinging on a uniquely American wilderness fantasy world, had been tweaked before – while working at

118

Kirkwood Ski Resort. I realized a few years after I'd chosen to resign my "permanent" (that is, year round) National Park ranger position in 1971, that the Craigheads were kicked out of Yellowstone for many of the same reasons I decided to leave, and at the same time. 1970 was the year of the so called "Stoneman Meadow Massacre," when some hippies in Yosemite Valley embarrassed the National Park Service so badly, over their incompetent law enforcement, that all other criteria for ranger training became secondary.

Stone throwing flower children refusing to leave their illegal and conspicuous occupation of a meadow in the crowded valley forced the publicly witnessed retreat of a hastily assembled cadre of rangers and maintenance personnel. This incident together with the increasingly urban visitors to the National Parks, and the budget cuts by Congress, precipitated the display of firearms by rangers, who chose to stay on, and the exit of many backcountry oriented rangers such as myself.

Cop rangers, ignorant of - and not inclined to learn natural history, and unable or unwilling to leave their patrol vehicles or offices, adopted "natural regulation" as an excuse for "letting nature take her course" in the backcountry. The stage was thus set for "police state wilderness," and the drift of our National Parks even further into the *Playing God in Yellowstone* dilemma that had plagued us, certainly before then, but stimulated the publication of Alston Chase's best selling book of that title, in 1986.

Ski huts and any backcountry structures thus became best known as the objects of bureaucratic arson. Even further budget cuts under the neoconservative Congress of the 1990's, early 2000's and the tragic George W. Bush administration, spread even the cop rangers so thin that car clouting became commonplace. The 2006 murders of two women hikers in the North Cascades set up a storm of

119

protest in the Northwest outdoor community, and the call for getting rangers back out on the trails. This may help explain part of the Democratic victories in the fall of 2006.

My intimate professional association with the realities of human impact at the Waterhole hut site, made mine almost as undesirable a message as the Craigheads' about Grizzlies and garbage. Yes, the routine clean-up of "toilet paper flowers" is just part of a ranger's duty. Park bureaucrats, and their loyal but ignorant, environmental constituency didn't want to even hear about such messy things, let alone face up to them. An academic ecologist friend, who was finishing up her Doctorate in alpine ecology at Duke University under Dr. Billings, in the mid-1970's, suggested that I might investigate this situation by tracking the Craigheads' influence through academia.

This I did, through the newly emerging theories of island biogeography back east, to the National Academy of Science report on the Craigheads' ouster at Yellowstone, and finally a private talk with that report's principal author, Dr. Ian McTaggart Cowan at the University of British Columbia. Dr. Billings was the foremost alpine ecological investigator at that time, and had attracted some of the best minds in that field. I also had a few other leads in the academic world, that helped expedite my search. So from Duke to, Morgantown West Virginia, then Bozeman Montana – where I finally obtained a copy of the report, I landed in Vancouver, British Columbia.

Dr. Cowan assured me that continued frustration was in store should I choose to either return to the bureaucracy, or enter the academic world, and that writing for the popular market was the most effective means to effect constructive change. Huts do very well in Canada, and especially well in the heli-ski territory of British Columbia. Finding myself stuck with American citizenship however, I moved as close to the Canadian hut scene as possible, guiding heli-skiers in the North Cascades. Huts were

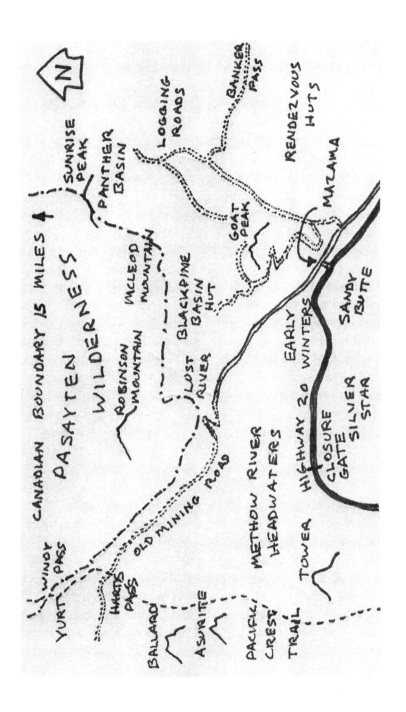

making some progress in my new home range, but were still up against many of the same prejudices that frustrated my attempts to change the American National Parks. The simultaneous invitations, in 1986, from two ski business friends living and working in Norway, provided the opportunity to trace the roots of skiing, including huts.

Norwegian ski huts proved as controversial as those anywhere, even though they don't need hut keepers to keep them clean. (New Zealand is apparently the only other country with such impeccable hut manners.) The wide variety of Norwegian huts was my real eye opener. They have everything from the simplest three sided shepherd's shelters to elaborate backcountry hotels, complete with maid service. Every single one was apparently fought over, just like at Olympic and North Cascades, and the same in Canada. Europeans are simply more used to fighting, and don't let it get in the way of worthwhile projects. As my Norwegian entrepreneur friends put it "You have to lean on the government pretty hard to get anything done." They were referring to both Norway and the United States, where they had personal ski business experience.

Rendezvous Outfitters, in the Methow – back in the Northeast Cascades, had been so successful with their groomed trail accessed huts, that when I returned from Norway we started once more to think about high elevation huts. We saw them as not so much dependent on helicopter access, but rather as a means of escaping from helicopter dependence. Norway had outlawed heli-skiing in most places and we could foresee it happening here too. Utah already was showing the symptoms of ski terrain overpopulation. In addition to this, the helicopter's weather dependence had also proved troublesome to the Methow's first high elevation hut, up north of Harts Pass.

Weather, and possible touring access by intermediate skill level skiers, pointed us toward the eastern half of the

Pasayten Wilderness boundary. Terrain there is not quite as steep and intimidating, as further west at Harts Pass. Flying weather is also more reliable than up at Harts Pass, and also on the Pasayten Wilderness boundary. The Wilderness edge at both locations provided protection from mechanized disturbances on at least half of our hut's potential ski touring area. Panther Basin's hut site, with logging roads stopping a few miles short, and therefore accessible by snowcat or snowmobile only that far, looked like our quietest location. Those last few miles, beyond the ends of logging roads, are steeply forested and side hilly enough to prevent even the newer snowmobiles from accessing the hut site or its ski terrain, but skiers could be guided in. The complex terrain also meant less likelihood of unguided skiers finding the hut. Forest Service permit conditions didn't allow a permanent structure, so we put in a yurt. Less initial cost was also a factor.

What we learned during the several years it operated was that yurts are too delicate, even in the relative snow shadow of our Northeast Cascades. High maintenance costs, primarily time on a shovel, plus time to ski in and out, or helicopter time - if guides couldn't be spared from the yo-yo operations, forced us to discontinue the Panther Basin yurt. At this writing, only permission to install a sturdier structure would make it worth trying again. The one yurt still maintained (as of 2007) by North Cascades Heli-skiing north of Harts Pass is lightly used and requires shoveling after almost all heavy storm cycles. It couldn't survive financially without being part of our lodge based heli-ski operation. The Methow Valley's next ski hut will likely be another groomed trail accessed structure, but probably with indoor plumbing, to try tapping into the market niche that's working just north of us in British Columbia.

Our Methow Valley huts were not the first ski huts proposed for the North Cascades, and certainly not the most famous. That honor belongs to "Hickel's Hostels," named after then Secretary of the Interior – Walter Hickel, and so notorious that they may explain why the scoping file for our little Cedar Creek hut proposal contained so much animosity. The fact that Hickel's Hostels were proposed for inclusion within the brand new North Cascades National Park, also probably contributed, which is why I included the background about the Craigheads, Yellowstone, and Alston Chase. The North Cascades original National Park proposal was only able to get past conservative political opposition by including both aerial tramways and huts. The good ol' boys in Washington D.C. envisioned something like the European Alps. Remember that this was back in the years of a booming ski lift industry, the 1960's, when America looked like it might indeed duplicate the ski business success story that followed the Marshal Plan's reconstruction of Europe after World War Two. Neither Hickel's Hostels nor the aerial tramways were built, but for political rather than practical financial or biological reasons.

Meanwhile back on the ground, in the North Cascades, my examination of the proposed locations for Hickel's Hostels revealed that all but one were in avalanche paths. These lovely flower meadows probably impressed some east coast based National Park planning expert with their Julie Andrews ambience. So maybe it's not so surprising that huts have an especially bad reputation in the North Cascades. Avalanches quite often get ignored whenever politics are involved, but in this case we had the additional complication of planning and management way too far removed from reality, a situation common to both the corporate ski industry and the bureaucratic National Park and Forest Services. Clifford's *Downhill Slide*, cited in my lifts chapter, examines this issue in detail.

The one good hut site picked by those Park planners, back in the 1960's, should still be built in this century if we can ever overcome the anti-hut legacy. That location is Bridge Creek, above Stehekin where that creek meets the Stehekin River and the old mining era road, towards Cascade Pass. A ski and hiking hut there could eliminate the controversial historic dependence on shuttle bus access for day hiking over Cascade Pass and the other spectacular day hiking possibilities that radiate from Bridge Creek. Part of the controversy revolves around a poorly located and engineered road which washed out on a regular basis. As of this 2007 writing the road has been officially closed below Bridge Creek, at one of the locations where it used to wash out ("car wash falls") , and the Courtneys are operating a tent camp above there – at Bridge Creek, exactly where the Hostel was proposed.

The other and more significant aspect, besides the too distant planners, is that Bridge Creek is in a National Park with all the national publicity and resulting overcrowding, wilderness permits, reservation systems for designated campsites, cop rangers enforcing all these regulations, and I've barely scratched the surface; in short it's police state wilderness. If you doubt what I've just written, you can visit Stehekin, without the hassle, by staying with the Courtneys at their guest ranch up valley from the boat landing. They've dealt with all this for two generations, and from before they got included into a National Park Service run "Recreation Area."

Water Hole, Panther Basin, and Bridge Creek are simply three examples of a problem common to almost all potential ski hut situations: fossil fuel consumption versus overnight structures for back country access. "Oh, but you can't have structures in Wilderness; it's illegal !" is the all too typically shrill urban environmentalist's response to hut proposals, and the reason I included EDGES as my third chapter. Edges are second, only to avalanches, in importance related to ski huts and skiing's other impacts on wildlife in the mountains. Away from mountains they are of primary importance. This includes by far the vast majority of snow country. Again, to summarize the case for huts: they are an effective means of directing impact to locations away from critical wildlife habitat, and where it is technically practical to absorb that impact, and they are overnight accommodations close to the prime recreational attraction, versus burning fuel to commute to them from lodging farther away.

Skiing figures into such situations because a hostel on an old roadway, like the possibility at Bridge Creek, makes an ideal ski touring destination. Even roads with shorter snowed-in ski seasons, than Stehekin's, fit this scenario. Remember Chapter Three's description of all the trailhead ranger stations, campgrounds, and lodges that would be an easy day's ski in, from down a road that would no longer have to be plowed. Snowplows make SUV's look like gas misers. Wilderness edges are the place for huts on the American, and many other snow country landscapes.

There are exceptions to the placement of huts on edges, not many, but when they occur they're pretty obvious. Camp Muir in Mount Rainier National Park, is the example most familiar to residents of the Pacific Northwest. This climbing hut, at the 10,000 foot level of our 14,000 foot high Washington State icon, is necessary for facilitating summit adventures. It's surrounded by active glaciers and steep alpine rock and snow. This is wilderness in the physical as well as the political reality, and the sanitary and public safety reality simply does not lend itself to the traditional American tent campsite. There are way too many people !

Pressure on places like Mount Rainier National Park can also be at least partly alleviated by huts to attract people away from the main attraction. Fortunately, for Mount Rainier, that is starting to happen along the western edge of the Park. This more easily accessed, and serviced, ski hut system promises to follow the lead of huts in the

Methow, Colorado, and Canada. I've left out many more fine examples, but perhaps that is best, until the political situation improves. Overcrowding existing huts before they have the opportunity to expand and provide for more users would not necessarily be helpful.

Sanitation is one of the principal reasons for building more, and upgrading existing facilities. The progression from outhouses to composters, and on to indoor plumbing, is necessary as usage increases. Not all situations need or allow this progression, but the helicopter outhouse is not the best solution. Neither is requiring recreationists to pack it *all* out individually, as an increasing number of American areas are doing. "Wilderness" in these crowded circumstances is a head-in-the-sand political joke. Huts with civilized sanitation are the obvious answer.

I came across the hut style I like best on the Canadian section of the historically famous Chilkoot Trail, into the Yukon from Skagway and Dyea, Alaska. Working as a backcountry National Park ranger for the Chilkoot Trail National Historic Park , for a summer, gave me lots of time to network with the Canadian Park Wardens. This was part of my regular duties making sure hikers on Alaska's most popular trail had a safe and enjoyable experience, plus an additional assignment to assess the avalanche situation so that there is a reasonable chance of avoiding a repeat of the infamous tragedy of 1898. The avalanche that killed all those potential gold miners on the American side, during the rush, could also come down on the Canadian side. These Saint Elias mountains can produce avalanches any time of the year, so I had some serious discussion time with the Canadian Wardens.

Canada does a much better job of managing their National Parks than the United States, from my perspective - and my curiosity as to why this could be, led me to spend most of my days off on the Canadian side. Wildlife is an integral part of Canadian culture – it is even featured on their money. Their dollar is called "the Loonie," because it pictures the Loon, (or "Diver" to Europeans) the water bird that many consider to be the voice of the North Woods - as much as the howl of the Wolf. Canadian National Park wardens, like the Mounties before them during the gold rush, run a tight operation and this includes a seemingly automatic awareness of what it takes to avoid wildlife problems.

Food storage is key to both visitor safety in bear country, and for maintaining endangered species in nature reserves that should allow all wildlife, endangered and otherwise, to avoid negative human interactions. A separate grizzly bear and rodent proof structure, handy to the sleeping hut and designated campsites, accomplished this all important service. Hikers allergic to snoring, or simply desiring more privacy, can set up tents that way, safely store food and other wildlife attractions, join with folks in the main hut for food preparation and socializing, and in this setting eliminate most of the problems associated with less sophisticated hut and campsite designs.

Herb and Pat Kariel have written guidebooks for the western Canadian huts that cover the history of each hut, complete with engineering and politically specific details. Colorado's huts, although not nearly as rich in history, have nevertheless been successful enough to provide lessons future hut builders should also study. The Appalachian Mountain Club has a long history of dealing with hut issues, and their *Backcountry Facilities Design and Maintenance* authored by Leonard, Spencer and Plumley is an excellent overall reference. It contains many lessons that newcomers to the hut scene out west can benefit from.

Skiing's impact on huts is to provide the year round use that makes more huts possible than could be supported without winter use. The impact of huts on skiing is to channel its impact, increase its safety margins, and allow increased use with less impact on wildlife than camping.

PACIFIC CREST TRAIL NORTH

CUTTHROAT PASS

HIGHWAY 20

CORRIDOR

SILVER STAR

CHELAN SAWTOOTH WILDERNESS AREA

TWISP RIVER ROAD

WASHINGTON PASS

HWY 20

RAINY PASS

NORTH CASCADES NATIONAL PARK

MOUNT GOODE

LAKE CHELAN NATIONAL RECREATION AREA

STEHEKIN

CASCADE PASS

GLACIER PEAK WILDERNESS AREA

PACIFIC CREST TRAIL SOUTH

BRIDGE CREEK HUT SITE

The benefits for wildlife are substantial enough that even nonskiers should support more and better huts. Park and Forest rangers' lack of understanding in regard to huts, and their reputation in the United States for burning them down, requires careful examination. The ranger is an American cultural icon, with symbolism that is vastly different from modern reality.

Chapter 8: RANGERS wildlife and wilderness managers, "snow safety," and "analysis paralysis"

"The other rangers are all *too busy* to help with the snow survey. You and I are it. Meet you at HQ, 0600?"

Deep fresh snow stopped our National Park Service truck the next day, down below the Deer Park boundary. It was raining hard at sea level, and snowing just as hard up in the forest, below Olympic National Park's steep northeast side. The rapid elevation gain we'd driven up was enough to dry out the sloppy snow most residents of Washington State's Olympic Peninsula regard as typical. Cold snow up where we parked however, dictated green climbing wax for the all day ski trek, which included a vertical mile of elevation gain.

Water runoff is predicted from snow depths and densities measured on snow survey courses all over the western United States. A long hollow aluminum tube is driven by hand down to the ground, and the resulting snow core weighed to get water content. Multiple cores, typically ten - for computational convenience, are taken along an established route - where the snow is not disturbed. It's a simple procedure, requiring only that someone of reasonable intelligence be at the designated sites, representative of the watersheds involved, once toward the end of every winter month, plus April which typically starts the runoff, in America's snow country.

Skiing obviously is the least expensive, minimum impact access, but demands some skill and decent physical condition. Predictably, modern rangers prefer helicopters or snowmobiles, or better yet – remote sensing. Satellite imaging and "snow pillows," big rubber bladders filled with antifreeze, can and have replaced many old snow survey courses. Satellites measure the geographic extent of snow cover, while the pillows register the weight, and therefore water content, pressing down on them.

Heavy falling snow thinned rapidly as we ascended the old fire look out dirt road. At about 4500 feet above sea level we broke out above the clouds, into sunshine of the famous Olympic rain shadow, which for us was a snow shadow. At 6000 feet the old ranger station had to be dug out, and made habitable before we could do the courses. This involved some extra serious shoveling to check the building's propane supply for possible snow creep damage and potential leaks. Propane explosions under snow can be especially dangerous because of the possible entrapment of large volumes of gas. Another gas, carbon monoxide, needs to be adequately vented out the top. Snow forces those touring over it, or living in it, to practice a unique set of skills to be able to avoid mishaps and work effectively. There's more to it than just staying out of avalanches and keeping warm.

The term "snow safety" is most often applied to avalanche monitoring and control work which, before neoconservative budgetary cuts, used to be supervised or actually performed by rangers. Wildlife habitat however covers vastly greater areas than the avalanche paths threatening ski areas, highways, railroads and other concentrated human activity. If rangers are to safely and effectively operate in snow country beyond the road corridors, their expertise must be broader, and include things like building fires in circumstances similar to those made famous by Jack London.

All these basic snow survival and winter housekeeping activities are necessary to monitor wildlife in winter, and the impact of increasing numbers of winter recreationists, plus the old fashioned poachers. A trip like this was a perfect training opportunity for rangers who might be required to go out in such conditions for rescues, when the weather doesn't allow helicopters to fly, or the terrain precludes snowmobiles.

The reluctance of rangers to acquire such skills was symptomatic of a decaying National Park personnel system in the 1960's. These were the tight budget years of the Vietnam War. Jack Hughes, my ski partner, and boss - as the Northeast District Ranger, was a veteran of the Korean War. His bosses had been in World War Two, or survived the even tighter budgets of those years. The "war on terror" is having a similar effect.

"You can always tell a ranger by that far away steely look in his eye, and the deft sure way with which he handles a garbage can." - is an inside joke in the National Parks. Thus, the federal bureaucracy has – at its top management levels, those who somehow survived the lean budget times. Their expertise lies in the realm of minimal maintenance, not skiing or wildlife habitat.

Above them are political appointees, often with little or no training or experience, or even interest, in wildlife, wilderness, or Park and Forest protection. Their agendas reflect the dubious needs of the political process that put them there. And that's why citizen watchdog groups have long called for separation of National Parks from that process, by a structure more like the Smithsonian Institution – reporting directly to the President. National Forests in turn have been periodically threatened with transfer to the Interior Department, along side the National Parks, instead of Agriculture, where they reside at this 2007 writing. Whether any of these sorts of reshuffling the bureaucratic deck might help is suspect, in my opinion. I think the ranger problem has deeper roots.

Sunshine and powder snow, above the low clouds enshrouding Puget Sound, are not uncommon, but few skiers know about this, because the weather below the clouds is so intimidating. This intimidation extends to rangers as well, as Jack and I sadly discovered. National Park planners for North Cascades, across Puget Sound from the Olympic Mountains, proposed aerial tramways as a way to get Park visitors above the clouds, as is done in the Alps. Skiing up 5000 vertical feet is fine, if our purpose is to keep a physically fit ranger force, but is completely unrealistic as a plan for the general public, especially those too young, or too old, too obese, or otherwise disabled. These are precisely the ones who most need exposure to the magnificence of our mountains if the wildlife they shelter is to survive. Reality in this regard includes rangers, stuck down below the clouds - emptying the garbage, collecting and administrating all the fees, writing the citations for those in violation of all the rules, appearing in court to defend those citations, and wondering how they got sucked into this, mostly indoor, boring office job.

My dream job, as a snow and sub district ranger for Hurricane Ridge, under Jack, lasted just two years. That was typical tenure for that era. My next two years, at Olympic, as Staircase sub district ranger, but a three hour drive around down to the Park's southeast corner, completed my own disillusionment. I too was rapidly developing "that steely far away look in (my) eye."

Snow ranger status, during the short winter ski lift season – while serving those two years at Staircase, did little to help me influence the direction of management at Hurricane Ridge. A new Park superintendent, who definitely needed an aerial tramway to educate him about mountains, proved to be a hopeless case. He abolished my snow ranger duties, transferred Jack to road patrol duty away from the Hurricane Ridge ski area, and painted over the beautiful historic natural wood interior of the Park administration building's reception area. Next, he offered me a promotion to a full time office job. I politely declined, and started applying for snow ranger jobs elsewhere. This was in 1971 when Stoneman Meadow in Yosemite, referred to in my hut chapter, kicked off the law enforcement era for National Park rangers. It was also when the Craigheads left Yellowstone.

No luck; the job I hoped for on the Eldorado National Forest, supervising the development of Kirkwood Ski Resort, in California's northern Sierra Mountains, went to a Forest Service veteran. He distinguished himself there by laying out the main beginners' hill ski trail off the fall line, so that snowplowers had to side hill for almost half a mile. His career went on to become a Forest supervisor, who fired a botanist – with the audacity to find, and then worst of all – report, an endangered plant in the middle of a proposed timber sale.

The professional ski patrol job, I opted for at Kirkwood, soured when corporate style management from Colorado's ski lift areas took over. Read Hal Clifford's *Downhill Slide*, cited in my lifts chapter, if you're not yet familiar with this problem. Kirkwood was born of a Sierra Club lawsuit, which failed to stop the lifts, or even site them optimally. The Canadian consultant, Al Beaton, suggested gondola access, instead of the multi-million dollar avalanche defenses that the poor California taxpayers subsidized at Carson Spur, on otherwise avalanche free Highway 88. Details like this held my interest for eleven seasons, even though I was unable to prevent the major mistakes. Meanwhile I had the opportunity to learn the avalanche game from some of the best in the business, principally Kirkwood's mountain manager, Dick Reuter.

The process of dealing with the first ski lift resort to come under the Environmental Policy Act was fascinating, while the disappointment of seeing another lovely alpine valley be mismanaged was heart breaking. If the people involved in decision making, like our off-the-fall-line snow ranger, or the Sierra Club litigators, had been more knowledgeable about ski trails and wildlife, things might have turned out better. That on-the-snow experience, in the 1970's, sunk very deeply into my consciousness, and

135

together with Dr. Cowan's advice to try popular writing, began the process leading to this book, and my return to the Pacific Northwest, full time.

Telemark instruction became my specialty at Kirkwood as guests, seeing the tracks I left coming down from snow safety explosive avalanche control routes on cross-country skis, wanted to learn how that could be done. This was before Telemarking became a separate branch of cross-country skiing, but it still proved to be my ticket to employment as a heli-ski guide.

So my first published articles in ski magazines like *Nordic World* (now *Cross Country Skier*), and *Powder*, were about how to control skinny touring skis in ungroomed snow. They helped kick off the Telemark subculture, complete with planned obsolescence of the latest equipment, plastic boots and ever wider skis, which you must have now or be branded as a hopeless "retro." I stuck with my comfortable soft leather boots, light wooden touring skis, and shifted to editorial subjects like the Mineral King case, at the request of the editors at *Powder*. These firmly established my reputation as a ridge runner, offending both developers and tree huggers.

Avalanches in Mineral King were not the politically correct issue for either of the warring factions. Monty Atwater, the first U.S. Forest Service snow ranger had similar problems. His book *Avalanche Hunters*, is as much about bureaucracy and politics as avalanches. Canadian, Sid Marty's book *Men For The Mountains*, probably does the best job of explaining the field ranger's dilemma, from an insider's viewpoint. He was one. Only in Canada of course, they're called wardens, but the same forces were at work. Frank Craighead's book *Track of the Grizzly*, looks at this from a researcher's perspective. His Chapter 11: *Bureaucracy and the Bear*, is a classic description of ranger behavior, that led to the Craighead brothers' 1971 departure from Yellowstone.

Free speech rights for rangers do not include job security. Jack Hughes stalled his career at Olympic by forming the first Professional Rangers Organization (PRO). Not a bad Park to be stuck in, and maybe Jack planned it that way. Anyway, we (Yes, I was foolish enough to join up, along with many other rangers and naturalists) tackled a whistleblower case in Glacier National Park, Montana. A ten year battle in the courts finally netted our ranger-whistleblower ten year's back pay, some of which went to our very patient and generous pro-bono attorney. Meanwhile our plaintiff resigned, rather than take an office job in Nebraska – sort of the Park Service equivalent of Siberia, for naughty mountain park field rangers, and picked up a PhD under the Craigheads. The final settlement for his case was half time reinstatement to Glacier National Park, - so he could continue teaching courses at the University.

Jack at least had a job in Olympic, one of the finest National Parks in the world, but little official influence, other than life tenure as spiritual leader of the good fight for sound biological management, and confidant to some of the best conservation writers in the business. You can read about him in Mike Frome's book *Regreening the National Parks*. The Association of National Park Rangers (ANPR) which arose from the ashes of Jack's PRO, has proven ineffective at reforming the Parks. A little problem with job security perhaps. The new Coalition of National Park Retirees may have better luck for the same reason former directors of the U.S. Forest Service: Jack Ward Thomas and Mike Dombeck have been able to go public with critiques.

The nicest result of all these attempts at reform from within, has been FSEEE: Forest Service Employees for Environmental Ethics, which publishes a monthly magazine of alternative views, simply titled *Forest Magazine*. It features articles by authors such as Thomas and Dombeck. Jeff DeBonis, the former Forest Service employee, who started FSEEE, went on to found PEER: Public Employees for Environmental Responsibility, which covers the other public land managing agencies, including the National Parks.

Overemphasis on "law enforcement" in the National Parks, and timber production on the National Forests, has left the ranger ranks in short supply of those physically and academically capable of monitoring ski trails and wildlife. Their incompetence blends with corrupt political influence, to create a bewildering mess of unique situations, which require the best efforts of citizen watchdog groups to figure out, and hopefully straighten out, with advisory boards, lawsuits, or Acts of Congress, whatever it takes, and it's a formidable challenge.

The ranger profession still attracts, and holds, a few good people. They live and work in an intimidating world however, so don't be surprised if they're slow to take you into their confidence. Political spies, including double agents, are everywhere, and they'll sell incriminating information to the highest bidder. It nevertheless is possible to establish contacts with some rangers, to work on projects with real substance, thanks largely to Jack Hughes, FSEEE, and PEER. Whistle blowers at least now have a chance to have legal representation, without having to pay for it out of their meager government salaries. Be aware however that each area is unique, as to what can be accomplished and how. Be discreet, and respect the lives of rangers and their families, who your actions may endanger. The divorce rate, even in the National Parks, the favorite wildlife viewing areas of the American public, was second only to the CIA, last I heard.

All this of course will be very convincingly denied, even by its victims, who are hostage to the personnel system. Casualties are not just confined to the ranger ranks either. Journalists too can have job security challenges. I think Mike Frome (now retired) may hold the record for being fired from the greatest number of supposedly "environmental" magazines, including: *American Forests, Field and Stream* (where he covered our Glacier Park case), and *Defenders* (the magazine for Defenders of Wildlife). *Battle for Wilderness* is another of his always fearlessly provocative books.

Where the Grizzly Walks by Bill Schnieder, was the first book to build on the Craigheads' research, in a way pertaining specifically to ski trails. Ski lift resorts' effects in, and around, the communities near Yellowstone are related to their impact on bears and all the economic and ecological multiplier effects that saving bears produces. Decisions for or against Grizzly habitat by National Forest rangers, adjacent to the Park, are compared to those by National Park rangers within the Park. Dr. John Craighead's contributions to the 1990's book *The Greater Yellowstone Ecosystem*, includes later studies that are even more specific about which wildlife populations are influenced by which impacts, but this is a scientific compilation for the very serious student. Bill Schnieder wrote a second edition, with the same title - in 2004, which includes much of this recent information, and almost completely rewrote his earlier book. Both editions however, make great reading for the non-technical wildlife enthusiast, who is also curious about ski impact.

Simplistic condemnation of rangers - as cops, misses the crucial point that they, like Grizzly Bears, are trying to survive in an artificial habitat. Parks, Wilderness Areas, and Wildlife Refuges are managed, often by default - but still managed one way or another, even if their rangers are required to preach the gospel of "natural regulation." If your kids want to grow up to be rangers, they'd best get a degree in law enforcement. If they're also interested in wildlife, they'd better also go to a school close enough to wild country that they, and their professors, can get some hands on, and skis on, field experience.

If citizen activists want rangers to be more than cops, we have to create habitats for them that require less time in the office and patrol vehicle. That means ranger residences close to wildlife, preferably right at the trailhead for surveillance of the parking area, to prevent car clouting, and monitor who's going into the woods. They need to be discreetly designed, just far enough away for reasonable privacy – and so the thieves or poachers can't discern whether they're being observed or not. Trailhead residences are the kind of perk that used to keep backcountry oriented rangers on the job. Being snowed in half the year is only attractive to those in love with skiing – ski touring that is, the kind required to monitor wildlife.

Until reforms can be accomplished, and old fashioned trailhead ranger stations rebuilt or refurbished, our best hope for wildlife is volunteers. The organizations are in place and only need some encouragement. First is the nordic arm of the National Ski Patrol which provides on-the-trail safety information and rescue when needed. This however is very rarely needed for nordic skiers, and usually is for snowmobilers or out-of-bounds alpine skiers and snowboarders. Ski patrolling gives tax breaks to their volunteers, and there are discounts provided by ski areas and equipment suppliers. Cop rangers on their days off, or their friends in watchdog groups, may be able to do what rangers should be paid to do, ski the backcountry to help enforce zoning of snowmobiles, apprehend poachers, and monitor wildlife photographers - that can potentially harass, and harm, wildlife whether on skis, snowshoes, or snowmobiles.

Violators would never know whether or not that skier, over on the distant ridge - with the spotting scope, is just a birdwatcher, or a nordic ski patroller with a radio, to call in the enforcers. Watching birds and other wildlife, and recording what's seen, could even be more valuable. Winter stress is often the most critical time for wildlife. Dr. James Halfpenny's *Winter: an Ecological Handbook* is just one of several excellent books out now, that home in on how wildlife survives the cold. Halfpenny's book just happens to be specific for the Yellowstone region, and therefore applicable to much of the American west's avalanche country. Most winter ecology books deal with the broader expanses of boreal forest, typical of the Canadian Shield. These resources are available now for nordic patrollers.

The second organization that can help is the Professional Ski Instructors of America (PSIA). It is largely made up of part timers who teach skiing more for their love of the sport, and its natural environment, than for any money they receive. So in a sense they also are volunteers. Much of their interaction with students is before or after the lesson hours they may get paid for. They do get deals on equipment, and free lift or cross-country trail passes, like the ski patrollers. None of this however makes ski teaching a profession that often qualifies as actually making a living, except for a select few - at an even fewer number of resorts. Even most full time ski instructors consider their pay status as "ski bumming" and usually they move on to "a real job," when family responsibilities come along. In spite of all this however, the fact is that PSIA and parallel organizations in other skiing countries, have more contact with the skiing public than the ski patrol, heli-ski guides, or snow rangers.

Snow rangers, like I was at Olympic National Park, started some of the first winter naturalist programs. These proved so popular that when budgets cut out the naturalists at many Parks and Forests, volunteers took over. Sometimes the Forest is still nominally involved, as a sponsor, like they are here in the North Cascades' Methow Valley, as of winter 2007. Many of our volunteer naturalists are school teachers or retired professionals, and many of us also teach skiing. Still we're usually on snowshoes, dealing with folks who likely don't ski, and otherwise might have little contact with winter natural history. Snowshoeing is a fast growing sport, but it doesn't come any where near reaching as many people as cross-country skiing does, and there is another quantum leap involved when lift skiing is compared to the self powered winter sports.

Ski instructors therefore have largely replaced rangers as the human face the majority of the public associates with winter. PSIA–Northwest, subtitles their news magazine *"Inspiring lifelong passion for the mountain experience,"* and that sums up what the net effect of alpine ski instruction really does, although nordic ski instruction obviously covers more of nature in winter than just mountains. If reforms ever get rangers out on the snow again, new recruits may come from the ranks of these two organizations, and meanwhile they are our best hope.

Mark Twain wrote a book which bears on our ranger dilemma. *The Prince and the Pauper* fantasizes about two similar appearing young boys who innocently switch clothes, just for the fun of it, only to be whisked off (by adults who don't bother to let kids communicate with them) to their polar opposite lives. This gives Twain a means of educating his readers about the perils of theocracy, giving kids too little credit, and concentrating wealth in the "upper" classes, lessons as applicable today as in old England. "Dressing for success" and "if you have an outfit, you can be (one) too," get equal play and this is what sheds light on our ranger problem. Putting rangers in neckties, badges, guns, and synthetic fabric uniforms, complete with military creases and shiny shoes, tends to attract and hold people impressed by such things.

The U. S. Forest Service has been less military in this regard, and recently let their public contact folks wear open necked polo style shirts. Their law enforcement types however, look as stupid as the National Park rangers, who have been referred to as "imperial" by some critics. Slow progress in the form of fleece jackets has softened the American Park rangers' image somewhat, but they can't yet seem to get away from synthetics. Canadian Park wardens lucked out, and get to wear a working man's curled brim Stetson – so they don't get confused with ol' Dudley Do-right, the Royal Mountie of the TV comedy spoof. Canada is way ahead of the United States in their use of, and attitudes about, military and police powers, in spite of (or perhaps because of) their loyalist royal tradition. Canadian naturalists in their Parks also have very refreshingly nonmilitary uniforms. All this probably will follow the generally slow, but hopefully steady, disenchantment with things military.

The sadly outdated assumption that military uniforms somehow make the public more respectful of authority is a problem much broader than Parks and Forests. Reality is exactly the opposite, for all except that same very vocal minority that still cling to other medieval traditions such as religious bigotry, superstition, and barbarism.

Switching clothes proved useful in my own career. When I started to feel that imperial syndrome making me behave as ridiculously as some of my fellow National Park Rangers - toward the end of summer, suddenly no more uniform, and I'm packing mules for the trail crew, or greasing sheave wheels up on some chair lift. Next it's a red jacket with a big white cross on the back. Costume changes like these tend to keep you on your toes. I know it gave me some healthy reality checks, and I suspect it could help other rangers. A cooperative jobs arrangement with the ski industry, to formalize and expedite such outdoor career paths could benefit all concerned. "Walking some miles in someone else's shoes (or moccasins)" and "wearing different hats" are popular expressions of the, I think, very accurately perceived need for discovering other viewpoints and other ways to deal with society's problems, especially our poorly understood ecological ones.

Park Rangers and naturalists, like I was in the Olympic National Park visitor center, get chewed out by the outraged public for what "we" did to the National Forest. The general public does not distinguish between Parks and Forests. To them it's all a big green confusing outback, full of bears and rattlesnakes. The Late Successional Reserves of President Clinton's Northwest Forest Plan suffer especially from this confusion, as judges and legislators try to take over forest management from the discredited federal agencies. They know very little of what it takes to manage forests, especially those really cold scary ones up in the mountains, and in Canada, where avalanches and forest fires compete with Grizzly Bears, Wolves, Lynx, and Spotted Owls for legal attention.

The unfortunate result, out on the ground, has been management by the 'ologists I introduced in the trails chapter. These specialists have taken over from foresters, as a consequence of problems caused by clear cuts and fire suppression. The mixed bag of good and bad outcomes has been almost as narrow minded as the previous regime run by timber beasts. "Can't see the forest for the saw logs," has been replaced with "can't see the forest for the owls or salmon," or whatever the latest court cases have tunnel visioned on.

Legal challenges, to just about any decision, are inevitable, because of conflicting legislation and legal precedents. In too many cases the Forest Service's restricted legal budget often precludes even giving permission to partnering organizations, for good projects – such as short loop trails, thinning trees at the Forest boundary, or reopening historically significant old ranger stations by private conservation education organizations.

"Analysis paralysis" has been the too often quoted result, for these wildlife and recreation issues as well as the more publicized timber wars. About all the United States government agencies can do anymore (2007) is crank out voluminous legal impact statements, full of repetitious nonsense, that few people have the time or patience to wade through. Those determined individuals that do read them find themselves almost as paralyzed by the process as the agencies and actions they'd like to change.

Ski areas suffer because what we do in the forest is confused with the more easily understood timber wars. The best wildlife habitat managers, as of this 2007 writing, are The Rocky Mountain Elk Foundation and The Nature Conservancy. Yes, the same two I introduced in the fire chapter. They are free from the public stigma surrounding rangers, and have the political and financial clout of hunters and birdwatchers, respectively, behind them.

Ski areas, fortunate enough to work with either of these organizations, will find very much more receptive ears. Bringing the public agencies, and their rangers up to the standards being set by these two outfits is just one challenge this book hopes to address, by helping to better inform both the skiing and wildlife activists.

The loss of credibility has hurt more than the ranger profession. The downhill ski industry, with their image of elongated clear cuts, has a parallel problem. Going green however, has special resonance for skiing in the era of global warming. The proverbial snowball's chances are shared by all winter snow sports. Attempts to educate environmentalists by both the ski industry, and their ranger landlords are often dismissed as "greenwash," and some of it is. The sad truth though, in the context of our wider social - political arena, is that environmentalists are the ones with the biggest credibility problem. "Locking it all up in Wilderness" is the all too prevalent popular perception, and misconception, among the opponents of wilderness. "Pristine wilderness, untouched by humans" is the racist myth still persisting for many others. These two equally erroneous views help perpetuate conflict.

Chapter 9: WILDERNESS – and the *urban* mind, the perils of environmental fundamentalism

Politics, religion, and sex are often subjects avoided to keep the dialogue polite and not offend anyone. So although I will do my best to supply an objective examination, illustrated with some personal experience, I must apologize in advance to those I am about to irritate. All three of these infamous irritants are central to the environmental–conservation movement, and avoiding them would be a disservice to the cause of restoration. Fundamentalism is a tough trail to follow, so once again please brace yourself – because these next two chapters are, of necessity, even edgier than the third.

Dealing with ignorance or dishonesty and the consequent loss of credibility, the essential roots of fundamentalism, is a very delicate undertaking. Humor is probably the most effective, but when issues are complex - stimulating curiosity also is required. Sometimes songs such as "It ain't necessarily so," "Imagine," and "We shall overcome" have succeeded in the public arena, and maybe even changed a few minds. "Canadian Sunset" can perhaps use romance "on that ski trail" to help restore our snow country trails and wildlife.

Clarence Darrow walking out of the conclusion to the Scopes Monkey Trial, in the movie *Inherit the Wind* , is my model for dealing with fundamentalists. The verdict is guilty, but Tennessee is the laughing stock of a secular audience all over the world. Clarence has just chewed out the wise cracking reporter, who appears to have no use, or sympathy, for Bible thumping true believers. Darrow's lecture to this extremely rude reporter suggests a more tolerant and ecumenical approach, and he concludes by tucking the Bible under one arm, and Darwin under the other, for his exit.

Skiing has become an issue similar to evolution, for environmental fundamentalists, and the result has been similar to the Monkey Trial. Sure, ski lift areas got stopped for 22 years, (until Idaho's Tamarack finally cracked the political log jam) and evolution is still not taught in many schools. The problem is that environmentalists, and Al Gore's "green jeans," became the laughing stock of the media, the same way religion is made fun of by many secularists, such as that Monkey Trial reporter. Neither environmental nor religious fundamentalism may be everyone's cup of tea, but both are very real undeniable components of human experience. Evolution and skiing are rejected in both cases, I believe, more because of ignorance than any inherent human defect, which leads me to hope that education is the solution. Maybe "Give me that old time (environmentalism)" will be the theme song for a new ski movie, imitating *Inherit the Wind*.

Skiing of course is only part of the green movement's problems, (just as evolution is only part of religion's problems), but symbolically they are both certainly very important parts. The general public's perception is that facts are too often being twisted, "like man – it *AIN'T* necessarily so." They aren't sure which assertions to believe because the subjects are usually far removed from their secular urban lives. Indiana Jones' lament in *Raiders of the Lost Ark* was "Didn't you guys go to Sunday school?" Of course they probably did not, and they also probably don't ski, hunt, or watch birds. And that is partly why many tend to discount both religion and the environmental movement. It should not be surprising that these two former enemies have lately begun to form alliances, an encouraging trend led by such notables as Harvard scientist E.O. Wilson, with his book *The CREATION An Appeal to Save life on Earth*.

Superstition however still thrives in the information age because it still makes a significant number of people feel

148

better. LasVegas, Disneyland, and televangelism are very successful enterprises. Environmental activism is also big business, and it makes most of its followers feel better too. "Those idiots may destroy our natural world, but at least we went down fighting," is a widely held sentiment. Carrots (i.e. good feelings) work better than sticks, and probably explain most of this activity, but sticks exist too.

Superstition is also the result of fear, and the green doomsayers preach a pretty convincing brand of hellfire and damnation. Are threats to the biosphere, as we know it, worth blowing up University research laboratories in the Pacific Northwest, burning down a beautiful natural wood ski lodge at Vail Colorado, or lying about where lifts are planned and the bed or lift capacity of a proposed ski resort in the Methow Valley, and if it's worth all that, does it really do any good ? Is it worth the loss of credibility?

Obviously some environmentalists think so, but the net result politically has been disastrous for conservation. Al Gore's new Academy Award winning movie *An Inconvenient Truth*, as of this 2007 writing, shows promise to slow or even reverse that loss of credibility. So does the capture, conviction, and one suicide, of the Earth Liberation Front criminals who apparently planned and carried out both the attacks on the research laboratories and the arson at Vail. The straw man tactics used at Early Winters are part of chapter 13, and still an uncomfortable legacy. Whether we can keep extremist, within the environmental movement, in check may determine the outcome of many conservation objectives. The parallel to attempts for an international peace process is apparent, and agonizingly frustrating.

Some wise person once said that "one should never attribute to malice, that which can be adequately explained by stupidity." That may be true for religion and politics, but in the context of conservation biology, (and probably religion and politics too) I would have to add ignorance.

Biology is more complex than we can even imagine, so it is little wonder that different people perceive it differently, depending on how much they know, and what aspect of it they're familiar with. For instance, Al Gore's movie popularizes the current conventional wisdom that Carbon Dioxide is a significant cause of global warming. There are at least a few courageous academics suggesting that rising Carbon Dioxide levels may instead be a result of, rather than a cause of, global warming. Their idea is that climate changes primarily due to solar input variability. If these "deniers" are right we may be headed for a cooling period. That's a nice thought for skiers, but climate complexity suggests uncertainty at best, and meanwhile it won't hurt to try and clean up the atmosphere - no matter what the climate does. The most productive course of action, in the light of this biological complexity, is to put more emphasis on education, rather than confrontation. Religion and politics could also benefit from less violent approaches.

Skiers, and especially professionals in the ski business, do much better with this strategy. Even though we are perceived as evil "developers" by many environmentalists, reality is that an in depth understanding of nature is essential to success in the ski industry. Snow farming comes closest to describing what ski areas actually do, out on the ground. We can teach the world a lot about snow.

Michael Pollan's best selling 2002 book *The Botany of Desire* quotes two famous literary giants on this subject. Pollan uses their quotes to help conclude his first chapter on the apple's coevolution with humans, from its origins in Kazakhstan, to Johnny Appleseed, then its struggles with religious fundamentalists, and now industrial agriculture.

"In wildness is the preservation of the world," from Thoreau, is his reference to the mid 20th Century conventional environmental wisdom. Wendell Berry, the modern proponent of sustainable agriculture, supplies the "necessary corollary" to Thoreau, for the 21st Century: "In human culture is the preservation of wildness." Pollan goes on to the Tulip, Marijuana, and the Potato, for one of the most elegant, and sexually explicit, romps through the sagas of *coevolution* in modern literature. His writing is a wonderful compliment to Dagget's *Gardeners of Eden*, the 21st Century new testament for restoring the biological integrity lost when Europeans invaded the Americas.

Organic snow farming is the image largely already achieved by the cross-country ski areas of North America. Downhill ski areas have a much tougher public relations challenge , even though what they do really only adds lifts and scale to what the cross-country areas are doing. Lifts concentrate human impact, and therefore make it more obvious, but from a biological conservancy view point this also makes impact easier to deal with, because it takes pressure off their surroundings, if they're well managed.

Heidi and Switzerland – represent our mythical alpine Garden of Eden. This powerful fantasy preceded Disney, even though his movies (Heidi and its sequel, with an extremely wild wooden ski scene) help perpetuate it. Swiss reality, including ski lifts, is still for many people an esthetic ideal for living with mountains, and has much that North America is hopefully learning from, (most notably how to use huts and public transit) but that romantic Heidi image is of a beautifully simple agrarian life style which is getting hard to find, and (like America's cowboy) is more a product of good ol'days nostalgia than historic reality.

American wilderness also has a powerful element of fantasy. Heidi and wilderness both tug on peoples' heart strings in ways that make them behave irrationally. If we wish to change their behavior for the benefit of nature as she really is, we have to first remember that they're having fun. Our suggestions to them need to hold out the possibility that reality might help them feel even better. It's the old Unitarian-Universalist strategy, that the truth

151

works best in the long run, even while recognizing how soothing and cozy the old myths are for many people.

The illusion of nordic skiing purity is one of those old powerfully comfortable myths. It is much more than a weird modern form of social Darwinism. It is part of a related dogma which the Craighead twins and Alston Chase refer to as "naturalism," that has led to the official National Park policy of "natural regulation," discussed in the ranger chapter. The root problem is semantic and illuminated by the fact, referred to in my introduction, that Native Americans had no words for wilderness. American "wilderness" was their home and their "garden", before Europeans messed it up. Dr. Roderick Nash explores this dilemma in detail with his classic *Wilderness and the American Mind*, now out in its 4th edition. Nash is not against Wilderness, quite the contrary, in fact. Rather he is explicitly realistic about its attendant fantasies, for the purpose of helping to better manage Wilderness. He's even on the advisory council of Wilderness Watch, the organization specifically focused on the management of Wilderness *areas*, as opposed to wilderness *fantasies*.

The truth can be expressed in the English language by admitting that what we in the western world call "pristine wilderness" is land which *appears* unaffected by our own mechanized western culture. "Naturists," a term not to be confused with naturalists, is a synonym for nudists, and the wilderness our ancestors conquered was inhabited by "naked savages." Nudity is taboo in much of the so called "civilized" world because of its sexual implications, and sex is the principle mechanism through which evolution operates. Sex is as much the reason Darwin is resisted, as of this 2007 writing, as is revulsion to the idea that humans and monkeys have a common ancestor. Sexual hypocrisy is the cultural obstacle which reaches its zenith in the United States and the Middle East, much to the amazement of the more secular Europeans.

That strange polarity, Christian and Muslim - with sex as its common denominator, may partly explain why those two cultures are the current (2007) focus for violence in the world. Violence and disease have served as a check on overpopulation since life began. Sex alone, without these lethal natural selection processes, would overpopulate the world with many species besides ours. Birth control has only recently emerged as an alternative to human violence or disease, and religious resistance to sexual change is at the root of continuing violence against "infidels," Protestants, Catholics, Jews, Grizzly Bears, Wolves, bugs, and all wild nonhuman nature. Religious and cultural warfare's dominance in worldwide media: bikinis vs. burkas, TV vs. libraries, nukes vs. small arms, and of course fundamentalists vs. scientists, is why conservation has been taking a back seat.

Jihad vs. McWorld, How Globalism and Tribalism are Reshaping the World by B.R.Barber supplied the following quote for the IUCN (International Union for Conservation of Nature) book *Securing Protected Areas in the Face of Global Change – Issues and Strategies*, edited by Kenton Miller – project director, Charles Victor Barber, and Melissa Boness.

"in shimmering pastels, a busy portrait of onrushing economic, technological and ecological forces that demand integration and uniformity and that mesmerize peoples everywhere with fast music, fast computers, and fast food – MTV, Macintosh and McDonalds – pressing nations into one homogeneous global theme park, one McWorld tied together by communications, information, entertainment and commerce."

The significance of this for protected areas, including those in snow country, is two fold. The first is that reality is not only global warming, but global distraction over sex and violence, which makes it difficult to get the conservation biology message heard above the noise of religious warfare and partisan bickering. The second is that the cause of religious violence is the same as the cause of environmental conflict and litigation. Overpopulation with conflicting ideas about how to address, or even recognize, it have led to lost credibility with its attendant mistrust and paranoia.

Coevolution of what westerners call "wilderness," with those "naked savages" which historians now finally admit fully inhabited the American continent before Europeans, smallpox, gunpowder, and the plow arrived, is resisted by many environmentalists the way *evolution* is resisted by the religious right in the United States. Dan Dagget's *Gardeners of Eden* is an explanation of *coevolution*, and the counterproductive resistance to it, by too many people. Humans and nature *coevolved*. Nature without humans, or "wilderness" in the minds of many "preservationists," has led to the displacement and loss of wildlife and the destruction of habitat needed for their restoration. Until the environmental community comes to recognize the need to manage wilderness as well as wildlife, restoration is going to have tough times. Wildlife needs the *habitat* that *coevolved* with humanity, those "naked savages."

"Letting nature take her course," the philosophical basis for "natural regulation" is really letting the monocultures and contamination produced by human overpopulation, and gross over consumption, destroy what's left of our biological life support system. Yes, nature can heal herself, but the way we're currently headed she'll likely have to get rid of most humans in the process, probably with a series of pandemics. Then the fly, Mark Twain's idea of God's chosen species – as described in his *Letters from the Earth*, or E.O. Wilson's ants, or Darwin's beetles may inherit the earth. This sort of scenario has been popularized in books such as Sam Harris's THE END OF FAITH – *Religion, Terror, and the Future of Reason*, and James Lovelock's *The Revenge of Gaia*.

Harris's book is especially valuable to this discussion, because he is critical of fundamentalist errors made by both the political left and, of course, the right - as his faith based title fearlessly proclaims. In it he takes on Noam Chompsky, the famous MIT professor and champion of the secular left. Chompsky is criticized by Harris for confusing intent and omission (malice and stupidity), not for his many eloquent and necessary illuminations of the failings of western society. Secular fanaticism is as dangerous as its religious counterpart, because it damages the credibility of the very intellectuals who have the education, skill, and experience to lead the way out of religious warfare and the related environmental quagmire. Harris was significantly back on the best seller list, at the end of 2006, with a new book: *Letter to a Christian Nation*.

Skiing is an evolutionary product of ice age stress which has proved irresistibly enjoyable, for a relatively small, but disproportionately influential minority. Sex, religion, war, alcohol, drugs, and wildlife, probably in about that order, will probably (and in my opinion – unfortunately) always be more popular. Snow skiing's rating on the fun meter however is much higher than environmental litigation – for all but another even smaller, but extremely influential minority. Both minorities would do well to realize that they can ignore the majority (Jihad vs. McWorld) only at their mutual peril.

It is not suprising therefore that ski areas have become refuges from the conventional urban and beach oriented cultures. We who gravitate to snow, and the wildlife associated with snow country, are regarded as strange and exotic by the teeming masses of warmer climates, including most of the United States. Canadians especially, suffer from this popular image. So it is also not suprising that ski areas have become mating grounds, "leks" in wildlife management jargon, for snow people. Some of us have even tried to nest there.

155

Raising a family in ski country inevitably seems to lead away from naturalism, toward the realization that post ice age nature coevolved with humans – hunting, fishing, gathering, burning, fighting, snowshoeing, and skiing. Maybe having to answer our children's questions, while surrounded by nature, makes it more difficult to lie. The *National Geographic Magazine* has made two generations of the Craighead families, in Jackson Hole, Wyoming, into internationally known advocates for the reinvestment of reason into wildlife management. The Courtney families in Stehekin, Washington, share a similar association with this maverick minority view of nature. These views put them at odds with the National Parks' natural regulation policy, and too many greens - who consider them anti-environmental.

Their views are typical of those of us still living and working closely with wildlife. We see the urgent need for hands-on wilderness and wildlife management - and restoration. The 1995 reintroduction of Gray Wolves to Yellowstone is the most dramatic successful example of the need for active management. Neglecting to make sure that an adequate prey base exists before trying to bring back a predator - for instance Red Wolves in the Smokies, is an example of failure. Grizzlies and Wolves without Elk may have similar problems. Heretics in wildlife matters are almost as outcast as religious nonbelievers, but history may yet prove that Galileo, Darwin, Leopold, the Craigheads, and Dagget were correct.

Wilderness is primarily an abstract concept of the urban mind, a beautiful spiritual fantasy that land managers try to satisfy as well as they can, given the constraints of our laws and political-bureaucratic pressures. The Wilderness Act, National Park Organic Act, Endangered Species Act, and so on, are all part of this reality out on the landscape itself. Some legal events however stand out with particular significance, and Mineral King is one of those.

Chapter 10: MINERAL KING - vs. the Sierra Club, preventing ski lifts there, while allowing them at Kirkwood

My own evolution to, what I conceive as, natural reality occurred at the first ski resort born of a Sierra Club lawsuit: Kirkwood, in the northern Sierra Nevada Mountains of California. Wilderness, with a capital "W"- that is legally designated Wilderness Areas, surrounds Kirkwood and provides the flavor for its skiing, summer recreation, and politics.

The 1970's were the time of Kirkwood's attempt to live with a judge's decision, that unlike other skiing targets of Sierra Club lawsuits - most famously Mineral King (in the southern Sierra), this one would be allowed to go ahead – providing it was included retroactively under the National Environmental Policy Act (NEPA). Plans for a mountain top restaurant, and year round tramway access to it, were scrapped. The golf course planned for the big central meadow was even sacrificed. See how I got sucked in ? Of course it probably helped that the peaks around where ski lifts were planned, had been where I'd learned to climb and ski tour as a high school kid. My younger brother drove the bulldozer that punched in Kirkwood Resort's first road. He tired of the ski lift resort game long before I did, and fled to Idaho - to shoe horses. During the time Kirkwood was in the planning stages however, he was wrangling horses for Kirkwood's stable, and quite naturally gravitated to the proposed new resort which promised to do things right, for a change. After all, a Sierra Club litigated ski area might not be all bad. Or could it? We were both curious and emotionally involved.

Up on the Kirkwood rimrock, I could hear cowbells in the central meadow 2000 vertical feet below, but I flushed

157

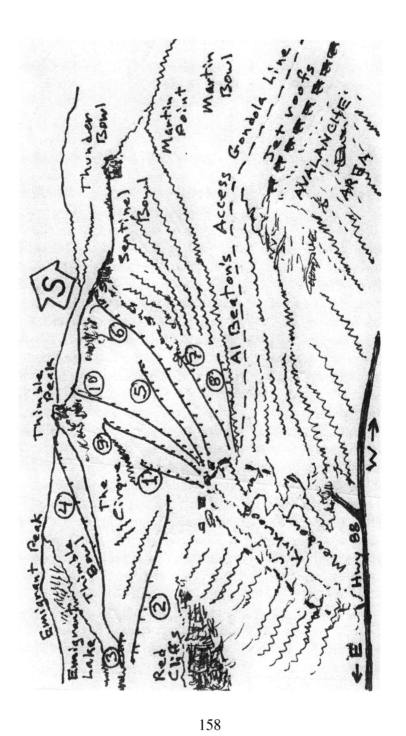

Thunder Bowl

Martin Point

Martin Bowl

Gondola Line

Jet roofs

AVALANCHE AREA

S

Sentinel Bowl

Al Beeton's Access

7

8

6

10

5

Thimble Peak

9

1

4

The Cirque

2

Emigrant Peak

Emigrant Lake

Thimble Bowl

3

Red Cliffs

W

E

Hwy 88

158

a big Mule Deer buck as I jogged past Martin Point. Canadian consultant, Al Beaton had shown me his idea for an up-and-over access gondola that could bypass the avalanche hazard on then summer only Highway 88. His gondola would have gone just north of Martin Point, so I checked the top terminal site to see if the terrain really allowed unloading in both directions; it did - so far, so good. The lift plan he'd laid out was supposed to blend in unobtrusively with the four miles of alpine ridge top. I was skeptical, and needed to look things over by myself, to see if this master plan was realistic. What I found was ski terrain of such high quality that it blinded me to the future problems my kid brother saw from a different perspective. As a forest recreation planner, who was both a skier and naturalist I wanted to see if Kirkwood could work, in both realms. It was a possible new approach to development.

Long talks with Roy Parker at Sierra Blanca (now Ski Apache) in New Mexico, flashed through my mind. A few years before I had skied there regularly, as a young National Park ranger assigned to Big Bend in Texas. Roy had advised that if I wanted to really learn about ski development I'd have to find a ski area at its birth, and work with it to adolescence. After that, he also cautioned, it gets relatively dull – because with all the amenities of our typical modern ski resorts, come the kind of people who need those amenities, and there goes the neighborhood. I wanted that total immersion field course, in what I knew was going to be the biggest source of impact on wildlife in the boreal forest. Kirkwood provided that opportunity.

My brother stopped playing his harmonica, and followed the big German Shepard's gaze out across moonlit Kirkwood Meadow. There were just four foreigners in snowbound Kirkwood that night, that we knew of: my wife and I, my brother and the dog. The Lodgepole Pine fire crackled a bit noisily, so we stepped out on the balcony of Kirkwood's first new home to listen. We'd taken a snowcat in 14 miles from the west, and it was 10 miles in over snow from the east. Snowmobiles and the occasional nordic skier came in, but whatever this was – only the dog could hear. We stood enchanted that April evening, scanning the glistening powder snow and straining to hear too. Finally a sound, unmistakable to us all, came rollicking across the meadow: Yap-yap-yip-yurr-rr-RHAH, and then an echo off of the red cliffs. We wondered how many more winters we'd be able to hear the coyote's lovely music across that meadow. Employee commuter traffic noise was the dominant sound at most ski resorts we knew. Coyotes would quietly thrive in any event, as they do in many cities. The ski industry's and the Sierra Club's credibility were the double elements of doubt in our minds.

Dust engulfed the large flatbed truck, loaded with ski lift parts, as I drove it into the base of #4 chairlift. Finding no one to help unload, and afraid to simply dump my future life support system, I hiked up the lift line to find the cable hauling crew. Puffing hard at that 9000 foot altitude, I realized I was getting even less aerobic exercise as a ski lift construction worker , than I used to as a ranger. The climb was pleasant though, through open glades of Mountain Hemlock trees, together with fields of sub-alpine flowers in peak bloom.

This bowl would have made a nice addition to the adjacent Mokelumne Wilderness, had this lift not been built. It was at the end of an uneconomical series of four chairlifts, leading out to within a mile of the Wilderness boundary. Wind exposed, above timberline, slopes meant that - even in normal years - the expansive Thimble Bowl, that this lift served, would be closed on over 30% of its potential operating days. Beating the Sierra Club to lovely Emigrant Valley apparently seemed more important than short term cash flow obtainable with a more compact lift system, or bypassing the avalanches on Carson Spur with an access gondola, north of Martin Point.

I bought into this concept in hopes of a warming hut, ski touring and hikers' hostel below Emigrant Lake, to take pressure off its fragile meadows. Longer term cash flow suffered too, as Thimble Bowl's windy day closures left the young ski area with no expert terrain. Consequently an expert's only lift (Cornice) had to be built, along with an intermediate skier's lift next to it, to attract the black diamond crowd. All this hardware was too far away from where an access gondola would have dropped skiers off.

Arriving on top I finally found the crew collapsed next to the ski patrol hut, having lunch, and discussing the lawsuit and debates about camouflaging the top terminal. "Yew zee dat r-r-road ovare dare?" the French foreman said with a wave of his sandwich toward Carson Pass, on Scenic Highway 88. "Eye am aeesthet–ickely oaf-ended by eet, ant eye teenk dey shood poot aye camoflage net ovaire eet." Obviously the Sierra Club had little credibility with this veteran of ski lift construction on two continents.

I did get to help Dick Reuter hide the ski trails and lift lines we cut after those first four lifts. No camouflage, just the chance to lay out trails and lifts under the watchful eyes of the most experienced mountain manager in the ski business. The environmental impact statement specified that the lifts and ski trails should not be visible from Scenic Highway 88. Dick pioneered over the snow logging on our ski trails to save both operating costs and prevent soil erosion damage. He taught me more about how ski areas operate than I'd bargained for, and convinced me that private enterprise was inevitable if the public was to get their taxpayers' money's worth on our National Forests. Kirkwood's first snow ranger provided the proof that government sources were not to be trusted, with his off-the-fall-line beginner's ski trail. Dick's avalanche teaching alone was worth the 11 winters I spent away from the

Pacific Northwest. Avalanches, it turned out, were key to the credibility of players in the first proposed ski area to grace the United States Supreme Court – Mineral King.

Kirkwood was far from perfect in spite of Dick Reuter's and the Sierra Club's best efforts. Yet the potential was there to make it much better. Where and how we failed to realize that potential will always haunt me. Ugly condominiums and overcrowded, poorly planned ski lifts were not what I had envisioned back when my brother drove us in on the snow cat. Of all the stories Dick told of other ski areas, the ones about Mineral King, the almost built ski area, fascinated me most. Preventing bad ski areas was clearly as important as building good ones, and avalanches figured into both.

Dick was also a timber faller of such skill and reputation that he sometimes made more money on his days off, from his mountain manager jobs, than he did at those ski areas. Thus it happened that he cleared the huge Mountain Hemlock stumps from the site of the Alpine Meadows Ski Area base lodge. I'd shied away from working there as my first ski patrol job, years before, just from the look of the slopes above that base area. Those stumps which Dick cut, had been sheared off at 8 and 10 feet above the ground by avalanches. In 1982, while I was still at Kirkwood an avalanche took out the bottom lift terminal and four employees' lives, including Anna Conrad's fiancé, and our friend Bernie Kingery – Alpine Meadows' mountain manager. Anna was the first live avalanche victim found by a search dog in America.

Mineral King exemplified the skiing versus wildlife and wilderness debate, which there became Disney versus the Sierra Club. No - those weren't the legal titles, but they're how the public perceived it. Dick had been part of a survey team that prepared a bid in competition to Disney's, for the Forest Service Permit to build Mineral King. His team failed to get the job because they had realistically planned for the avalanche hazard – that the Disney corporation's plan underestimated. One Disney team member was killed by an avalanche on site, and the stories told about snow surveys there are legendary within the avalanche profession.

Mineral King's case didn't go all the way to the United States Supreme Court because of avalanches however. The issue before the Court was the Sierra Club's right to sue on behalf of Mineral King's natural objects; their "legal standing." A similar case, as far as its public's perception is concerned, at this 2007 writing, is the Arctic National Wildlife Refuge (ANWR). Mineral King, like ANWR, became a political football.

Two books have been written about Mineral King, the most famous of which is *Should Trees Have Standing* by Christopher Stone, referred to briefly at the end of my lifts chapter, as a segue to trails. In it he thoroughly explores the dissenting opinion of the late Supreme Court Justice – William O. Douglas, from Yakima in Washington State. Douglas was a famous outdoorsman and prolific author, in addition to his long and illustrious career on the Court. His opinion was a dissent, because the Court majority ruled against the Sierra Club. Justice Douglas was also a key player in setting up the Arctic National Wildlife Refuge, the largest legal Wilderness in the United States.

Mineral King is now better known among conservation lawyers than skiers. The second book however details events out on the ground itself, including avalanches and misunderstandings about them. It's by John Harper, and titled *MINERAL KING, Public Concern with Government Policy*. The resolution there was finally political - with legislation adding it to Sequoia National Park, including the specific prohibition against "any permanent ski facilities." This last detail was added because Sequoia already had ski lifts, as did several other National Parks.

Avalanches are the real reason Mineral King should never be serviced with lifts, but few people know or care. Many skiers regard it as their greatest single defeat at the hands of preservationists. If the Disney planned ski resort had been built it would only have been a matter of time until a European scale avalanche disaster struck. Many skiers still don't want to believe this, in spite of the articles I and other avalanche technicians wrote for national magazines like *Powder*. I remember our off-the-fall-line snow ranger at Kirkwood casting doubt on avalanche consultant Norm Wilson's "loyalty," when he dared to write the truth about Mineral King.

That the Disney Corporation happens to have helped perpetuate the folly that was Mineral King, is probably just coincidence, as is their rise to be a leading corporate power. Much more important to the world, and wildlife especially, is the Hollywood-New York inbred urban cultural axis of media monopoly on what gets broadcast and published. My wildlife photographer friends in the Olympic Mountains told me horror stories about what happened to their footage, when it went to the Los Angeles cutting rooms. The Olympic Elk was one of the few films that made it through to release without being butchered. It received, and deserved, an Academy Award. Later films in Disney's *True Life Adventure* series got progressively worse. The Lemming scenes in *White Wilderness* not only perpetuated the long standing arctic myths about mass suicide, but also infuriated animal rights groups, when word leaked out about how those scenes had been faked.

"The Disney Version" is now a generic term applied to wildlife pornography, among other things, produced by a world wide network of companies and individuals. An annual wildlife film festival is hosted in Missoula Montana, and there have been partially successful attempts to clean up the industry. Good wildlife films do exist, but not enough to counter the now long established

164

myths, or restore credibility to the industry. The recent deaths of photographers and presenters, who got too close, (to Grizzlies and Sting Rays, lately) have cast further doubt on their credibility. Honest photographers now routinely state whether captive animals or digital alterations were used to produce what is published.

Bambi and all of Smokey's cute little forest friends, are also instruments of the urban media's brainwashing. Bambi and Smokey, like Jesus and Jonah, have become icons for lost credibility, and the unfortunate fact that too many people still believe that these metaphorical myths are literally true. Canadian naturalist John Livingston has written books, including *The Fallacy of Wildlife Conservation* and *One Cosmic Instant* that tried to warn of these problems. Livingston's ideas, about why much of conservation is sadly failing, anticipated the publication of *The Death of Environmentalism.*, by Shellenberger and Nordhaus. This more recent book is getting much wider attention, perhaps because of the much more obvious conservation defeats and wildlife setbacks engineered by neoconservatives under George W. Bush.

Another Canadian, Shane Mahoney, puts these conflicts into clearer perspective with the 2006 release of the DVD *OPPORTUNITY FOR ALL; The Story of the North American Model for Wildlife Conservation* by the Rocky Mountain Elk Foundation and Conservation Visions. The need for organizations like the Rocky Mountain Elk Foundation is the result of the failure of government processes alone to adequately conserve and restore wildlife. Success is incremental, and most biologists and naturalists, such as Livingston, see the need for a much greater educational effort in the face of *"The Population Bomb."* The fact that too many famous, (and way too influential), political neoconservatives are still blind too overpopulation and the need to limit growth – is "the fallacy of wildlife conservation." The fact that North American wildlife and

Wilderness have been able to hold out, as well as they have, against overpopulation pressure is a beacon of hope for the rest of the world.

Skiing and the all-season resorts originally built for skiing, have the best chance to accomplish the cultural deprogramming needed for wildlife restoration. Snow country reality is seen by the most people through the lens of ski resorts. National Parks come in a pretty close second, but are politically, budgetarily, bureaucratically, and geographically limited. Mineral King's southern California location, closer to the L.A. market than Mammoth Mountain Ski Resort, on the east side of the central Sierra, was seen by the Disney Corporation as an obvious opportunity. Opponents to Disney's plans saw an equally obvious need to keep the antithesis of all things natural as far away from Mineral King as possible.

The Sierra Nevada, Klamath Mountains, Cascades, Southern British Columbia, Laurentians, Adirondacks, and New England, in particular, lie adjacent to the population centers most brainwashed and at risk for perpetuating the destabilizing effects of our "McWorld." Professional naturalists shudder to think of where many of their visitors may have just come from. L.A. and New York City are the poles of our urban media "axis of evil," but spinning around them are other cities filled with electronically hypnotized multitudes with little direct wildlife experience. Even country inns in very nonurban locations, such as the Methow Valley, need to have "wireless" electronic cocoons to shelter their city slicker guests from a potential overdose of nonvirtual reality.

Disneyland and LasVegas are only the most famous theme parks. They are being cloned at an alarming rate, and the wiser heads in our ski industry are advising that we not try to imitate them. They remember the trouncing the ski industry and U. S. Forest Service took at Mineral King. Our best marketing strategy is to provide unique alternatives to "McWorld." Some snow people come to ski areas specifically to escape the mass mediocrity engulfing them back home. Cross-country ski areas have benefited most from this trend, but many of my ski school students would enjoy lifts too, if they didn't come with so many unpleasant side effects. British Columbia's Silver Star and Sun Peaks are proving that both kinds of skiing can coexist, based out of the same resort village. Such resorts provide the opportunity for a cultural progression from the "extreme sports" scene, hot tub sex fantasies, and glamorous restaurants - that may have initially attracted most guests, to things like a naturalist led walk on snowshoes or cross-country skis – looking at wildlife tracks and birds.

National Parks simply don't have the capacity to handle all the urban pilgrims seeking a "wilderness experience." Wilderness Areas are even more limited in what they can legally provide. Ski areas, especially ski lift areas, have the facilities to handle the big crowds. They are certainly not wilderness, but that doesn't change the fact that they give their patrons an opportunity to view wilderness from the comfortable surroundings which most of them require. That first step is absolutely essential, and we naturalists who seek to regain credibility with today's voters, would do well to pay more attention to what's happening around ski lifts. Why? Because that's where the people are !

Mineral King's defeat gave a much needed pause to the ski industry's frantic expansion in the 1970's. It may even have helped defeat the Early Winters and other ski lift area proposals. Disney proceeded much more cautiously in evaluating alternatives after Mineral King's demise. The public also was at least a little more cautious about anything with the Disney label. This mix of skiing and the public's perceptions of wildlife and wildlife habitat, most notably the "pristine wilderness" myth, just happens to

167

revolve around Mineral King and the fantasies of both the skiing and wildlife constituencies.

Alston Chase and many other critics of the environmental movement, make some very valid points. Chase's chapter titles in *Playing God in Yellowstone*, such as "Hubris commandos" and "California cosmologists" tell of the ongoing struggle within the environmental community to throw off "The Bambi Syndrome," and the popular images of many environmentalists as irrational "tree huggers." Religious leaders, even the Mormons and a few evangelicals recently, are starting to support conservation, but we can hardly blame them for being a little cautious yet about environmentalism. The "E" word is tainted with too much intolerance and mythology. It has become too much like the religions it replaced, for too many of its true believers.

Sam Harris's *The End of Faith* spells out the strangely unpopular lessons that centuries of religious warfare have taught us. Skiers and environmentalists thankfully have largely avoided the gruesome tactics of religion, but dishonesty and ignorance still persist as the all too obvious credibility gap embarrassingly demonstrates. The ski industry is currently making more obvious efforts to close that gap, but positive examples can be found in both realms: religion and conservation.

Patrick O'Donnell, the CEO of Aspen Ski Corporation, is leading the ski world with highly visible environmentally friendly operational policies and practices. He happens to be uniquely qualified as his resume includes the top management jobs at: Badger Pass ski area in Yosemite National Park, Kirkwood, Keystone, The Yosemite Institute, Patagonia, and Whistler.

Tamarack, the new kid on the block in Idaho, is following the Canadian lead of Silver Star and Sun Peaks by blending nordic and downhill skiing into one seamlessly integrated whole. Tamarack's architecture is also setting high standards for the use of natural stone and wood in the best tradition of National Parks and the old CCC (Civilian Conservation Corps). The National Parks themselves are also finally seeing the architectural light. Mount Rainier is in the process of replacing the ugly concrete and glass monstrosity of a visitor center at Paradise with a structure to match the old classic Paradise Lodge, which also will be retained and renovated.

Robert Redford is leading both the skiing and environmental industries with his tastefully understated Sundance ski lift resort in Utah, and as the most famous board member and spokesman for, the Natural Resource Defense Council (NRDC) tackling some of wildlife's most formidable antagonists, including the U.S. Navy. Perhaps because Redford has a foot in both worlds he is viewed with suspicion by some environmentalists I've run into.

Redford isn't the only peacemaker with this problem. Audubon, The Nature Conservancy, and naturally the Rocky Mountain Elk Foundation (hunters after all !) have been most conspicuously accused of "disloyalty." This sort of "us vs. them" polarized mentality reminds me of my old off-the-fall-line snow ranger, and America's two party political polarizing system. Somehow the truth has to break through this irrational tribal feuding tradition.

The Sierra Club used to be the leading environmental organization. They, and many of their allies in the timber wars, could regain the credibility they once had, during the Mineral King era (when David Brower was running things) if they could renounce their "no commercial cutting on Public Lands" policy. Reality is that the politically conservative urban majority is not going to pay for the forest fuel reduction needed to keep the boreal, or any other, forest from going up in smoke, methane and carbon dioxide. Sustainable forest practices have to pay for themselves, and wood is a renewable resource that can be responsibly managed.

Mineral King was about trees, and "public concern with government (forest) policy" - in its most lasting legal legacy. Forestry is slowly regaining its credibility as foresters are increasingly finding employment with NGOs, and as consultants to the new owners of forest lands. These newly acquired holdings are often cut-over forests that the old traditional timber companies can no longer afford to keep, in the face of escalating land prices and tax structures. Land Trusts, resort developers, and distant speculative corporations may compete or cooperate in managing these new ownership structures. The forestry profession has the knowledge to help them manage for either profit or restoration, but ideally both - if the new owners are smart enough to realize that, in the long run, the two have to go together.

Tree huggers and cow haters have to give up their cherished mythologies, and admit that wood, meat, and milk are part of the human life support system, almost always have been, and probably always will be, because they are renewable. Population control will still be needed, even if the whole world went plastic and vegan. Try that on the Eskimos or Sami ! Wilderness advocates will have to give up their "natural regulation" myths too. They need to quit fighting constructive developments adjacent to Wilderness and wildlife reserves – such as ski areas that support wildlife restoration.

Ski trails, paid for by the logs removed to create them, can help restore America's National Forests and Canada's Crown Lands to the more wildlife friendly habitats, once managed by Native Americans. "Vegetarian is an old Indian word meaning lousy hunter," and the truth behind this hunters' joke relates to why fire was used for millennia to thin the forest. Steve Arno and Steven Allison-Bunnell put it neatly in their *Flames in Our Forests* book: "We need to become high-tech hunter-gatherers." This too however, is an over simplification - because hunting and gathering cultures can, and have led to the extinction of wildlife, Mastodons being the most dramatic example.

Dan Dagget's and Wendell Berry's inclusive message of *coevolution:* humanity and wildlife habitat, equally - and once again - working together for their mutual benefit, can be the new strategy for environmentalists. The restoration of credibility is needed for both the ski resort industry and the champions of snow country wildlife. Of the two however, it is the wildlife, and wildlife's friends – such as hunters especially, who are the least understood and hardest to explain to a population several generations removed from any intimate contact with the land, either as farms and ranches - or wild country.

Mineral King finally gave trees legal standing. It is skiing's somewhat reluctant gift to conservation, and it has revolutionized conservation law. It's southern California location, next to the Sierra Club's power base, and the persuasive dissenting opinion of Justice William O. Douglas from Washington State, give this almost ski area's case a special western social credibility that will outlast it's misguided attempt to be a ski lift area. Many other ski areas that got their lifts, such as Kirkwood, bear the responsibility for proving that ski lift areas can be good neighbors for wildlife and Wilderness. Ironically it is Mineral King, the almost ski area that never became the feared "Disneyland in the Sierra" that gave us the legal key to saving and restoring wildlife habitat.

171

FISHER

Chapter 11: LYNX – and the keystone wildlife

Ten chapters have concentrated on trail related human factors bearing on wildlife restoration. Essential as these are however, I think this is the place to take a closer look at some of the animals themselves. The Lynx just happens to currently be under the endangered species legal spotlight and therefore perhaps the most famous, or infamous - depending on your orientation. Many others deserve our attention, and some are certainly more important. Those thought to deserve the most attention are often referred to as "keystone" species.

The capture, tagging, radio collaring, and release of a young female Wolverine near Harts Pass, above the Methow, during the winter of 2006, made the front page of our local paper. Letters to the editor were universally sympathetic for the Wolverine, and very critical of the interference with her life. When she went to Canada and her collar quite moving, many feared the worst. Her later return to Harts Pass with a boyfriend - who was also captured, ear tagged, radio collared and released, dramatized the Canadian connection and the need for international cooperation. The winter of 2007 got another duo radio collared near the easternmost tip of North Cascades National Park, just south of the Methow Valley. One of the females was also pregnant. Wolverines have a fierce reputation, and are almost as widespread and thoroughly adapted to the boreal forest, as the Lynx.

The return of a Wolverine to the Wolverine state (Michigan) made headlines there. They are not yet on the endangered list, but it seems inevitable, that they're headed that way. My closest encounter with a Wolverine occurred on one of the routine ski patrols that I voluntarily performed during the winters of 1983 to 1987, in North Cascades National Park. The aging roof of the old snow survey cabin, which was my summer backcountry patrol headquarters in the Park, was in eminent danger of being collapsed by snow. (It was torched by the Park in 1988.) Skiing in to shovel it off was a nice quiet counterpoint to my noisy winter job, guiding helicopter skiers in the adjacent Okanogan National Forest. On this occasion I'd invited my fellow ski instructor, heli-ski guide, and commercial cross- country ski entrepreneur, Don Portman, to come along.

The two of us made quick work of shoveling the roof, so we were free to check out some new potential heli-ski runs immediately adjacent to the Park. Fresh Wolverine tracks caught our attention as we ascended toward the National Forest boundary, and since they were going up too, we followed along. Two ski instructor/guides, on top of their form, can easily catch up with a Wolverine, as we soon discovered. This Wolverine seemed simply curious about us, as we observed from a respectful distance. Certainly there was no hint of its famous ferocious behavior. We then continued to ski up the mountain on what we guessed would be our path of least disturbance to our gracious wilderness host. As good as the skiing was, and it was great, our close encounter of the wildlife kind was the highlight of that ski trip.

The International Wolf Center in Minnesota is also in superlative cross-country ski territory. It is the leading organizations dedicated to educating the public about predation ecology. Wolves are the most important keystone species in boreal forests, because their hunting tactics and leftovers effect all other life. Yellowstone's Grizzlies have been only the most obvious beneficiaries. Wolves and their ecological influence, have given cross-country skiing there additional interest too. More cross-country skiers means more citizens witnessing the obvious noise and air pollution from snowmobiles. The planned phase out of snowmobile use, within Yellowstone Park, has incidentally been helped by this very successful Wolf

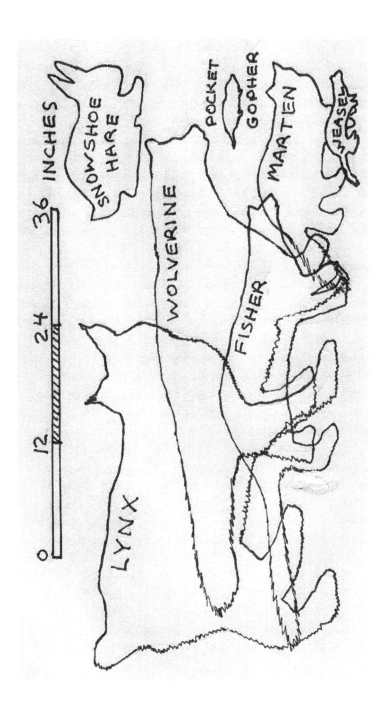

SNOWSHOE HARE

POCKET GOPHER

MARTEN

WEASEL STOAT

WOLVERINE

FISHER

LYNX

INCHES

36 24 12 0

reintroduction. Wolves share with Lynx and Wolverines the distinction of being important original native residents of circumpolar boreal forests. Why one species or another catches more public attention is often a product of complex events, such as criminal actions.

The successful reintroduction of Lynx to Colorado, financed in part by Vail Ski Resort, toned down some of the anti-skiing environmentalist sentiment that may have led to the arson at Vail. The arrest and prosecution of those guilty of this and other crimes with "environmental" motives has helped somewhat to heal the embarrassingly tarnished reputation and credibility of the environmental community.

Restoration is possible, as these two, and other dramatic examples illustrate. Cross-country skiers tend to love wildlife, and many of those other, lift riding conspicuously consuming, downhill skiers favor wildlife too. Put a bunch of ski resorts and second homes into a valley like the Methow anyway, and the wildlife will be much safer than they ever were with the hook and bullet folks. At least more of the hooks are barbless and some of the guns are shooting tranquilizers for wildlife research. Not enough hunting or natural predation around all these new houses is an additional complication. Overabundant deer, Elk, and Moose can consequently become more than a nuisance. Safety problems involve both these large animals themselves and the predators that eventually follow them. Banff is a classic case of the former, and Boulder Colorado of the latter. Fortunately many of these new land owners tend to support local land trusts and conservancies to protect their new investments and life style choices. Unfortunately their experience with, and knowledge of, wildlife is often quite limited.

These days, guests at our country inns and lodges in the Methow tend to avoid hunting season. Hunters used to be a very major source of revenue for rural communities.

Now they mainly occupy a couple weeks in October, when the majority of our guests then are asking about trails in the National Park .

Hunters still do more to support wildlife than any other class of wildlife enthusiasts. This is true, even in the liberal enclaves surrounding ski areas, although many of these recent urban refugees may not realize it. The North American model for wildlife conservation was initiated by hunters such as Teddy Roosevelt and Aldo Leopold. The taxes hunters pay on their sporting equipment, and the organizations they support, are the financial backbone of wildlife conservation. Regrettably shooting road signs from the backs of oversized pickup trucks, firearms accidents, and tossing beer cans and bottles for the rest of us to pick up, has done for hunting what clear cuts did for forestry. Prudent hunters don't parade around ski towns in their camo outfits anymore. Conversely some ski resorts have learned to advertise for hunters, during the hunting season, because many of their regular clientele are staying away.

A few years ago much was made of Vail's expansion into Blue Sky Basin, as an impingement on prime Lynx habitat. A whole hundred acres were said to be at risk, according to one account I read. Whether or not 100 acres, or 1000 acres, would make any real difference, misses the symbolic significance of the very extreme irrationality surrounding lift skiing. Actually any small opening of the boreal forest probably enhances habitat for Snowshoe Hare, the favored prey for Lynx. A 1000 acre clearcut however is far different from 1000 acres of ski trails with their productive edge habitat for wildlife. Maybe those "100 acres" surrounded a new day lodge. Vail's ski trail map for Blue Sky Basin denotes areas off limits for skiers, to protect wildlife.

Lodgepole Pine, which burns frequently or succumbs to insect attacks, or both, is the boreal forest component most likely to supply the early successional stages favored by the forage plants which Snowshoe Hare prefer. Spruce and fir trees tend to cycle more slowly or be replaced, after a fire, by Lodgepole Pine. Anyway it happens, disturbance of one kind or another, on a schedule that keeps snow bunnies well fed, also keeps Lynx well fed. Ski trails will do just fine, as long as the Lynx aren't being trapped, shot, or otherwise harassed.

Equally important for Lynx might be the competition supplied by other carnivores, and much has been made of this possibility by the opponents of snowmobiling. The theory as expressed in the U.S. Forest Service guidelines for management of Lynx habitat is that the firm snow provided by any "recreation" trails may allow Cougars, Coyotes, and Bobcats to compete with Lynx up in the deep snow country. These guidelines admit that the theory is unproven, but the Forest Service uses it anyway to justify a policy of no new trails in snow country. The problem with this is first, that it's probably not valid as explained in my introduction, and second that more recreation trails are needed to manage the impact away from the critical habitat for lots of other species. Trail design and maintenance as zoning tools, for an alternative to "police state wilderness" is the theme of my trails chapter. What the Lynx habitat controversy illustrates is that different animals have different needs. Some of these other species are more important than Lynx to over all ecosystem health, and therefore indirectly help Lynx survival. These are often called keystone species.

Like the keystones in the arches of traditional European stone masonry, these species occupy essential places in the structure of wild lands. Beavers are perhaps most obvious and easily understood, because of their effect on water tables. Much less obvious, but equally important, is their geological effect, further flattening the bottoms of valleys already gentle enough to allow them to build the first dams. Multiple generations of dams and the Aspens, Cottonwoods, or Willows necessary for both food and construction material, weave a complex multilayered mosaic of silted up dams turned to meadows as trees are used up, then back to riparian forests, and back to dams again, and again, over and over, for thousands of years. "U" shaped glacial valleys can by this process have riparian habitat extended closer to their steep sidewalls.

Riparian areas obviously are the richest wildlife habitat. What's not so obvious, at still another ecological level, is what it takes to maintain forests that will sustain Beavers, and therefore keep water tables at the levels with which other species, such as Lynx evolved. Yellowstone has been beautifully demonstrating that Beavers depend on Wolves, and other top carnivores to keep the Elk populations low enough, and moving enough, to allow the riparian forests to grow sufficiently to sustain the Beavers and their dams. Predation by Wolves which thins the beaver populations also sometimes helps their trees recover. Management guidelines that focus narrowly on one species, or even some group of species that happened to get listed under the Endangered Species Act (ESA) are doomed to failure. "It's the (habitat), stupid" is the often paraphrased political slogan, that possibly can work for wildlife.

The increase in large and artificially intense, wildfires, due to fuel buildup, misplaced trail priorities, and a warming climate, meanwhile erodes the habitat for old growth species such as Spotted Owls, the endangered species that spawned much of the habitat dilemma. Using Lynx as an excuse to stop ski trails is perhaps ironically appropriate. Fewer trails means less fuel fragmentation and reduction, which in turn creates the indirect effects of more stand replacing insect epidemics and crown fires, which then bring on the early successional vegetation stages favorable to Hares and Lynx. Too bad about the

179

owls, and other species favored by late successional forests. Which endangered species wins, is the new game.

The *Wilderness Management Handbook* by Hendee and Dawson, and available from the Fulcrum Press in Colorado, is in its 3rd edition, and one of the very best references for those desiring to see the whole picture. It is written by and for professionals, but comprehensible to anyone reasonably familiar with the outdoors. Recognized expert authors contribute chapters in their respective fields, from fire ecology to recreation impact. It's expensive, $65 U.S. in 2007, and hard to find on either local library shelves or your local Forest Service office, but there's no harm in bugging both, before you finally may decide to order it yourself.

The handbook's authors assume a certain knowledge base, so for instance if the reader is not yet familiar with the Lynx – Snowshoe Hare 10 year cycle, they may want to check out some basic wildlife and forestry primers. Much of this stuff has been around for centuries, because our interaction with wildlife and boreal forests - including written records, goes back to the fur trade which opened up the North American Continent to European settlement. The Hudson Bay Company account books are the classic documentation for the dependency of Lynx on Snowshoe Hare. Ten years happens to closely match sun spot cycles, but recent research points to a vegetation impact and recovery cycle as the governing factor, with obvious but complex feedback loops, involving the Lynx, fire, insects, and all the other predators.

"Charismatic megafauna" is the term often used to describe the effect big furry animals, such as Lynx, have on the politically influenced wildlife agency budget funding and regulatory processes. Research currently is showing that some of our keystone species may not fall into that popular category, bees for instance, or bark beetles. Some of the most critical species may even turn out to be plants or lichens. Managing these first involves research of the type pioneered by none other than the U.S. Forest Service, through their research division.

Forest research personnel and budgets have been cut back severely during the Republican dominated years since the neoconservatives gained prominence in 1994, but still survive at a token scale. Publications originated by the Forest Service like the *Wilderness Management Handbook* have been taken over by NGOs (non government organizations), and an argument can be made that this is actually an improvement. Certainly there are fewer political and bureaucratic constraints to publishing the truth. Retired forest research scientist, such as Steve Arno (fire), Jack Ward Thomas (Elk and owls), and Mike Dombeck (fisheries), may be contributing more effectively to wildlife and forest management now that they are freed from the politically dominated government service. Thomas and Dombeck also served successively as heads of the United States Forest Service. The buildup of years of frustration may help too.

The best role for government is always open for debate, and the training which professionals like myself gained in government run agencies can perhaps lead to better service in our retirement, than if we'd never been through all that "official" training and the school of hard knocks. Critics of the enlarged role NGOs are taking on, argue that the lack of accountability to the broader public can also be a liability. Most NGOs answer to their members and funding sources, not the general public. Snow country involves many different kinds of cultures, sovereign states, and political systems, with different ways of organizing the management of wildlife, parks, wilderness, and commercial skiing.

Whatever their ideal role may be, reality in the early 21st Century is that collectively NGOs currently are the largest influence on wildlife, in terms of money, political influence, management, and research. The Switzerland based IUCN (International Union for the Conservancy of Nature), is the main organization attempting to provide communication and coordination world wide, among the vast array of NGOs which are evolving to fill the voids left by shrinking government appropriations for wildlife.

Their approaches to wildlife conservation are as many and varied as their respective constituencies, but so far they have tended to pattern their best efforts on the Canadian-American model of wildlife and wilderness reserve management. This is what established wildlife as public property, dramatically restoring most of the wildlife populations that had been nearly wiped out during the ethnic cleansing of North America.

Canadian and American National Parks also inspired the non hunting public to support wildlife conservation and restoration biology. So what started out as an effort primarily by hunters, is now almost equally supported by non hunters, "birdwatchers" and other urban come-lately followers of John Muir. Wilderness management, still struggling for acceptance on the continent that invented it, is nevertheless now being applied in many other parts of the civilized world. It even has its own periodical: the *International Journal of Wilderness*.

Conserving Forest Biodiversity – A Comprehensive Multiscaled Approach by Lindenmayer and Franklin (2002) takes these North American inspired concepts from a less crowded past century and attempts to apply them to the 21st. Its principle contribution to the debate is the concept of *matrix management*, meaning that management of the landscapes surrounding the Parks and other nature reserves, is as (or more) important than the reserves themselves, or the corridors recently conceived as the means of encouraging continued genetic transfer and therefore continuing evolution.

Wildlife, and birds especially, tend to not confine their activity to our narrowly conceived reserves, or even the migration corridors between them. These fauna, and even the wind, carry the seeds and spores of flora both ways across reserve boundaries. Wildlife management has the advantage of very much wider public acceptance than wilderness management, and also happens to largely control, along with fire and range management, what goes on in the matrix landscape. Whether Elk or cows, or deer or sheep, or Moose, are chewing on the flora out there, makes a big difference on what's available to burn in the next forest or range fire, what's available for birds to eat, and the winds to blow, and therefore what is available for animals such as Snowshoe Hare and Lynx to eat.

Wide ranging charismatic megafauna, such as our Lynx, dramatically carry the message of matrix dependency. Birds do this on a world wide scale, and have the advantage of being accessible and attractive to the fast growing "sport" of bird watching. "Birdwatchers" is the generic term often used to describe this usually non hunting wildlife constituency, who may in fact be as concerned with Lynx, Wolves, or Grizzlies, as with birds. Many neotropical migrating birds nest in the boreal forest, so the tie-in is hardly unexpected. Birds are simply the urban accessible charismatic mini-fauna that are most likely to hook city people into supporting wildlife NGOs, or voting for and supporting political candidates that promise to take care of nature.

Lynx share the boreal forest with an assortment of other wildlife that, although lesser known, are equally important to snow country ecosystems. The term keystone species oversimplifies what actually happens in nature. The concept however is useful for the purpose of allocating scarce resources in wild land management, and certainly some species are more important than others, and are capable of carrying others along with them. Which species

183

may be discovered to be important next is hard to predict, so it's useful to introduce some of those less famous.

The Fisher is one of two members of the weasel family to have the honor of a book devoted specifically to him, in this case - a young male. *Winter of the Fisher* by Cameron Langford may be hard to find, but is well worth the effort if you enjoy novels about the Northwoods. The other book *Ring of Bright Water* by Gavin Maxwell, about Otters, is much more well known, but less illustrative of boreal forest ecology. Many members of the weasel family are widespread in the boreal forest, and together occupy an important position in keeping the rodent populations in some sort of sustainable balance with vegetation. The Fisher has been successfully reintroduced into its former range in the New England States to control Porcupines, which can damage conifer plantations. Olympic National Park is in the process of studying the possible need to restore Fishers, simply for biodiversity, and the complex accompanying multiplier effects.

All the weasel family members are specialized for somewhat different ecological niches, primarily provided by the even more diverse rodents and other animals or fish that they prey on. I've watched a Marten, for instance, take a Snowshoe Hare out beside a ski trail in the North Cascades. The Hare was about twice as big as the Marten, but that was not a problem in *that* snow condition. Certainly however, in *softer* snow, smaller rodents such as Red Squirrels are usually more convenient for a Marten, which can catch them in the tree tops, a tactic less available to the much larger Fisher. The Fisher also can pursue prey through the tree tops, but is at a disadvantage with smaller prey because of its heavier weight and smaller feet which also are a disadvantage in soft snow.

Of all the rodents in the Northeast Cascades, probably the one most deserving of the keystone title, other than the Beaver, would be the Pocket Gopher. Ermine, the little weasels that turn white in winter, are one of the few predators that can move freely through narrow Pocket Gopher tunnels, in the snow - at ground level in winter, and underground in summer. These Gophers are nature's rototillers, moving and mixing tons of soil. Their backfilled snow tunnels make those sinuous dirt mounds seen on the surface of mountain meadows. Little is known about the predator – prey relationships of these two little animals, but we do know that soil is the basis for wildland health, and every inhabitant of the forest and adjacent meadows, including the insects and flowers.

Wildlife is the basis for plenty of "nature faking," as Theodore Roosevelt used to call it, and predators get some of the worst. The *International Wolf Magazine* often runs a column titled: "Don't Believe Everything You Read". It features press statements sent in by readers that they know, or suspect, are false, alongside the scientists' explanations. *Never Cry Wolf* by Canadian author Farley Mowat is the target for repeated criticism because what was represented as a first hand account, was actually fiction, and also because his book left many readers with the impression that Wolves are primarily mousers.

The Disney movie of the same name got much of the same bad press reviews, but nevertheless helped spread Mowat's books to the far corners of the world, translated into many languages. I thought the movie was maybe better than the book because its protagonist is a nerdy wildlife student out getting his field education the hard way, like falling through the ice. Mowat's books still sell well and have probably recruited millions of people to the cause of nature conservation, even if they do contain some biological flaws.

Canadians are reasonably tolerant of naturalists that take liberties with reality, and the most famous of all actually presented his Beavers very accurately to his international audiences with on-stage performances,

185

dressed up as a Canadian Indian and holding his little Beaver kits. Grey Owl was the name he used on stage, as an author, and as a hunting guide. Actually he was an Englishman, and that's what got him in trouble with the critics. His books also still sell very well and he, and his Canadian Indian wife, are credited with educating the world about the keystone role of Beavers, and therefore finally getting better trapping regulations that let Beavers, water tables, and lots of other wildlife recover. Grey Owl also was the subject of a movie by that name, starring Pierce Brosnon, the actor more famous as a recent James Bond, the intrepid agent 007, but his Mohawk wife was a lot cuter. Grey Owl was also the inspiration for one of the most beautiful books, published recently (2002), about the boreal forests of eastern Canada: *In the Footsteps of Grey Owl – Journey Into The Ancient Forest* by Gary and Joanie McGuffin.

Predation as an ecological function, has probably been most understandably presented in a book with a title which almost tells the story by itself. *Why Big Fierce Animals Are Rare*, by Paul Colinvaux, also explores some other biological myths equally well, such as why blue water isn't necessarily better than green. When big fierce animals are not rare we suspect problems with public safety and ecological health. *The Beast in the Garden* , by David Baron examines the fatally tragic consequences of misunderstanding predators, using Cougars and the new age community of Boulder Colorado as his example.

The Okanogan National Forest is home to one of the largest remaining Lynx populations in the lower 48 states. Private efforts recently raised the money necessary to stop logging on the Loomis Forest owned by the state of Washington, adjacent to Okanogan National Forest on the east, and to Canada immediately to the north. Lynx was the symbolic wildlife involved, and also prompted the Canadian designation of the Snowy Protected Area, just east of the existing Cathedral Provincial Park, and immediately north of the Loomis Forest. Canada is currently (2007) pursuing the possibility for a new National Park in this area, their southern Okanagan. And yes, they really do spell it with three "a"s. National Park status in Canada might help establish an international peace park, similar to the Waterton and Glacier Parks on the Alberta, British Columbia, and Montana border.

During the fall of 2006, the massive "Tripod" forest fire spread into the Loomis, and will probably renew its Lodgepole stands. Two other lightning caused fires were simultaneously doing the same for Lodgepole and Lynx within Okanogan National Forest further west: one in the Pasayten Wilderness up by Canada's Manning Provincial Park, and the other in our non-Wilderness but roadless, and very rugged heli-ski permit area. So rugged, in fact, that it's safe from snowmobiles and was judged unsafe for firefighters to get in close to the fire itself, initially. This is how "Late Successional Reserves" get changed to *early successional* forest stands. It is also how people, including bureaucrats and politicians, get ever so slowly educated about fire and wildlife. Recently blackened moonscapes don't look much like old growth (late successional) forests, and the voting public notices these things.

The forest fire that burned in our heli-ski area opened up terrain that previously was somewhat tight skiing in the bottoms of two of our favorite bowls. It is has also thinned forest stands just below there, suited to Scandinavian style ski touring, touched on in the huts chapter, and fire fighters finally did a little thinning along the firebreak clearing down below, at Early Winters. Some of our local greens of course wanted the fire line "restored," while our cross-country skiers saw a good start toward more groomed ski trails. The inseparable relationship of wildlife and fire is still reflexively resisted in even the most liberal and otherwise well educated elements of society.

Our local District Ranger wrote an excellent guest editorial for the Methow Valley News which attempted to present the complex reality of both the biological and political processes involved. Hopefully this fireline will eventually become the recreation trails that allow us to thin, prescribe burn, and actually restore the forest, as opposed to setting it up for the next stand replacing fire.

Wildlife and people can interact and coexist positively in spite of all the misconceptions still prevalent about wildlands, and especially snow country. Those of us who are convinced that restoration is possible and desirable have to devote more of our time and effort to education and the political/bureaucratic process. It's slow but very rewarding work and there are an increasing number of excellent NGO's devoted to this task. We are not alone!

Here's just one sample of my attempts at responsible participation in the process, beyond signing all those petitions from the NGO's. Personal letters, preferably neatly hand written, get more notice than mass mail generated responses or e-mails, or even computer printed letters sent by snail mail. Don't bore them with stuff they already have read from other sources, over and over.

Field Supervisor
Fish and Wildlife Service, Montana Field Office
100 N. Park Ave., Ste 320
  Helena, MT 59601   July 30th 1998
Dear Wildlifers,

Congratulations on finally getting the Lynx "proposed" for listing under the ESA ! Please count this letter as in favor of listing the Lynx as endangered, not just threatened.

I'm well aware that politics will still endanger the Lynx, even after listing. In fact, it's almost guaranteed that green bigots, both outside and inside agencies like Fish and Wildlife, will use the listing against the best course of action – biologically. Yellowstone's Wolves are the most famous similar example, but I'm still convinced that it is better to list, than not to.

I live surrounded by Okanogan National Forest, adjacent to the Loomis, so this hits close to home. Forty years of work, either for or, with government wildlife managing agencies, has taught me that most real progress in wildlife matters comes from better informed voters, rather than through any bureaucratic processes. That's why this letter is the trailer to the Lynx chapter in a manuscript titled: *Ski Trails and Wildlife.* This political reality is also why I won't trouble you with any more details about why I think the Lynx deserves ESA protection. I help pay Hank Fisher, (then) with the Defenders of Wildlife, to do that.

Sincerely,   Eric Burr

Lynx are missing from Olympic National Park, because of its isolation during the last ice age. More visitors see it from Hurricane Ridge than any other part of the Park. It also happens to be a ski lift area within a National Park.

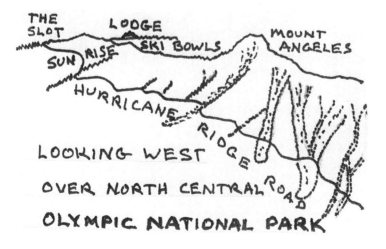

Chapter 12: HURRICANE RIDGE – in Olympic National Park where ski lifts and Wilderness coexist

This is a paradox for many Americans: 'paradise paved with a parking lot,' but its millions of visitors hardly notice that, or the little Poma ski lift tucked back into the Subalpine Firs, and both surrounded by one of the world's more spectacular flower meadows. When they round "the slot" where the access road cuts through the ridge itself, the view of the interior mountains is so staggering that most find it even hard to notice all the wild flowers.

That's summer, but in winter this meadow sprouts a couple old fashioned rope tows that take downhill skiers over to the Poma, and lets ski school students gaze out at the same view which dazzled the summer folks. Cross-country skiers take off along three different ridge lines radiating out from the day lodge, keeping a close eye on the weather which can all too quickly demonstrate how this ridge got its name. I'd first seen Hurricane (locals leave off the "Ridge") during my trail crew employment in 1959, before they'd even paved the road. By fall of 1967 it was paved, but there was no Poma lift, and I'd just accepted an offer to work as a snow ranger there.

Out of habit from Boreal Ridge, in the northern Sierra, the chair lift ski area I'd just left, I parked my little VW Bug where I could watch its ski rack from the breakfast counter. Even though it was just a little past 7 AM the counter was nearly full. Most of its customers this November day seemed to be loggers, log truck drivers, or mill workers, just getting ready to go on shift. There were also a few business man types, in suits and ties. 1960s eh !

Port Angeles was a busy little seaport, serving the vast commercial and National Forest that surrounds Olympic National Park. It was also headquarters for the Park, where I was to check in that morning. The sky was typically gray with a low overcast, and looked like it

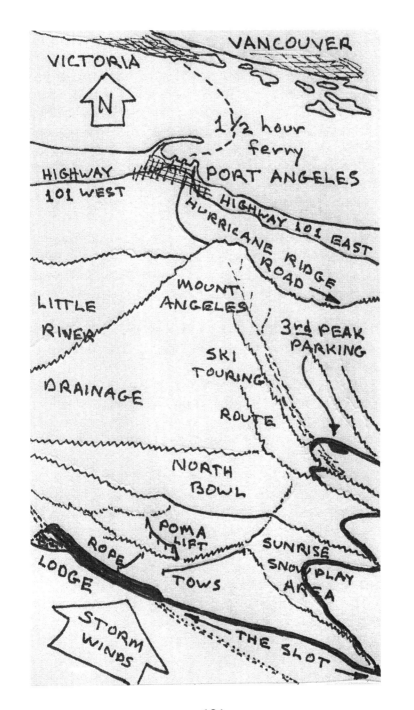

should rain or snow soon. Seattle was two and a half hours driving and ferry riding to the east, and Victoria, British Columbia, Canada, was an hour and a half ferry ride to the north. So far I knew that the Park's steep colorful old rope tows were overdue for a change, and that there was pressure to upgrade, along with preservationist pressure for removal. While eating I overheard a conversation, among the suits and ties folks, that went something like this.

"You're crazy, the Park won't let you build real ski lifts."

* * *

"If they're not serious about upgrading, then why are they hiring this new snow ranger? I hear he's got a professional skiing background, and that one of his jobs will be to survey the entire Olympics for ski terrain."

* * *

"Hey, don't get your hopes up, they probably just hired this guy to make it look like they're investigating the possibilities."

A seat opened up next to this conversation, and I asked if I could join them. Another round of coffee later and they seemed to think that maybe I was ready for the attempt at brainwashing they were sure must inevitably follow when I hit the Chief Ranger's office.

Did they know I was a double agent, a ski instructor and card carrying member of the Sierra Club, from back when ski mountaineer David Brower was running things? Did these local downhill skiers and Park critics realize how paralyzed the Park was by politics, and that the so called "they" actually represent far more people than just the local Park personnel ?

"Hurricane Ridge is like the Alps before the people came." is a thought frequently expressed by European visitors to Hurricane. I heard this often as a ranger and naturalist, but my ski business experience led me to suspect that this would soon change, and that the people would be coming sooner than the Park's infrastructure would be ready to handle them.. That experience also indicated that solutions to future crowding would be similar to some of those already tested, and now working, in the Alps. The name "Hurricane" comes from the wind exposure common to many timberline situations, but this one lets enough people sample such conditions that "Hurricane Ridge" soon replaced the old shepherds' "Big Meadow" place name, from before the Park and the road.

More skiers would know those winds if it were not for the avalanches which frequently close this 1950's built access road. The late Senator Henry Jackson found the taxpayers money to build that road across 10 major avalanche paths and through 3 tunnels. Sightseers and snow players outnumber skiers even in winter. Nordic skiers began to equal alpine skier numbers in the 1970's, just after I decided to leave.

Ski trails and Wilderness overlap very generously at Olympic. This forced me, as a young sub-district ranger to face the problems addressed in this book. When I left the full time National Park ranger ranks in 1971 to rejoin private enterprise in the ski business, most of those problems were still unresolved. I could not forget them however, and as my experience with skiing as a professional accumulated, so did possible solutions to those problems. When the pieces began to fall into place, I wrote letters to the Park staff, returned as a seasonal mountaineering ranger, and then as a naturalist at Hurricane, all the while discussing ideas with any one who was interested. Many a seasonal or year round ranger and/or naturalist, snowplow driver, trail crew laborer, research scientist, avalanche technician, ski instructor and/or patroller, heli-ski guide, and Park or ski area planner has contributed to these ideas.

Olympic surpassed Mount Rainier National Park in total visits per year during the 1980's, thereby joining the big

193

international Park mainstream tourist circuits. Banff up in Canada, and Olympic are now often included on the same European visitor's itinerary. United Nations Biosphere Reserve status was added to help protect its relatively intact ecosystem. Only the Wolf had been eliminated, and the Mountain Goat added. Unlike Yellowstone, the Elk herds appeared to be within the range capacity available, and not displacing other ungulates or Beavers. Wolf reintroduction is not as obviously needed, as it was in Yellowstone, and neither does it appear to be as potentially controversial.

The exotic Goat population started to explode on my watch as the Hurricane sub-district ranger. Although Bruce Moorhead, the equally newly hired biologist, and Yellowstone veteran Jack Hughes – my boss as District Ranger, could see an obvious problem, the "naturalism" true believers in charge did not. It wasn't until after resigning my full time ranger job that I was able to match up a new PhD (from Duke University) with a National Wildlife Federation grant, to start the first Goat habitat research in the mid 1970's. She had been studying Red Heather, comparing timberline meadows in the Olympics with similar meadows in the northern Sierra Nevada, adjacent Kirkwood and my summer Wilderness rangering.

I returned to Olympic, as a seasonal mountaineering ranger quite by chance, but very conveniently, because a C-141 military transport jet had crashed into cliffs above a glacier on Inner Constance, one of the higher areas of my old Staircase sub-district. It also is one of the most scenic, above Home Lake, with a trail through classic timberline meadows. The wreckage made an ugly mess out of this, so the military was persuaded to fly out everything, but we needed mountaineers to first safely peel it off the cliffs.

"Eric, can you take a long distance call at the top of Chair #2 ?" It was Jack, and he needed someone uniquely qualified, who could come on early in the spring. Ski areas can be pretty flexible sometimes, and Kirkwood was able to let me go early with no hard feelings, luckily. So I was able to also help Dr. Olmstead set up her exclosure plots and Bruce keep track of Goat numbers on my 4 days off from crash cleanup duty, every 2 weeks.

The research was ongoing the next summer, so I signed on as a naturalist. I wanted to again help with the goat business, and I was curious about the naturalist programs. They are what I, and many other National Park veterans, consider to be one of the most important jobs in the Parks. Naturalists are conservation biology's front lines for educating and gaining public support. I also knew that retired ski bums might not be able to hire out as mountaineering rangers or guides, and so maybe I'd be wise to try out this naturalist business as preparation for my geriatric years.

Ski touring is superb in the relatively dry rain shadow of Olympic's northeast corner. Alpine lift skiing potential however, is severely limited by the rapidly increasing dampness and decreasing snow, below timberline. Snowshoe Hares and Weasels in fact, do not even change to white in winter, because most of their predator – prey selection occurs down where it's green. High snow covered ridges are usually relatively narrow fingers of white, separated by vast lower valleys of green. It was here I confirmed that skilled naturalists need few snow surveys to ascertain snow depths and cover durations. Plants and animals give many excellent and obvious indications of average snow conditions.

In these ways I learned that commercially viable vertical for lift skiing was limited to about 300 meters or 1000 feet. Olympic's planners, at that time, set aside an enclave of non-Wilderness down off the north side of Hurricane excluding twice that much vertical from their Wilderness recommendation. Most of Olympic National Park is roadless and has since been protected as legal Wilderness,

195

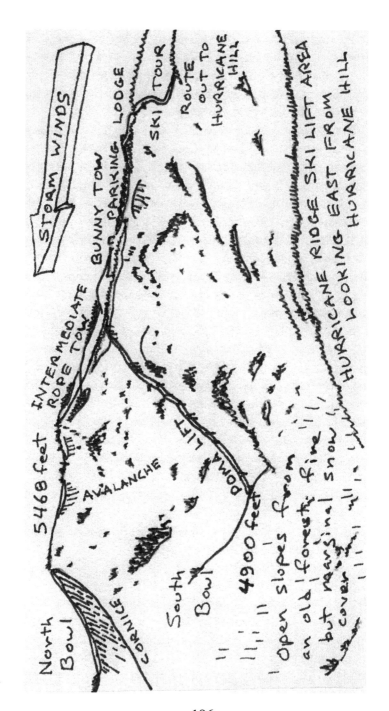

STORM WINDS

5468 feet

INTERMEDIATE ROPE TOW

BUNNY TOW

PARKING

LODGE

SKI TOUR

ROUTE OUT TO HURRICANE HILL

HURRICANE RIDGE SKI LIFT AREA
LOOKING EAST FROM HURRICANE HILL

North Bowl

CORNICE

AVALANCHE

South Bowl

POMA LIFT

4900 feet

Open slopes from an old forest. Fine but marginal snow cover.

including the area around Hurricane. It wasn't until 1988, however, when Wilderness was finally legally designated, that my friends on Olympic's planning staff were able to tighten that boundary up to the bottom of the Poma lift installed in 1971. That Poma was a compromise between the chairlift the local skiers wanted, and the removal of all ski lifts from National Parks called for by the National Parks and Conservation Association. It replaced two of the steepest, and least safe, rope tows operating when I arrived in 1967.

Only five National Parks included ski lifts back then: Yosemite and Lassen with chairlifts, Sequoia (at Wolverton not Mineral King), Olympic, and Rainier. The Poma at Rainier was soon moved to Sequoia's Wolverton, as ski lifts were eliminated from Paradise. No, that's not an intentional pun on Joni Mitchell's famous song, about how "you don't always know what you've got 'till it's gone; they paved paradise and put in a parking lot." Paradise is the real name for the most popular alpine meadow at Rainier, and it still has a parking lot. Rocky Mountain National Park had ski lifts up until 1991. Official policy does prohibit any new ski lifts, while allowing established ones to continue. New or replacement lifts at these old areas must be subject to public environmental review. Lassen National Park was able to upgrade to a chair lift by this process, but the approval document stated that ski lifts were subject to removal if and when alternative lifts became available nearby. Most of these lifts in National Parks started out being the only downhill skiing opportunity for locals, and local support for Parks is crucial for their success. Crystal Mountain and White Pass made Rainier's lifts unnecessary, and Steamboat took care of Rocky Mountain's locals.

Ski lifts referred to in this policy are wire cable or rope tow installations, not oversnow shuttle buses. Yellowstone is in fact encouraging oversnow shuttle buses, but these are for nordic skiers and sightseers. Oversnow vehicles can of course be used to transport alpine skiers as is done at Mount Bailey just north of Crater Lake National Park, and at several areas in British Columbia. We use passenger snowcats on 4000 feet of vertical in the Northeast Cascades when weather prevents us from using the helicopter. At Hurricane oversnow shuttle buses would let alpine and cross-country skiers ski back down the snow covered roadway, freeing the buses to transport sightseers both ways in the late morning and afternoons. The roadway is wide and gentle enough to safely allow both skiers and the buses simultaneously if, but only if, it's groomed. The snow needs to be soft for easy skier control.

Meanwhile snow players, sliding down on inner tubes and other toys, at Hurricane have increased to the point beyond which the one lodge can contain them, without interfering with skiers and sightseers. Additional space has been provided back down the road a half mile, just behind "the slot", and out of the wind often, but with no shelter for warming and no sanitary facilities. The terrain does have good runouts for relatively safe tubing and sledding. This site is an extremely picturesque flower meadow in summer, that is illustrative of the type of plant communities adapted to deep snow areas.

Being out of the wind during most storms, but immediately in the lee of the ridge, it receives very heavy snow deposition, and is subject to wind slab avalanches. I used to routinely ski off the cornices there, producing small but potentially deadly slides. This was just part of my regular snow ranger duties, during my four winters at Hurricane. In summer and fall this very accessible little meadow is used by small natural history classes, but as a Park naturalist I avoided it in the busy summer season to prevent trampling. There are no trails there yet (2007) to absorb such impact, as there are up next to the parking area and lodge. This little meadow also happens to be the closest and safest entry and exit point for ski touring out to Obstruction Point and that controversial little ski hut at Waterhole halfway out.

The half mile of roadway from this new overflow snow-play area to the existing lodge is referred to as "the slot" because it becomes just that after a few snow storms. Most of the snow removal money, and of course fossil fuel, goes into maintaining this half mile in safe condition for conventional rubber tired vehicles. Each new storm repeatedly fills in the ever deepening "slot" and more and more snow must be removed as the winter season progresses. Much of the rest of the snow removal budget goes to front end loader time clearing avalanche debris from the ten major, and a few minor, avalanche paths that cross the road. And yes, this is the subject of my 1976 presentation to the International Snow Science Workshop.

Part of my 1960's snow ranger assignment was to look for alternatives to what in 1970's dollars was often $100,000 or more a season, on just 17 miles of road, for snow removal costs. This seemed extravagant to some of the Park's critics, and struck me as bad ecology also.

None of the alternative potential ski lift sites were any better than Hurricane, and all but Mount Townsend are now in legal Wilderness. Mount Townsend is too windy for ski lifts. Hurricane has at least a few lee side, relatively protected bowls that hold snow well and are operable on snowy days. The key to Hurricane is access, and the existing paved road is what we're stuck with, even though hindsight, from European experience, indicates that a cableway up Little River may have been a better choice. Such a cableway would have been out of the storm winds, but still would have presented many of the engineering challenges of any access through steep terrain. On the other hand new technology may actually redeem those 1950's road engineers, as I indicated in the chapter on lifts.

The original road access to Hurricane was up an old single lane dirt fire road, from the Elwha River now famous for its dam removal/Salmon restoration project. The electric power line comes up from there, but the roadway itself is closed to vehicles. A cable tramway up that side would be subject to the direct impact of storm winds. That old roadway and underground powerline are now in Wilderness, but legal under exceptions allowed "for the administration of the area." Little River is also in Wilderness.

Senator Jackson was very specific in his desire for an overnight lodge on Hurricane, but none was built. Instead what evolved was a kitschy day lodge, half chalet – half cutesy imitation totem pole style decorated, ramshackle, leaky roofed, maintenance nightmare. It was, and still is, hopelessly crowded to overflowing during the high seasons of summer and winter. Its roofline has finally, after thirty leaky years, been reconfigured to authentically clean and simple alpine chalet, snow, water, and ice dam, shedding configuration. Hurricane winds still blow fine snow particles through the walls, which melt inside, so the leaking problems aren't quite solved as of 2007.

From the top of the little ski hill, above the meadow, Hurricane Ridge Lodge looks, and always has looked, pretty good from that distance, with Mount Carrie and Mount Olympus for a backdrop. Its latest remodel, which cleaned up most of the kitsch, and finally finished off the sidewalks, even makes it respectable looking, up close. The main problem is exposure to Hurricane's namesake winds. They can, among many other problems, make for very challenging evacuation situations, if a storm comes in too suddenly, and they often do. So it was actually good that an overnight lodge was not built on that site. The question remains of how to graciously and safely handle the weekend crowds.

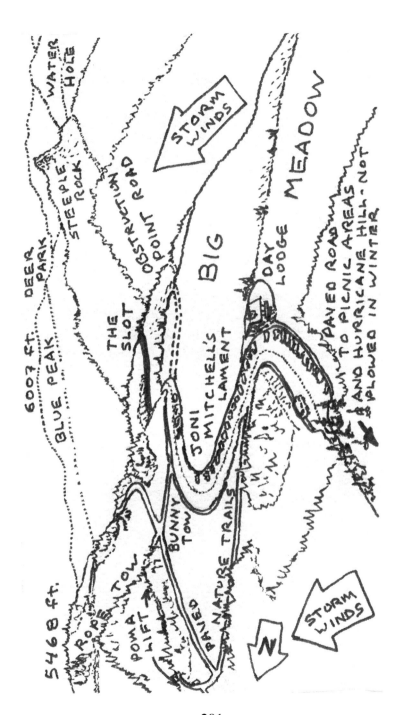

Hurricane's name supplies the answer: *get out of the wind*, and especially get private passenger vehicles out of the wind. The newly refinished parking lot, next to the existing lodge doesn't look bad empty, or with a few cars or shuttle busses. Adding some more benches and picnic tables would spruce things up even more, if only there weren't so many cars. It really does look like Joni Mitchell's lament when it's overflowing with cars.

Shuttle buses should be a no-brainer. Reconfiguring the facilities to accommodate them takes a little more thought. The American habit of using cars as our principle shelter is almost too obvious to notice. One reason there are more huts, lodges, and shelters in the Alps, is that without cars people need alternative forms of shelter. As my hut chapter attempted to illustrate, shelters of all sorts are a very effective non-coercive way to manage people. Build it and they will come, out of the wind - in this case.

Those shelters which are already exposed to the wind, and which should stay there because of the views in nice weather, need to be brought up to European alpine standards, and that means the chalet configuration. All doors and most windows need to be under the gable ends of a gently pitched simple two sided roof. That roof needs to be oriented to the storm winds and sun so that the combination of wind and sun have the best chance to keep at least one gable end free of snow with a minimum of shoveling.

The chalet evolved and survives because after centuries of shoveling snow and fixing leaky roofs, alpine builders finally figured this out. What happened at last to the existing lodge, needs to happen to the little restrooms out at the picnic areas near Hurricane Hill. They need to be two stories high to get above the snow, and that second level needs to be a picnic shelter for use in all seasons when tough weather strikes. This is where folks could comfortably and safely wait for the shuttle buses.

202

Wind dictates that no more development should occur out where it's not really needed, so how to take care of all the snow players, and what about Senator Jackson's long overdue overnight lodge. One of my least pleasant duties was shooing visitors off Hurricane at night in nice weather. The sunsets and sunrises are complete with alpenglow and the light quality is a photographer's best wild fantasy. Many an evening I closed the road late to let visitors enjoy that last magical lighting, and sometimes I'd let a photographer know if I could open the road early so they could follow me up. Many times I tried to explain why Jackson's overnight lodge didn't exist, and why the Park didn't even allow camping up there.

Sunrise is the name for the nice little wind sheltered meadow which has become the snow play area, by default, with no shelter or restrooms. It's well named for the view it offers to the northeast, not quite as spectacular as Mount Olympus, but not bad – especially when views to the west are socked in. A lodge for Sunrise meadow is obviously as needed as the existing one out on Big Meadow, around the corner and up at the other end of the slot. This Sunrise Lodge could be built right out at the beginning of the slot, so that its access is behind the ridge out of the storm wind, but with some windows looking out southwest toward the Park's interior, and some out toward the sunrise.

This could be an "overnight lodge," but reality includes avalanches as well as storm winds. Hostel might be a better description of what this site could offer realistically, and hut might fit it even better – warming hut, where in a wilderness threshold setting, the glory of the full day's light, including moonlight and starlight, could safely be experienced. The luxury that the term "lodge" implies can be better, and more safely, supplied lower down, and outside the Park itself, as is being done around the North

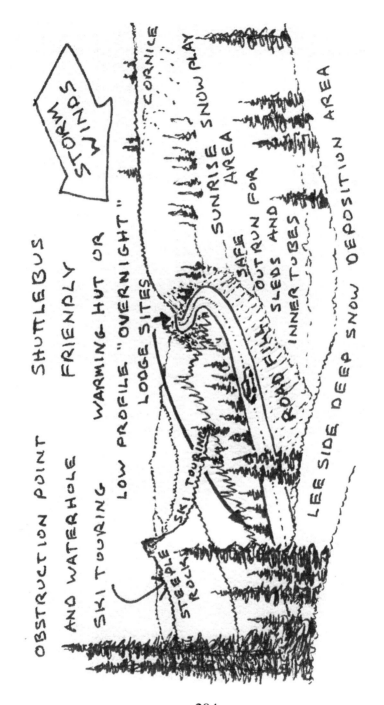

Cascades National Park, and on the west side of Olympic at historic Lake Quinault Lodge.

The term "day lodge" however seems to be accepted at both Rainier's Sunrise area and for Hurricane's Big Meadow "lodge" above its Sunrise. So perhaps we could at last finally have Senator Jackson's "overnight lodge," even though its capacity would be more accurately described as a "ski hut." The European ambiance of ski lodges close by the slopes could be satisfied at least in a token manner this way, while the oversnow shuttles would extend the "ski slopes" down to the tunnels during most of the ski season. Light snow years or early and late season would shift this transfer point up to the Double Parking or Third Peak parking areas.

Locating such a structure out at the beginning of the slot would subject it to many of the same wind problems currently compromising the existing day lodge. Dropping back to the bottom of the sledding hill makes more sense. This location would also fit the needs of alpine skiers better. They could ski the powder off the top of the lift serviced slopes, down to this new lodge for a ride back up on the next shuttle. The hot chocolate or latte they enjoy while waiting would help shorten the lift lines.

But what about camping? The picnic areas out toward Hurricane Hill could be also used this way, assuming the second story warming shelter level is added to the existing restrooms. Then when the wind blows down (or blows away) the tents, our campers can discover the European hut style of overnight facility, and a shuttle bus means there are no cars to dig out in the spring. Bear and rodent proofing are requirements too. Shuttle buses need to have oversnow capability for this to work, but Yellowstone and Canada have already pioneered that one, and it's probably the best primary winter access up to Sunrise and the Big Meadow anyway.

I know, the picnic area views of Olympus are not nearly as good as back at the Big Meadow lodge, or Sunrise and the slot. In fact if we really want the best views, the Obstruction Point Road is the place to go. Back in the late 1960s, during my sub-district ranger years there, plans were on the books and survey stakes were in place, for a loop road connection over to Deer Park. Somehow the survey stakes and loop road plans disappeared, but there's no denying that the views are better out there.

Waterhole has plenty of room for sheltered camping with those better-than- the Big Meadow's -views, but Elk Mountain, where the loop road was proposed to go, is in legal Wilderness now. Obstruction Point, that got its name from a rockslide area which slowed down the road engineers, has wind and marmot problems. These cute rodents like to chew the tasty rubber things under cars. Some hikers in Canada carry wire fencing to place around their cars, but shuttle buses are a better solution for marmots and windy snow storms, especially since they're needed anyway as the primary high seasons access up the paved road from Port Angeles.

Waterhole melts out about a month earlier than Obstruction most years, June or July maybe. The Obstruction Point road's last four miles make a great hike in early summer, as do the spur ridges radiating out from there, including an old burn now in classic vegetative recovery. Remember that ideal hut configuration I described back at the end of the hut Chapter ? I think Waterhole would be the perfect spot for that. It would need shuttle buses and rangers that ski cross-country, and know avalanches, but I also think those are good ideas.

If Scandinavian style ski touring ever becomes popular in America, Waterhole could be *the* - overnight lodge," but I suspect that is unlikely. Telemarking has substantially replaced ski touring for the American market, and like skating – is effectively keeping most skiers out of the real backcountry and remote wildlife habitat. Telemarking skis are too heavy and fat, and skating skis are too light and short for skiing any real distances in ungroomed snow. Touring skis were, and still are, specifically designed for long distances in ungroomed natural snow. The tiny existing Waterhole ski hut no longer needs a reservation system, as it did in the 1970's and '80's. Touring is not dead; it's just a smaller segment of the slowly, but steadily, growing nordic ski scene. A much larger Waterhole ski and hiking hut and adjacent formalized campground, with adequate sanitary facilities, are therefore something that definitely needs to be planned for the not too distant future.

This scenario would also greatly help reduce the need for Wilderness Permit restrictions for Grand Lake, as has occurred by closing the road above Staircase, leading to overly popular Flapjacks Lakes. The Sunrise Lodge would be the entry and exit point for ski tourers and early season hikers headed out to Waterhole. It could serve as the warming hut for them to wait for the shuttle buses. It would provide a safe and comfortable destination for sightseers when weather and/or snow prevent access to the existing Big Meadow lodge.

The half mile walk, snowshoe, or ski out to the Big Meadow lodge from Sunrise is a very scenic experience. It's much more sightseer friendly than driving, when only the backseat passenger on the valley side has an unobstructed view. When that half mile can't be plowed, for whatever reasons, fuel costs maybe, it could be groomed over the snow, by a snowcat with a blade on the front, and thereby get a start on moving snow out of the slot toward its summer reopening. If fuel costs and public consciousness about using fuel ever become limiting factors, a Sunrise Lodge could allow that scenic half mile to simply melt out, or alternatively delay plowing until June, when the big visitation season starts.

Grooming cross-country ski trails as a management tool could be useful too at Hurricane. Grooming limited to where there are facilities to safely handle the people, means fewer "NO" and "DO NOT" signs. It also helps people learn to ski, makes snowshoeing safer around steep slopes, and can move snow safely away from the sides of buildings with dangerous roof drop offs, for kids who otherwise will inevitably climb up on roofs. Grooming out to the picnic areas, and down the snowed in road to wherever the wheeled shuttle buses are transferring passengers to the over snow shuttle buses, certainly makes sense. The beauty of snow grooming is its flexibility to meet changing conditions. Therefore ideally Hurricane's management guidelines, and physical facilities, would allow rangers to take advantage of that flexibility, to give Park visitors a safe, enjoyable, and environmentally educational experience.

Grooming also compacts snow, so in a National Park Biosphere Reserve it should be minimized and primarily confined to paved roads. Not grooming at all forces ski, snowshoe, and boot traffic compaction onto more sensitive unpaved areas. The ideal is managed grooming for both wildlife habitat conservation and visitor safety, education, and satisfaction. Olympic's deep and dense snow makes snow compaction a less crucial factor than at areas with less depth and natural compaction, but it still is a factor, especially on windward slopes where the snow is less deep, even at Olympic.

Warming huts for shuttle bus stops would also be needed at those transfer points down the road: just below Third Peak, (to avoid the avalanche runout) Double Parking Area, the Tunnels overlook, (although the tunnels themselves offer some shelter) and Heart O' the Hills.

I know all this sounds terribly European, but remember that the cost of petrol has been much higher there for many years. Hurricane was indeed "like the Alps before the people came," but those days are gone; the people have come, and we can learn from the Alpine experience.

Once in place all this allows oversnow shuttle buses to serve as ski lifts. When I was snow ranger there I'd often lead the kids who liked to ski untracked powder off toward Mount Angeles from the high point of the rope tow, just at closing time. These kids of course were on alpine skis with their heels held down, so we didn't do a lot of hiking, but we could easily access a lovely powder run, (Maggie's) after leisurely viewing some different scenery, and learning something about avalanches. The timing worked out nicely for their parents to be waiting in their cars at the foot of the run. Today's Telemarkers and Randonee skiers have much more freedom for similar, but even longer excursions, if a shuttle bus could pick them up at one of the transfer points on down the road.

Shuttle buses have another advantage, unrelated to skiing, except that skiing may help facilitate the inevitable eventual switch to mass transit. Road killed wildlife is a fact of life wherever city people are allowed to drive their cars, and it's not just collision damage. Antifreeze spilling out of thousands of radiators in a crowded Park setting attracts deer and other animals to lick it off the pavement. They love it, just like dumb kids love crack and meth', and it has a similar unhealthy and sometimes fatal effect. Junk food fed to wildlife, from cars usually, also has classic bad side effects, including visitor injuries. Shuttle buses are good for wildlife and people.

Hey, but what about our chairlift ? Pomas are better than rope tows, but they're high maintenance, and the upski line under the cable impacts the vegetation by compacting the snow more than anywhere else on the hill. Compared to all the other changes needed at Hurricane, replacing the Poma with a chairlift would be insignificant. Most visitors would never know the difference, since the towers for both types of cable lift are tucked back in the forest and its shaded little bowl away from the principle view. Both have towers and a loop of cable, but the chairlift has chairs dangling off the cable. Paint these black or dark green and the comparative visual intrusion is minimal. If a chairlift does go in, serious consideration should be given to running it in the summer for hikers, who would access it from gently descending loop trails on either side. This would provide a little taste of wilderness style hiking otherwise out of reach for visitors who are physically challenged.

Compared to the vast terrain available for Telemarking, snowshoeing, snowboarding, backcountry skiing on either alpine or steel edged cross-country skis, and Scandinavian style ski touring, the little ski lift area is miniscule. It does however provide a place for local kids to learn to ski, and groomed tracks would encourage more cross-country skiing. Even cross-country skiers go down hills, and ski lifts are a great place to learn. At Hurricane they don't just learn to ski either. Small as it is, it still has avalanches. Recognizing and dealing with them is a significant step toward learning about the ecology of steep mountain slopes. And ecology is certainly part of what National Parks are all about.

Forest ecology, apart from avalanches, is also part of the reality at Hurricane. Ribbon forest glades described in my fire chapter, and detailed in Arno and Hammerly's *Timberline* book, are only one of the patterns evident around the Big Meadow. The Big Meadow is in fact getting smaller as trees slowly but inevitably close in. Pre-Park grazing and post-Park fire exclusion may be some of the factors at work, and of course global warming could also encourage forest encroachment. Whatever the causes, the result is less skiable terrain and the obvious need for some forest thinning and meadow maintenance if skiing, wildflower and wildlife viewing, bird watching, sight

210

seeing, and photography, are to continue as they have traditionally.

National Parks, even with their supersized parking lots, are still good for wildlife and people. Even lift skiers, who don't mind the lack of big lifts in American National Parks, can benefit by their brief exposure to nature in winter. National Parks bring people and nature together more effectively, and in greater numbers, than any other development in the boreal forest except ski resorts. National Parks, important as they are for inspiring and educating, still make up a relatively small component of the available ski trails, and potentially available future ski trails.

Alpine ski lift resorts reach far more people, and that first experience away from the boob tubes, and other electronic pacifiers, is crucial to their potential for realizing what winter is really all about. Writing off lift skiers as not worth the time, money, and effort to try and expose them to more of nature would be a huge lost opportunity. Many of my cross-country ski school students are former alpine lift skiers or snowboarders. I know also that many naturalists, some of whom occasionally ski on lifts, disagree and consider lift skiers to be hopeless. My long career in skiing has obviously convinced me otherwise.

Hurricane Ridge is a tiny ski area in a huge Wilderness National Park. Its concessions to lift skiing are a very small, but very important, part of an even more important and much bigger, but parallel, picture. The opportunity to ease our obese overly mechanized population away from their cars, computers, snowmobiles, and ski lifts presents itself most significantly at developed ski areas with groomed trails. Most of these are also serviced with lifts, but however and wherever winter recreationists are visiting in concentrated numbers, their experiences will shape the future of snow country. National Parks like Olympic are crucially important because of their iconic symbolic significance. It is therefore important that they be carefully planned and managed, even though they reach fewer people than the large ski area complexes such as Whistler-Blackcomb and Aspen.

National Forests in the United States, and Crown Lands in Canada, are the major future of snow skiing, and the frustrations of many lift skiers have been nowhere better observed than at Early Winters. Mineral King was and is relatively remote, tucked up at the top of its extremely torturous steep narrow winding road, even though it was more famous before it got included into Sequoia National Park. Early Winters by contrast is serving cross-country and helicopter skiers in slowly but so far (2007) steadily increasing numbers. Solutions to many of our ski trail and wildlife problems are also being pioneered there.

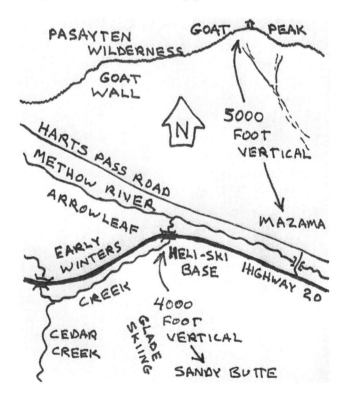

Chapter 13: EARLY WINTERS – on Okanogan National Forest, where nordic skiing quietly eclipsed a thirty year ski lift saga

ENTERING GOD'S COUNTRY

Next Secular Area 73 Miles

This would be an entirely appropriate roadside sign for Early Winters. But of course it must be mounted on a respectfully rustic National Park style peeled log and rock base, and the sign itself must be on a real wood slab with routed or hand carved letters. None of this cheap plastic Disneyland fake wood or painted plywood junk the U.S. Forest Service has been too often putting up lately.

Why such a traditionally historic style sign, and why the faith based reference are appropriate to this setting is a long story, and not all of it is germane to ski trails and wildlife. Other writers have explained this in fascinating sociological detail, and my bibliography will get those interested a good start at understanding the spiritual significance of the North Cascades.

The wording of the above sign is not original, but rather appeared as a cartoon in some ski magazine I read, and then forgot about, until events here jogged it out of the memory file. Probably it was in "SAM" (Ski Area Management). The natural old National Park style sign is something I started doing for clients here in the Methow Valley twenty some years ago, and has now reached its apex with the big WILSON RANCH entry arch Bruce Morrison carved for the Freestone Inn at Early Winters, and the ARROWLEAF trail sign I did for TPL (Trust for Public Land) across Highway 20 (the North Cascades Scenic Highway) from the Wilson Ranch. Bruce is just one of many local artists and sculptors who ply their crafts in this very unique valley.

Early Winters sits at the uppermost, and westernmost, end of the Methow Valley, and serves as the eastern sunny-side entrance to North Cascades National Park and the complex of National Forest and National Park Wilderness, Scenic Highway Corridor, and Recreation Areas, that make up what many people of many different spiritual and religious persuasions consider to be "God's Country." For all the political fighting that has gone on over this spectacular hunk of real estate, one thing almost all factions seem to agree on is: that it is sacred ground.

Early Winters campground sits across Early Winters Creek from the Wilson Ranch, with its rustic Freestone Inn, 15 rental cabins, and a few private vacation homes. The Arrowleaf Conservancy's 1100 acres, just up valley from the campground, include five discreetly hidden private homes, about 10 miles of public cross-country ski and summer use trails, three miles of prime riparian habitat, and the remains of four old homesteads with their fields interspersed between recently thinned Ponderosa Pine and Douglas Fir forests. The trails are part of, and connect to, the MVSTA (Methow Valley Sport Trails Association) web of similar trails connecting the entire upper valley.

Bears, Bobcats, Lynx, Cougars, Marten, and Coyotes are regular visitors from the surrounding Okanogan National Forest. White-tailed and Mule Deer, Snowshoe Hare, Red Squirrels, and other small game are the attraction for these rather shy predators. Moose and Wolves are much less common, simply passing through on their way to more secluded or otherwise more desirable locales. The Early Winters saga is only the latest battle in a wilderness preservation conflict that spans about fifty years. Luckily for the combatants, the wildlife, and the scenery, most of the action has taken place in court, in public hearings, and in the hallowed halls of legislatures.

Early Winters serves as a refuge for people too, from most of the "outside world's strife". The ski wars have been declared over, and cross-country skiers have decided it's safe to move to the Methow Valley. The distortions of developers' plans, by their opponents, have been largely forgotten or forgiven. Environmentalists are still distrusted, but that's a problem larger than Early Winters. Many of these sophisticated newcomers are working hard now to make sure we don't become a National Park gateway slum like Gatlinburg, Tennessee, outside the Smokies. They're doing it by inclusion rather than exclusion, by building alliances with the broad range of stakeholders. Whether we will actually be "the first purely nordic ski area to trash a beautiful alpine valley" remains to be seen. We are the first major nordic ski trail resort that is also isolated from any major alpine ski lift resort. We are a new experiment, being closely watched by the whole ski industry. The Early Winters catalog changed owners, and finally changed its name, as the hoped for but now extinct, ski lift resort no longer captured the public's attention, as it did in the 1980's.

Two alpine skiers were getting drunk, and one of them was carrying on about "how what a shame it was that the Early Winters (ski lift) resort was never built." His companion tried to console him by having him remember back to his childhood, when he discovered the truth about Santa Claus. Next it was those college bull sessions when they decided that "God was dead." Finally he said: "Somehow you survived those psychological traumas, and life goes on, right? Well now it's time to face up to the reality that Early Winters (ski lift resort) is also dead."

So, now two environmentalist are getting drunk, and one of them is carrying on about how snowmobilers and helicopter skiers are taking over the North Cascades, and why we failed to create the international peace park. The "death of environmentalism" is very debatable, and the international park is still possible, but the mentality illustrated by this old joke, and its recent variations, is the "no compromise in defense of": mother earth, alpine skiing, or whatever your favorite cause is, syndrome. "Compromise" is the relevant issue here.

Early Winters' main claim to fame, besides being the other (besides Mineral King) *almost* ski lift resort to go all the way to the U.S. Supreme Court, is its 30 year endurance record as an active environmental controversy. Whether the North Cascades should be in a National Park, and the companion debate about whether to build the North Cross State Highway, were even more intense. But these were quite sporadic with many decades-long- lapses, when the stark reality of how physically difficult the Highway undertaking actually was, sunk in. The overall wilderness preservation conflict is a much longer but also intermittent story, partly because the Wilderness Act didn't get passed until 1964, and also because the North Cascades are so rugged that few folks worried about them as much as all the more easily accessed wild areas that were much more vulnerable to getting clearcut, roaded, or otherwise "compromised."

Aspen Ski Corporation pulled out of Early Winters in the late 1970's, when it became obvious to them that the new environmental laws were going to take longer to get through than the two years (under the then-existing Capitol Gains tax law) they had to invest their parent company's (20'th Century Fox) windfall profits from Star Wars. They wisely took their marbles to Canada and helped bring Blackcomb on line to produce North America's biggest ski lift resort. Smaller players carried on with lift plans until the R.D. Merrill Company bought the property on the court house steps, and announced that ski lifts were not in their plans. Aspen's ski lift proposal provided the wake up call which probably deserves credit for saving the Methow Valley.

Readers interested in more details can find them in Sally Portman's Mazama Ski Wars chapter, in her Methow Valley history book *Smiling Country, 2nd* edition. Less available, until its second edition comes out, but far more detailed, is Doug Devin's *Mazama – The Past 100*

216

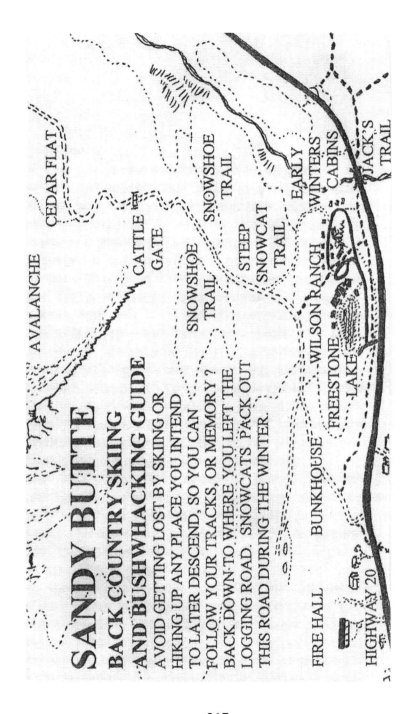

SANDY BUTTE
BACK COUNTRY SKIING
AND BUSHWHACKING GUIDE

AVOID GETTING LOST BY SKIING OR
HIKING UP ANY PLACE YOU INTEND
TO LATER DESCEND, SO YOU CAN
FOLLOW YOUR TRACKS, OR MEMORY?
BACK DOWN TO WHERE YOU LEFT THE
LOGGING ROAD. SNOWCATS PACK OUT
THIS ROAD DURING THE WINTER.

CEDAR FLAT

AVALANCHE

CATTLE
GATE

SNOWSHOE
TRAIL

SNOWSHOE
TRAIL

SNOWSHOE
TRAIL

STEEP
SNOWCAT
TRAIL

EARLY
WINTERS
CABINS

JACK'S
TRAIL

WILSON RANCH

FREESTONE
LAKE

BUNKHOUSE

FIRE HALL

HIGHWAY 20

Years. The upshot is that the entire upper Methow Valley, from Winthrop to Early Winters, has become one of the premier nordic resort complexes in North America. Rather than concentrating its ski trails around a single lodge or resort village, it is spread over a twenty mile long stretch of the upper Methow Valley, and includes dozens of small lodges, country inns, B&Bs, and hundreds of individual residences, rental cabins, ski huts, and yurts. Its 200 plus kilometers (nordic skiers prefer metric trails) cover almost every type of terrain except the timberline parkland glades on top of Sandy Butte, and up Highway 20 to the west. The factors which brought this about, and the vision towards which many of us are working, is the subject of this chapter.

Back in 1979, the Ruby Mountain Tramway was still on the drawing boards – over in the Park, while the Methow ski wars were just warming up. As a professional skier, I was curious about what this tramway had to offer in the way of skiable vertical, and incidentally whether or not it had the potential to take the ski development heat off the Methow. Eleven years earlier the Methow had imprinted on me when I came over from Olympic for my refresher training as a smokejumper. It happened to me the same way many other Methow junkies have gotten hooked. After work, the Forest Service jumpers invited me up for a beer at the newly completed Sun Mountain Lodge. The North Cascades frame the pastoral valley in such an appealing way from Sun Mountain's vantage point, that it's really not fair at all. I was in love, and didn't even know it.

Then in the mid 1970's my Mountain Goat researcher friend dragged me away from the Olympics to help her do some Mountain Goat and Mule Deer habitat work for the University of Washington. I remember staying at the Early Winters Campground, and wondering if this lovely spot was really destined to be the base area for a ski resort. The

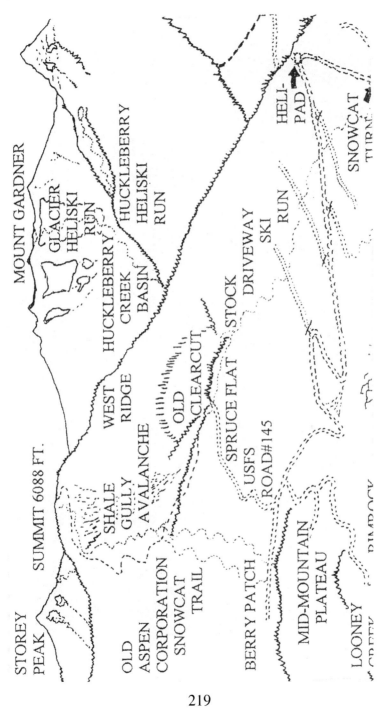

MOUNT GARDNER

STOREY PEAK

SUMMIT 6088 FT.

GLACIER HELISKI RUN

HUCKLEBERRY HELISKI RUN

HUCKLEBERRY CREEK BASIN

WEST RIDGE

SHALE GULLY AVALANCHE

OLD ASPEN CORPORATION SNOWCAT TRAIL

OLD CLEARCUT

SPRUCE FLAT

USFS ROAD #145

STOCK DRIVEWAY SKI RUN

HELI-PAD

SNOWCAT TURN

BERRY PATCH

MID-MOUNTAIN PLATEAU

LOONEY

219

ski magazine write-ups at that time were rather vague: something about a gondola being needed to transport intermediate skiers up to the gentler terrain higher on Sandy Butte. About all you can see of this "butte," from down at Early Winters, is 1000 feet vertical of cliffs. I'd already been burned by a ski lift resort that promised to do things right (Kirkwood) and was highly skeptical.

Anyway, whether I realized it or not, the Methow was already in my blood by 1979, as I followed a compass line up Ruby Mountain. That summer I was a "backcountry" ranger for North Cascades National Park, because it hadn't yet been designated as Wilderness, with a capitol "W." Wilderness and backcountry ranger duties are identical for all practical purposes. As such - I worked ten days on, with four days off, so Ruby Mountain was day one of a typical field ranger's holiday. The most skiable vertical I could find was about 1800 feet, and that was pretty wind exposed up at the top. Getting sightseers to the best views of the Park's biggest glaciers would require even more wind exposure, with consequent shut downs during the short fog free summer season. I was not at all impressed, but nevertheless drew up the most feasible gondola profile, along with my analysis of why it shouldn't be built, to send in to the Park's planners.

The next day I'm following another compass line up Sandy Butte, the way its access gondola would have to go to bypass the cliffs and accompanying wind exposure. Its top 3000 feet vertical is classic Colorado style intermediate skier terrain, so I could see why Aspen Corporation was attracted to it, however the bottom thousand feet vertical definitely needed a gondola. There are some skiable ways down around the cliffs, but they're all black diamond, except for the one logging road and one pretty narrow and advanced intermediate run. Black diamond means experts only, or unhappy intermediates if they've been misled into thinking that was the best way down.

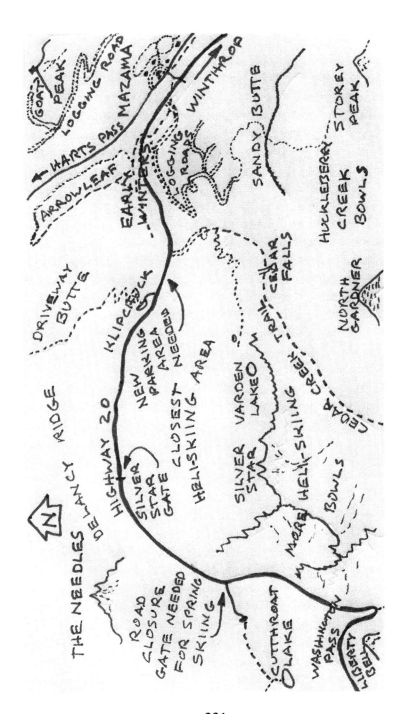

221

Why, I wondered, did Aspen choose this little (by North Cascades standards) 4000 foot vertical hill, when Silver Star, just right across Cedar Creek, has 6000 feet vertical with multiple wide open glacial bowls and plenty of tree skiing for windy and foggy days. That much vertical requires gondolas in any case, but at least Silver Star had an easy intermediate way down the Varden Creek drainage, to the same base area at Early Winters. Revelstoke, British Columbia, is planning to start lifts up 6000 vertical feet this year, 2007.

The answer, I was informed by local guide service entrepreneur Eric Sanford, was political. He was already scoping out the possibilities for helicopter skiing, and had arrived in the Methow Valley in the employ of Aspen Ski Corporation. Steve Barnett, the author of *Cross Country Downhill,* had suggested that I contact Sanford about the ski hill. Steve was opposed to the resort proposal, and was curious about what I thought of it. Steve was not alone in this opinion, but to Eric Sanford and me their chances for stopping it looked slim to desperate. Nevertheless the opposition was significant and putting the first lifts on little Sandy Butte seemed wiser than proposing them up in terrain that many considered to be worthy of later addition to the Park or a Wilderness Area.

Next I headed up Cedar Creek, behind Silver Star, and south to Stehekin for a return loop over famous Cascade Pass and the salt mines of the National Park's "police state wilderness." If this last term seems extreme, try moving backpackers who have not made it to their designated tent sites because they were too tired, or too wet and cold, and their stove quit working so they built an illegal camp fire. Anyway the Park was into crisis management mode, getting their new revegetation program going, and not receptive to anything proactive. A Ruby Mountain tramway was still considered inevitable, just like the proposed Early Winters ski lifts, but my contorted mind

222

was coming up with alternatives, even as I dutifully watered the "reveg" plots at those overused backcountry campsites all over the Park's "western side." The "east side" was the separate Stehekin District, and somehow the fact that Park visitors would gravitate naturally to the sunny east side of the Cascade divide and Okanogan National Forest, by the easy Highway 20 route, rather than boating, flying, or hiking into Stehekin, didn't seem to register with Park or Forest planners. After all they worked for separate branches of the federal government, and Highway 20 is run by a state agency.

Coordinating such widely disparate bureaucratic functions was not within the thought boxes of that era. Okanogan National Forest has 300,000 acres of spectacular non-Wilderness backcountry where we helicopter ski and mountain bike, and groups with over twelve sets of eyes are allowed. There is still plenty of wild backpacking territory, and reopening the many abandoned trails would allow even more dispersion of backpackers from the Park's overcrowded west side.

Trying to get Park regulations posted on Forest Service trailheads, leading into the Park, was a nearly hopeless undertaking. Still I tried, when I was hired on in 1983, as a backcountry ranger for the Stehekin District, and in 1984, '85, '86, and '87, with little success. We started up our helicopter skiing operation from Mazama in 1983, so the Stehekin job had me patrolling the backside of the same mountains I guided heli-skiers down in winter. This arrangement gave me a unique perspective on the whole Park visitor access business. Why put up an expensive tramway on Ruby Mountain, at taxpayers expense, that would be fogged in - or shut down by wind, much of its potential operating days, when a ski lift resort over on the sunny side could pay for one with private funding, and get some summer revenue from their lift system in the bargain. Kirkwood had given me the school of hard knocks graduate course in wind closures, and inefficient lift system design.

Helicopter skiing may smell bad and be even noisier than snowmobiling, but the skiing part is heavenly beyond description. A helicopter is also handy if someone needs a rescue. So even though the National Park dropped me as a hopeless troublemaker, I stayed on in the Methow Valley. Working for the Forest Service or in the construction trades, during the snowless months, meant many more opportunities to interact with local skiers. Being closer to Early Winters also allowed me to work for, or with, the ski developers. Sometimes I'd be laying out potential nordic trails for them as the representative of MVSTA (Methow Valley Sport Trails Association), while on other occasions consultants might need to be guided around the mountain. This kind of intimacy with a succession of developers helped inform my opinions about the possibilities, and the compromises that gradually unfolded.

Compromise has so far been good for the Methow. The one recommendation I made that has actually happened, thanks to some very talented and dedicated Forest Service folks, was the Maple Pass loop trail. Maple Pass shares its ridgeline with the National Park, and the loop trail was my idea to mitigate the impact from the old dead end spur trail by providing an incentive to move on easily to ever more attractive scenery. The Ruby Mountain Tramway also got dropped, but I don't know who to thank for that one. I like to think it was some dedicated and talented National Park employees, maybe even rangers.

Snowmobiles mostly stay up on the north side of the Methow Valley, which usually allows the cross-country skiers and snowshoers to enjoy some peace and quiet. Helicopter skiers base out of the Wilson Ranch near the very tip end of the upper Methow Valley at Early Winters, so they over-fly few residences or lodgings, except Lost River (five miles northwest of Early Winters) which is still popular with snowmobilers, those strange creatures that love noise. They even have an airstrip for light planes.

Most of the "backcountry" skiers and snowboarders our one helicopter flies over, are using snowmobiles to access their play areas. The helicopter ski guides often do the same trick on their days off from flying, so they know most of these snowmobile skiers personally, and avoid the places folks are skinning up to ski.

About the only two really serious avoidable conflicts we haven't worked out very well, as of 2007, are Highway 20 parking and short loop trails, with some vertical, in the upper valley. There are lots of lesser problems, but many of those could fall into place if upper valley trails and parking were solved.

Parking cross-country skiers, snowshoers, and snow-mobilers in the same lot is just plain asking for trouble, yet this is what happens in big snow years, like 2006 and 2007. Light snow years are not as much of a problem, because the state plow crews are able to, within budget, clear up 7 miles above Early Winters for snowmobile parking at Silver Star Creek. Obviously what's needed is snowmobile parking farther below Silver Star gate, but high enough above Early Winters to dissipate the noise and blue cloud and stench of two cycle engine exhaust fumes.

Just two miles up Highway 20 is the Cedar Creek trail access, popular with many snowshoers, and Klipchuck Campground, used for groomed trail skiing early in the season when valley trails still lack adequate snow. Between these two trail access points is one of the few flat spots on highway 20 that would lend itself to another parking area and winter plowing terminus. There isn't enough room to use it however, unless either the roadway is widened or a parking lot constructed just off the road way, which would be the more aesthetic solution. Making this happen unfortunately requires two separate bureaucracies, to communicate: The United States Forest

Service and the Washington State Department of Transportation. This is a challenge we're working on, as of 2007. Other closure points: at Cutthroat for spring skiing, and both passes – for when rock slides close the west side, but our east side is accessible, would also make sense if we're serious about helping the economy. Expanding the parking at Cedar Creek however, is the most critical.

At Hurricane Ridge in Olympic National Park we had the advantage of a single government agency to deal with. On the Highway 20 Scenic Highway Corridor, we have one Federal and two State: the U.S. Forest Service, the Washington State Department of Transportation, and the Washington State Highway Patrol. That third one is prone to giving parking tickets to the visitors unable to find adequate legal parking spaces, because the other two agencies haven't provided them. Vacation choices are often made on the basis of hassles anticipated, and we strongly suspect that the Methow has lost a few potential repeat customers by this lack of cooperation, and neglect or ignorance of the skiing public's needs .

Early Winters has some of the most scenic flat ski trails in the entire valley. The one area above the valley floor that isn't a cliff or a slope too steep to ski, is where the ski lifts were going to go. It also is where the thickest forest fire fuel hazard exists, threatening the entire Early Winters complex. Short loop ski trails on Sandy Butte and adjacent Driveway Butte would allow thinning this forest of its small diameter trees, providing both fire protection and badly needed groomed trails at the intermediate skill level. It would also allow us to link up the two miles to Klipchuck so that there would be less demand for parking there. Although only one agency is needed for this project, "analysis paralysis" has (as of 2007) this one stopped as cold as the Cedar Creek parking and Cutthroat gate.

The Early Winters Ranger Station has been closed ever since the Bush administrations came in and decided they had higher priorities. The latest threat was the possibility of it being sold, along with other "surplus Forest Service properties." Its classic old CCC architecture is listed on the historic register, so the buildings can't legally be torn down. They can, however, and are - being neglected and prevented (by the Forest Service) from being cared for by a coalition of nonprofit organizations, that volunteered to take them over as an environmental learning center.

This is just one example of the minor issues that also include the need for more user friendly parking at the existing Silver Star road closure gate, and alternative access from a second trailhead, including a climbers' hostel, for the increasingly popular Liberty Bell Mountain and Early Winters Spires. Climbers are impacting the meadows around these spires, and regularly overflowing the existing parking lot which is also popular with day hikers going to Blue Lake. Two illegal and also abandoned campfires were found at Blue lakes during the 2006 summer hiking season. I put one of them out myself. Designated fire resistant campsites would only put an insignificantly small dent in this classic overused area. Like Waterhole in Olympic, it's the logical site for a hostel and campground along tested Canadian design lines that I introduced in the hut chapter.

All these minor problems however add up to the much bigger recreation management crisis that is not, and will not be, resolved with more trailhead fees, restrictions, and enforcement. These Bush era fees are substantially eaten up by their administrative and enforcement costs, and are mainly producing public resentment and outrage. This is growing to join clear cutting and trail neglect as further incentives to do away with the Forest Service altogether. Renegade citizen trail crews are building their own trails, and opening old ones. Cars often ignore the fee parking trailheads, and instead park on the shoulder just short of the fee required signs. People know that it's really their

Forest, and they're not about to surrender to police state wilderness quietly.

This situation is obviously much bigger than Early Winters and the North Cascades, but I'm hoping that these local examples can help illustrate the more abstract presentations in the preceding chapters. Looming over all this is the old ghost of the downhill ski lift resort, and the Ruby Mountain sightseeing tramway. Their legacy has substantially increased the bureaucratic hesitancy to get involved in any proactive recreation development. They tried that thank you - and got burned badly, all the way to the Supreme Court, not just once – but twice, and both times revolved around lift assisted skiing.

Robert Redford's Sundance ski lift resort, in Utah, has proved that a small environmentally responsible lift system is possible. Back in the 1980's however, when I and others proposed such a limited development for Sandy Butte, it was rejected by the developers as an unproven alternative, (which it was back then) and by the resort's opponents as an unacceptable compromise. "Let them put even one lift in, and where will it stop ?" – was the thinking. The base village area has since been placed in conservancy by TPL, so the threat of another corporate mega-resort is dead. What's not dead is the ever rising price of fuel, and the steadily increasing population of the valley, both lodging guests and residents – full and part time.

Sandy Butte has a neglected logging road up the first 2400 feet of vertical. Like many Forest Service roads, it has been neglected because, in the era of limited budgets, there were higher priority roads to maintain – and maintaining it could possibly be interpreted by some litigious environmentalists as reviving that ski lift thing again. Better to just let it deteriorate and finally wash out enough so no one can drive up it anymore, even though it's not officially dropped from the road system. Such is the political legacy of Early Winters.

North Cascade Heli-Skiing's permit allows snow cat skiing on Sandy Butte when either weather or avalanche conditions prohibit flying. This is for alpine skiers or Telemarkers and snowboarders, using the snow cats as the ski lift. The snow cats follow the logging road and then a trail, cut by the Aspen Ski Corporation back in the 1970's that is passable only by oversnow vehicles, to the summit at 6000 feet. This summit is just high enough that the forest gives way to timberline gladed meadows leading over to Storey Peak, Mount Gardner, and Virginian Ridge, (named after the Owen Wister novel) all superlative hiking terrain, and some of it is potentially groomed cross-country ski trail terrain.

The top 1600 vertical feet of this Butte are steep enough that snow cats had to winch themselves up back in the 1970's and '80's. Modern snowcats don't need to winch up this mountain anymore, and their performance generally has improved significantly – as I detailed in the lifts chapter. So for practical purposes now all that would be required for a stand-alone snow cat skiing operation is thinning the forest enough to enlarge the glade skiing terrain and prevent a "big burn." Snowmass Colorado has had a great time with their Big Burn ski trails, but their hill isn't as steep as ours. Their Big Burn's wide open slopes provided variety often lacking on Colorado ski trails.

Sandy Butte's problem with a big burn is that it has old avalanche tracks that a stand replacing fire would likely allow to run again, and this would in turn complicate access through the steeper slopes of the lower mountain. Of course, without thinning, a big burn is what we're most likely to get, and the resultant wide open skiing might be pretty good. Personally, I would much prefer glade skiing, sheltered from wind and avalanche, where the forest has been thinned by competent ski trail planners. This must include biological competence, so that the resulting forest can be maintained with prescribed burns to restore optimum wildlife habitat as well as nice skiing. "Little burns" are a better option.

Rendezvous Huts, accessed by groomed cross-country trails, are across and just slightly down the valley from Sandy Butte. They use grooming snowmobiles to haul freight to their five huts, but their customers ski up almost as much as the 2000 foot vertical it would take to run a similar operation on Sandy Butte. Left over from the ski lift saga is a well at mid-mountain, that would give hut builders a leg up to put in a hut with indoor plumbing. Logging roads at the 4000 foot high, mid-mountain plateau could easily be looped into a higher altitude ski and mountain biking/hiking trail system. The Nordic racing team would love to have access to such a hut to provide a training area at an altitude comparable to those of the teams they race against. Sleeping at altitude, for athletes, is as important as skiing and running at altitude.

What is really unique about Sandy Butte is its very skiable upper 2000 vertical feet above this hut site. Its steepness would condition our athletes to the more sophisticated downhill sections increasingly being found on today's cross-country race courses. Relatively few cross-country skiers would use that top 2000 vertical, but everybody would talk about it. The subalpine meadow trails over toward Storey Peak and the ski touring out and down Virginian Ridge, together with the ski mountaineering on Gardner would be further frosting on what is primarily a huge cake of intermediate skiing, exactly what the upper valley lacks at this 2007 writing.

All this assumes that lifts are really dead. What if, however, gas goes to $10 a gallon, and the Methow continues to build more beds? Sandy Butte could also provide an energy efficient way to access the high country, an alternative to the steep, scary, crowded, and dusty old

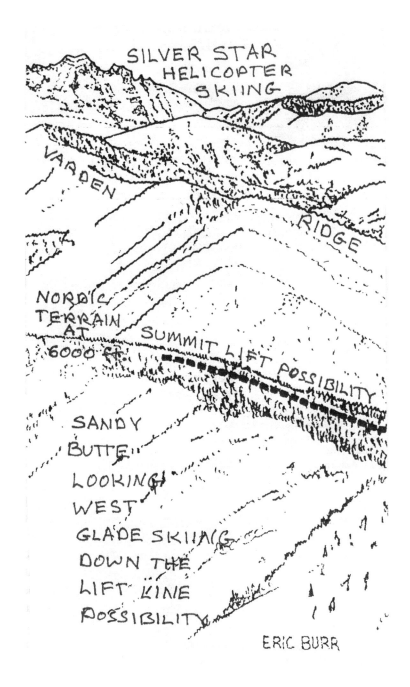

SILVER STAR HELICOPTER SKIING

VARDEN RIDGE

NORDIC TERRAIN AT 6000 FT.

SUMMIT LIFT POSSIBILITY

SANDY BUTTE

LOOKING WEST GLADE SKIING DOWN THE LIFT LINE POSSIBILITY

ERIC BURR

231

Harts Pass mining road, or the much less scary - but still equally dusty and washboarded logging road up to Goat Peak. Both these dirt road accesses to high country max out their parking on busy days. A Sundance style ski lift resort is physically possible, and could provide that access without the mountain top parking lot and fossil fuel consumption. Mazama, not Early Winters would be the closest bed base, save for the few rooms and cabins at Wilson Ranch, so shuttle buses would be needed to bring alpine skiers to the base gondola, just up from the existing MVSTA parking area. Cross-country skiers could simply ski over on the existing Community Trail, and by then - they might be the majority, which brings up the possibility of access designed specifically for nordic skiers.

That, to me, is a very much more attractive compromise than lifts designed primarily for alpine skiers. The thought of cross-country skiers having to watch out for careless alpine skiers and snowboarders while descending 4000 feet of vertical, after a full day over at Storey Peak, is not attractive. But I'm obviously an old school nordic skier. This nordic lift alternative would simply access both the summit and mid-mountain plateau with a gondola designed primarily to transport sightseers and cross-country skiers. The first leg would be 8000 feet long with 1880 feet of vertical, and the top section 6000 feet long with 1800 feet of vertical. The two cableways could share a common mid-station. There still would be some shuttle bus traffic, but not nearly as much as with a lift system designed primarily to accommodate alpine skiers.

Alpine skiers could use such a gondola, it just wouldn't be as attractive for them as chairlifts closer to the fall line. This gondola line would be down below tree top level, for wind protection and views out to the scenery framed by trees, rather than the typical downhill ski lift's view of skiers on the slope below. That's partly why it would stop 152 feet vertical below the wind exposed geographic

232

SILVER STAR

SANDY
BUTTE

A-STAR

summit. The other reason is that nordic skiers would welcome the 152 vertical feet, up an extremely scenic one kilometer ascent, as a nice warm up. Then they could comfortably take in the summit scene before starting down the very gently rolling ridge top meadows over toward Storey Peak and Virginian Ridge.

Which of these scenarios will happen is anybody's guess, and it's entirely possible that it could escalate from nothing to the proposed ski lift resort fought over for 30 years. Compromise comes in many forms, and personally I like the idea of a ski hut or two, with freight service and snow cat rides available for non skiers, but something less than a stand alone snowcat downhill ski operation. Since we can only guess at what the future may bring, it's prudent to leave as many possible future options open as reasonable. Ski huts don't preclude gondola access, if say for example, an earthquake smoothes out Dead Horse Point, on Harts Pass Road, into an impassable cliff.

For the North Cascades as a whole, I can see any of the presently possible upper valley developments as an asset, taking pressure off the backcountry. What I don't see as helpful is expanding either the North Cascades National Park or Wilderness Areas. The existing compromise, arrived at by some pretty tough negotiations, back before 1968 when the National Park and Pasayten Wilderness were established, is working surprisingly well, with different strokes for different folks, and a minimum of hassles. The Canadian attempt to create a new National Park adjacent to, and perhaps including, existing Cathedral Lakes Provincial Park and the Snowy Protected Area, might finally lead to an international peace park, and I see no harm in that, as long as they keep the Cathedral Lakes Lodge. This lodge predates the Park, is accessed by its exclusive use, extremely steep, 4 wheel drive road, and takes pressure off of the Park's popular backcountry. The 1990's attempt at an international park failed because of

234

the lack of credibility by the American organizations involved. Their 1999 Pasayten Wilderness Report was so inaccurate that it will be a long time, and take more than name changes, to regain credibility. The Canadians seem to be proceeding smoothly so far with their proposal. If they're successful it could help take pressure off of North Cascades National Park and its eastern gateway Early Winters.

None of this changes the fact that the Methow is a wonderful place for cross-country skiers who also enjoy self propelled summer sports. Quieter snowmobiles, better parking and closure practices on Highway 20, together with short loop trails, some more huts, and "firewise" forest thinning are my idea of improvements, in the Methow. MVSTA (Methow Valley Sport Trails Association), The Methow Nordic Club (primarily racers with a terrific kids program), The Methow Conservancy, and the Methow Institute Foundation, are the principle organizations making all this happen. Their memberships overlap, and there are many additional individuals working, in their own unique ways, to further the community wide vision of continuing to make this one of the best nordic ski resort complexes, and an example also of both sustainable agricultural, and light manufacturing development. Small diameter natural wood furniture and flooring, artists and musicians of many persuasions including kids, and of course anything that can bring income in with a computer, are all flourishing.

Elk are the obviously missing wildlife component in the Methow, and while not necessarily applicable to other National Forest areas, they are probably essential to restoring the browsing patterns and prey base for Wolves. This looks like a good candidate for a Doctoral thesis in wildlife management. Augmenting the high country Beaver population ties in with this, especially after the recent findings of how Wolves, Elk, Willows, Aspen, and Beaver interact in Yellowstone.

More important than what happens in the Methow, however is what happens outside the Methow and the North Cascades. As the Methow approaches build out under the current land use zoning, we need copy cats, to take the pressure off us. "Build out" means no more dwellings, and that the limits to growth have been reached. It is admittedly a relatively new, and perhaps local to the Northwest United States, but most certainly controversial concept. Canada is doing a good job with their ski industry, both alpine and nordic. Their Parks and Crown lands forestry practices obviously need some work, but Canada's larger ski population is being taken care of pretty well, and poses no immediate threat to overwhelm us with skiing refugees. They are more worried about what we do, or do not do, and for good reasons. Aside from Tamarack in central Idaho, the United States has produced little in the way of additional ski resort capacity. It is particularly short on quality groomed trail cross-country development. This is one reason the Methow Valley is approaching build out so fast. Selfishly we'd like to see more groomed cross-country ski trails on the east sides of Stevens, Snoqualmie, and White Passes.

As a retired National Park ranger I know of many other Parks and Wilderness Areas, all over the continent, that need alternatives to crowding ever more people into our limited system of wildlife reserves. The best way to restore snow country wildlife is with sophisticated trail developments adjacent to, but outside those reserves. So please come and visit the Methow, but don't expect to buy a place here, we're about full. Instead look us over, and take some ideas back to snow country close to where you live. You don't need lifts either. You certainly don't need to waste 30 years of litigation expense and angst like we did in the Methow. One of my hopes for this book is that it might let other ski areas avoid what we had to go through to finally arrive at a satisfactory compromise.

Cross-country skiing and other cardiac friendly sports are the wave of the future. But lifts aren't necessarily bad. Used wisely they can be part of the mix that saves energy, and introduces city folks to the world of winter, including its wildlife. This book is only intended to scratch the surface of what's possible, using areas I've come in contact with. There are many more success stories out there, and I'm hoping my annotated bibliography will lead those already interested into a new, more enlightened era of wildlife appreciation, conservation, and restoration. At the same time I also hope to encourage the fun possible with skiing and other winter sports, which are that crucial first step, for snow country newcomers, toward restoring its wildlife. Fun in the snow is absolutely essential.

Education is only possible if we can first instill an appreciation and love for nature in winter. I hope that Early Winters' long trip to the Supreme Court will have provided the political will to continue to make the Methow Valley a showcase for responsible ski development that includes both wildlife and people. Legal tools like those produced by Mineral King are certainly necessary, but getting a critical mass of politically active voters, who have accurate information about wildlife in our cold snow dominated habitats, is even more important.

Accurate information is necessary to mitigate the all too human, but destructive, paranoia regarding the dreaded "developers," who actually are the best hope for wildlife, because they have most of the power to make needed changes for restoring wildlife habitat. They need the help of dedicated naturalists who are informed enough to counter the misinformation too often used to frustrate responsible trail development.

Wildlife and ski trails are the keys to snow country restoration and the boreal forest life support systems.

BIBLIOGRAPHY

This will only get you started. Many of these references have excellent bibliographies of their own, so I've tried to not unnecessarily duplicate information readily available elsewhere. The ones here are listed in the order they are mentioned in the text. Many related but unmentioned publications are also listed
.

Chapter 1: SKIING

Johannsen, Alice E. *Jack Rabbit Johannsen* A history of ski development in Eastern Canada and New England, plus the industrial revolution by the famous skier's daughter

Tejeda- Flores, Lito *Breakthrough on Skis* The book that revolutionized ski instruction, construction, and sidecut

Barnett, Steve *Cross Country Downhill* The pioneering text that kicked off the Telemark renaissance

Parker, Paul *Freeheel Skiing: Telemark and Parallel Techniques for All Conditions* 3 rd Edition

Hindman, Steve *CROSS-COUNTRY SKIING – Building Skills for Fun and Fitness* 2005 standard reference

Petersen, Paul and Lovett, Richard A. *The Essential Cross-Country Skier – a step by step guide* This is slightly older than Steve Hindman's, but still applicable

McFee, John *Encounters with the Archdruid* The classic work about wilderness advocate David Brower

Eiseley, Loren *The Unexpected Universe* Ice age evolutionary classic, just one of his many books

Gawthrop, Daniel *Vanishing Halo –Saving the Boreal Forest* Around the world's, spruce and fir, snow country

Clifford, Hal *Downhill Slide – Why the Corporate Ski Industry is Bad for Skiing, Ski Towns, and the Environment* The Sierra Club side of the story

Fry, John *The Story of Modern Skiing* - 2006 This view from the industry is also listed under the lifts chapter, and it does have one short chapter on cross-country skiing.

Lost People Films LLC *The Lost People of Mountain Village* - 2005 DVD from Telluride, Colorado, but only 15 minutes long, so newcomers to ski culture may have to first read Clifford's or Fry's books (previous page) to understand the plot

The Ski Industry *SAM – Ski Area Management* The magazine for professionals in North America

Howarth, David *We Die Alone* - Scandinavian ski and reindeer culture during WW2 - non fiction

Berton, Pierre *Why We Act Like Canadians* - The famous historian's shortest (but arguably best) work, which explains to an American friend what's going on up in Canadia, and includes material explained more fully in his *The Invasion of Canada* – about the war of 1812

The X Country Ski Industry *Cross Country Skiing* and *Trax* - American and Canadian magazines, respectively

Chapter 2: AVALANCHES

Leopold, Aldo *Sand County Almanac* - the old (1948) testament of the conservation movement, and although dated – still applicable to the 21st Century's main problem

Fredston, Jill *Snowstruck – In the Grip Of Avalanches* - an Alaskan professional's view for the 21'st Century

Tremper, Bruce *Staying Alive in Avalanche Terrain* - practical survival for skiers, by a Utah based professional

Armstrong and Williams *The Avalanche Book* Colorado based introductory book, OK for nonskiers too

Daffern, Tony *Avalanche Safety for Skiers and Climbers* – the Canadian book of practical advice for recreationists

McClung, David and Schaerer, Peter *The Avalanche Handbook 3rd ed.* - the source for professionals, by two Canadians from British Columbia, an academic and Peter, the Swiss field engineer, who pioneered highway defenses at places like Rogers Pass on the Trans-Canada Highway, and who makes this book the ultimate blending of theory and practical application.

Chapter 3: EDGES

Natural History Magazine An objective apolitical view of nature, including human nature

Schieckel, Richard *The Disney Version* The early history of the American icon of sanitized "family entertainment"

Mander, Jerry *Four Arguments for the Elimination of Television* and *In the Absence of the Sacred – The Failure of Technology and the Survival of Indian Nations* - One of the earliest predictions of the actual dumbing down effect of the boob tube on western society

Postman, Neil *AMUSING OURSELVES TO DEATH – Public Discourse in the Age of Show Business* 1985 originally, but substantially updated in 2005 by Andrew Postman to include the latest electronic distractions from biological and sociological reality

Rocky Mountain Elk Foundation *The Bugle – Elk Country and the Hunt* The best magazine for hunters

International Wolf Center *International Wolf* The best popular magazine about wildlife's star performer

The Nature Conservancy *Nature Conservancy* magazine for the international pioneer in conservation biology

winterwildlands.org *Winter Wildlands Alliance* The only advocacy group focused on quiet winter sports

Schulz, Florian (photographer) with authors Bass, Chadwick, Heur, Kennedy Jr., Kerasote, Porter, Quammen, and Suzuki *Yellowstone to Yukon – freedom to roam* - large format spectacular look at the wildlife and wildlands of the longest genetic corridor yet proposed, including Jumbo, in B.C. - where a ski area is also being considered

Clarkson, Guy *Shining Mountains* – a Canadian DVD (2005) in French and English versions, that presents the Yellowstone to Yukon (Y2Y) corridor story with dramatic cinematography. It's especially good at explaining the buffer, matrix, and conservancy concepts.

Chadwick and Gehman *Yellowstone to Yukon: National Geographic Destination Series* (2000)

Romano, Craig and Johnston, James (photographer) *Columbia Highlands – Exploring Washington's Last Frontier –* smaller but similar companion book to *Yellowstone to Yukon* (previous page) explores the biological connection possibilities and personalities between the Rockies and the Cascades (2007)

Hilty, Lidicker Jr., and Mereniender *Corridor Ecology: The Science and Practice of Linking Landscapes for Biodiversity Conservation-* 2006 book for professionals

American Wildlands *On the Wild Side* - quarterly out of Bozeman, Montana, dealing with corridors in the Northern Rockies www.wildlands.org

Mountain Home Lodge 8201 Mountain Home Road, Post Office Box 687, Leavenworth, Washington State, U.S.A., www.mthome.com - a working example of using winter road closure to enhance recreational experiences

Chapter 4: FIRE

Arno and Hammerly *Timberline* The beautifully illustrated definitive book about the montane boreal forest

Atwater, Monty *Avalanche Hunters* by the first U.S. Forest Service snow ranger, about how bureaucracy gets funded, which applies to all disaster management

MacLean, Norman *Young Men and Fire* The tragic account of Smokejumper fatalities in the Man Gulch Fire

Fuller, Margaret *Forest Fires* A thorough examination of the field for nonprofessionals

Arno, Steve and Allison-Bunnell, Steven *Flames in Our Forests* 2002 introduction to fire ecology

Arno, Steve and Fiedler, Carl E. *Mimicking Natures Fire – Restoring Fire Prone Forests in the West* - This is the nuts and bolts, practical application case studies

Chase, Alston *Playing God in Yellowstone – the Destruction of America's first National Park* The bestseller that exposed the consequences of mismanagement of wilderness by the public's favorite bureaucracy

Kieter and Boyce *The Greater Yellowstone Ecosystem* Dr. John Craighead's contribution is referred to in my text

National Parks and Conservation Association *The Gordon Report* 1989 update on *The Leopold Report* by Dr. Gordon of Yale University, confirming Leopold's work

Leopold, Starker and co-authors *The Leopold Report* The 1963 "blue ribbon" document commissioned by the U.S. National Park Service to guide their management

Craighead, Dr. Frank *Track of the Grizzly* The firsthand account of the first radio collared Grizzly research

Dagget, Dan *The Gardeners of Eden* This is the new testament for explaining conservation ecology and psychology, building on Aldo Leopold's *Sand County Almanac,* for conditions in the 21st Century

Deur, Douglas and Turner, Nancy J. (editors) *Keeping It Living: Traditions of Plant Use and Cultivation on the Northwest Coast of North America* - local details of Dagget's thesis, documenting use of fire and hunting also

Mann, Charles *1491: New Revelations of the Americas Before Columbus* – blows the "pristine wilderness" myth out of the fundamentalists' holy water, historically based

Vale, Thomas(editor) *Fire Native Peoples and the Natural Landscape* - 2002 compilation of writings by a variety of authors with opinions and research about how much of the North American "wilderness" was actually the product of pre-European culture; also see Dr. Vale's chapter in the Wuerthner's *WILDFIRE: A Century of Failed Forest Policy* – next page

Cohen, Stan *A Pictorial History of Smokejumping* The best way to appreciate this unique access to fire ecology's hidden effects up in the boreal forest beyond roads

Taylor, Murray *Jumping Fire – A smokejumper's memoir of fighting wildfire* A popular account from 2002

Stone *Stehekin: Glimpses of the Past* including vivid accounts of forest fires around upper Lake Chelan

McConnel *Stehekin an Island in Time* A firsthand account from a Sierra Club refugee in the wild Northwest

Barker, Rocky *How the Fires of Yellowstone Changed America* An historical account of fire events and the social psychology that sadly set back fire management, but simultaneously stimulated more public awareness

Stanturf, John A. and Madsen, Palle *Restoration of Boreal and Temperate Forests* - ideas for international professionals and academics by U.S. and Danish authors

McLean, John N. *Fire on the Mountain – the true story of the South Canyon Fire, Fire and Ashes – On the Front Lines Battling Wildfires,* and *The 30 Mile Fire: A Chronicle of Bravery and Betrayal* - three books by Norman McLean's son, examining our most recent tragedies and reexamining old ones – including Man Gulch, the subject of his father's *Young Men and Fire*

Wuerthner, George – editor *WILDFIRE: A Century of Failed Forest Policy* - 2006 coffee table book with spectacular photographs and some excellent contributing authors, but unfortunately faulted by the editor's inability to see much beyond the environmental fundamentalist's conventional wisdom, including an especially weak grazing section, see Dagget (previous and next page) Wuerthner is not alone in misunderstanding grass.

Apostol, Dean and Sinclair, Marcia (editors) *Restoring the Pacific Northwest: The Art and Science of Ecological Restoration in Cascadia* 2006 including Steve Arno, Jerry Franklin, and many others – sponsored by the Society For Ecological Restoration International ser.org

Peluso, Beth *The Charcoal Forest: How Fire Helps Animals and Plants* – 2007 children's book including a very up to date reference section for naturalists, parents, and teachers, with Canadian, American, and web site resources

Chapter 5: LIFTS

Dagget, Dan *Beyond Rangeland Conflict – Toward a West That Works* The book that makes sense of cow hatred, grass ecology, and solutions to overgrazing; check Houle's *Prairie Keepers,* referenced under the ranger chapter, for more on grazing and attitude problems

Harper, John *Mineral King – Public Concern with Government Policy* - see chapter 10 for more detail

Stone, Christopher *Should Trees Have Standing* - also about Mineral King - see chapter 10

Jerome, John *On Mountains* Philosophical reflections on ski country and skiing culture

Cummins *Ski Patroller* First hand description of the sport that requires a first aid crew standing by at all times

Wingle, Peter *Planning Considerations for Winter Sports Resort Development* 1994 U.S. Forest Service handbook

Fry, John *The Story of Modern Skiing* - 2006 historical account by the long time editor of the most widely read ski publications in North America

Chapter 6: TRAILS

Birkby, Robert *Lightly on the Land – The SCA Trailbuilding and Maintenance Manual* 2nd edition - The best yet as of 2006 and clearly illustrated

Washington Trails Association (WTA) *Trails Magazine* formerly *Signpost Magazine*

Proudman and Rajala *Trail Building and Maintenance* The Appalachian Mountain club's 1981 2nd edition and still good, although geared to eastern North America

Vogel *Trails Manual* California based, for horse trails primarily, but that makes them easily skiable too

SE Group (Sno-engineering) www.segroup.com 3245 146th PL SE, Bellevue WA 98007 -- Tamarack Resort's ski trail planning, showing feathered edges and glades

Wiesel, Jonathan and Frado, John *Cross Country Close to Home: A Ski Area Development Manual* - from the Cross Country Ski Areas Association xcski.org

Spagna, Ana Maria *Now Go Home* – *wilderness, belonging, and the crosscut saw* - Stehekin and the North Cascades are the setting for a very personal account of one lady's adventures with trail crews, environmental fundamentalists, urban tourists, and back to the land homesteading, by a southern California refugee.

Chapter 7: HUTS

Kariel, Herb and Pat *Alpine Huts in the Canadian Rockies,Purcells, and Interior Ranges of British Columbia* This book is about construction and politics. They also have a separate guidebook for the hut's users.

Scott, Chic *Powder Pioneers: Ski Stories from the Canadian Rockies and Columbian Mountains* - including exploration, huts and helicopter skiing, to ski resorts

Appalachian Mountain Club *Backcountry Facilities Design and Maintenance* This club also put out a good trail design and maintenance manual, (see previous page)

Dawson, Louis W. the 2nd and Ohlrich, Warren (editor) *Colorado's 10th Mountain Huts and Trails: The Official Guide to America's Largest Backcountry Hut System*

Litz, Brian *Colorado Hut to Hut* - two volumes

Beck, David *Ski Tours in California* - Hut descriptions for Shasta, Peter Grub, Ostrander, and Pear Lake, along with an account of avalanches destroying cabins at Mineral King in 1969 during the ski lift controversy.

Reifsnyder, William *Hut Hopping in the Austrian Alps, Footloose in the Swiss Alps,* and *High Huts of the White Mountains: Nature Walks, Natural History, and Day Hiking Around the AMC* (Appalachian Mountain Club) *Mountain Hostels*

Lieberman, Marcia and Philip *Walking SWITZERLAND – the Swiss Way: From Vacation Apartments, Hotels, Mountain Inns, and Huts, 2nd edition* - also – *Walking the Alpine Parks of France & Northwest Italy*

Hurdie *WALKING AUSTRIA'S ALPS: Hut to Hut, 2nd edition* - yes, ski huts actually get more use in summer !

Winter Wildlands Alliance: www.winterwildlands.org For an up to date list of North American huts, in addition to extensive advocacy information and resources

Reynolds, Kev *Chamonix to Zermatt; The Classic Walker's Haute Route* - 2007

Chapter 8: RANGERS

Powder magazine – originally a fresh approach and attempted return to skiing's roots, but lately (2007) just another big air - " extreme" photography showcase

Off Piste - a Northwest based backcountry skiing newspaper has taken over the innovative journalism niche

Marty, Sid *Men For The Mountains* Canadian National Park Warden organizational history, a personal account

Frome, Mike *Regreening the National Parks* - positive suggestions for getting back on track (see below also)

Behan, R.W. *Police State Wilderness* in the February 1974 *Journal of Forestry* - the professional magazine for the SAF (Society of American Foresters)

FSEEE (Forest Service Employees for Environmental Ethics) *Forest Magazine* - forestry's alternative voice

Frome, Mike *Battle for the Wilderness, The Forest Service, Strangers in High Places,* and his most widely read - *Whose Woods Are These* - are all classics

Defenders of Wildlife *Defenders* - quarterly magazine by the lead NGO for bringing Wolves back to Yellowstone

Schnieder, Bill *Where the Grizzly Walks* – actually two separate books by the same title, both good - but the 2nd edition is almost completely updated

Halfpenny, Dr. James *Winter: an Ecological Handbook* - the only western based snow country wildlife book, as of 2006 – see Baron's *Beast in the Garden* (Chapter 11) for more about Halfpenny, a principle character in that book

Twain, Mark *The Prince and the Pauper* - THE classic on how clothes change people and influence behavior

Peter and Hull *The Peter Principle* - THE classic on how organizational structure can lead to disaster

Houle, Marcy *The Prairie Keepers* Mainly about hawks, cows, and ranchers, but her ranger types are very accurately portrayed in this narrative about grazing

Evans, Nicholas *The Loop* - a novel about wolves, ranchers, and wildlife professionals by the author most famous for *The Horse Whisperer,* and like Marcy Houle's book, above – it's a portrait of wildlife managers' stress. This one however takes gross artistic liberties to provide the gut wrenching details, which make many quit the job.

Heinrich, Bernd *Winter World – The Ingenuity of Animal Survival* - just the latest of several excellent books out now concerning snow ecology in eastern America

Marchand, Peter J. *Life in the Cold – An Introduction to Winter Ecology 3 rd Ed.* - probably the most available

Coalition of National Park Retirees - no publications yet, but info at www.npsretirees.org

Farabee Jr., Charles R."Butch" *National Park RANGER – An American Icon* - Not much about wildlife, but an excellent history of the profession and its evolution from generalist to law enforcement specialist

Society of American Foresters *The Greatest Good: A Forest Service Centennial Film* - in DVD and also a book (2005) with revealing interviews from many perspectives, including critics from both the left and right, but mainly an attempt to present a balanced history

Chapter 9: WILDERNESS

Tracy, Spencer and Robards, Jason *Inherit the Wind* - Two separate movie versions of the Scopes Monkey Trial

Phillips, Kevin *AMERICAN THEOCRACY The Peril and Politics of Radical Religion, Oil, and Borrowed Money in the 21st Century* This 2006 update on the Monkey Trial is a good primer for anyone not yet familiar with the challenges still presented by religious fundamentalists.

Wilson, Edward O. *The CREATION An Appeal to Save Life on Earth* - solutions to the theocratic dilemma by this Century's foremost biologist - 2006 publication

Gore, Al *An Inconvenient Truth* Both a movie and a book, following up on his *Earth in the Balance* best seller *The Attack on Reason* - 2007 is his latest book

Korten, David *The Great Turning: From Empire to Earth Community* - just his latest, with a refreshingly balanced perspective on religion and technocratic problems

Pollan, Michael *The Botany of Desire* - Best selling myth buster about our actual subservience to plants. His 2006 *The Omnivore's Dilemma*, and also a best seller, even got the attention of Britain's conservative *The Economist*

Nash, Dr. Roderick Frazier *Wilderness and the American Mind ; 4th edition* - The classic work examining wilderness as product of European minds transplanted to the new world.

Wilderness Watch *Wilderness Watcher* - quarterly from Missoula, Montana - wildernesswatch.org

Barber, B.R. *Jihad vs. McWorld, How Globalism and Tribalism are Reshaping the World*

Miller, Kenton with Barbor, Victor and Boness, Melisa editors *Securing Protected Areas in the Face of Global Change – Issues and Strategies* The IUCN effort to guide conservation and restoration biology, on the land and sea

Hamilton, Lawrence and McMillan, Linda (editors) *Guidelines for Planning and Managing Mountain Protected Areas* – the IUCN's companion book to Miller's (previous page) http://www.iucn.org/bookstore

Twain, Mark *Letters from the Earth* - by an archangel sent to our planet by God to see how things are going

Harris, Sam *THE END OF FAITH – Religion, Terror, and the Future of Reason* - a 2004, but equally serious update of Mark Twain's two works: one cited above, and the second for the Ranger Chapter 8 - *Letter to a Christian Nation* is Harris' 2006 best seller

Lovelock *The Revenge of Gaia* Sequel to his best seller that postulated our planet as a self regulating organism

National Geographic - the magazine that educated the emerging secular culture, after World War Two, about the Craigheads and nature, from Cloud Gardens in the Tetons to their pioneering work with Grizzlies in Yellowstone

The Wilderness Society – founders of The Wilderness Act of 1964 and focused on establishing new preserves, based in Washington DC www.experiencewilderness.org

The WILD Foundation *International Journal of Wilderness* - 3 issues per year - ijw.org They also sponsor current printings of *Wilderness Management* the guide for professionals cited under chapter 11 Lynx

Wildlands CPR *The Road- Riporter* quarterly, also from Missoula, but focused on road restoration and defense of roadless areas – wildlandscpr.org

Petersen, Thomas Reed (editor) *A Road Runs Through It* A collection of essays by writers such as Barry Lopez and David Quammen, about Wildlands CPR's mission (above)

Baldwin, Dwight Jr. ; De Luce, Judith; and Pletsch, Carl (editors) *Beyond Preservation: Restoring and Inventing Landscapes* - 1994 compilation of many authors

Chapter 10: MINERAL KING

Stone, Christopher *Should Trees Have Standing* The book that turned environmental law into an instrument for change, and transformed the conservation movement. Cited also under chapter 5 Lifts

Harper, John *Mineral King – Public Concern with Government Policy* The events behind Stone's book and Justice Douglas's dissenting opinion are less famous but equally important. Cited also under chapter 5 Lifts.

Turner, Tom (text) and Carr, Clifton(photography) *Wild By Law:* The Sierra Club Legal Defense Fund and the places it has saved. Mineral King was their first case. This book relates Mineral King to its impact on other critical events and places, such as the Redwoods.

Livingston, John *The Fallacy of Wildlife Conservation* and *One Cosmic Instant* - Canadian books that predate, but parallel, the recent *The Death of Environmentalism* by Shellenberger and Nordhaus. Both books are available together under the title *The John Livingston Reader* (2007) with an appreciation by Canadian novelist Graeme Gibson, and an interview with Farley Mowat (see the Lynx chapter) which reveals their mutual anti-hunting bias.

Mahoney, Shane *OPPORTUNITY FOR ALL; The Story of the North American Model for Wildlife Conservation* – a 2006 DVD available from the Rocky Mountain Elk Foundation - elkfoundation.org See also chapter 11

Rosenzweig, M. L. *Win-Win Ecology - How Earth's Species Can Survive in the Midst of Human Enterprise 2003* - introduces the concept of "reconciliation ecology"

Hampton, Bruce and Cole, David *Soft Paths* The best book on minimum impact backcountry techniques, including winter applications

Ehrlich, Paul R. *The Population Bomb* - the 1968 bestseller that foresaw traffic gridlock in even rainy Seattle

Newman, Nell and D'Agnese, Joseph *Newman's Own Organics Guide to a Good Life – Simple Measures That Benefit You and the Place You Live* 2003 – the best reference on minimum impact front country techniques

Kingsolver, Barbara *Small Wonders* - nonfiction by the author of best selling environmental novels like *Prodigal Summer* and *Poisonwood Bible* - This may be the best little book explaining why *Jihad vs. McWorld* is crucial to conservation biology and why we should be familiar with Newman's and Harris's books, (above) and chapter 9

Dankmeyer, Ingrid (writer) and Harrington, John (editor) *WASHINGTON – Renewing the Countryside* - beautifully illustrated with color photography, similar to Dagget's books, and including examples from the Methow Valley, near ground zero for Early Winters

Durbin, Kathie *TREE HUGGERS – Victory, Defeat, & Renewal in the Ancient Forest Campaign* Including photos of the lead players in the Pacific Northwest, for an insider's take on this historically significant saga.

High Country News - unaffiliated with any advocacy group, this newspaper gets the highest credibility marks

Chapter 11: LYNX

Mahoney, Shane *OPPORTUNITY FOR ALL; The Story of the North American Model for Wildlife Conservation* - DVD available from the Rocky Mountain Elk Foundation, call toll free at 1-800-CALLELK or elkfoundation.org

Hendee and Dawson *Wilderness Management 3 rd Ed. – Stewardship and Protection of Resources and Values* The definitive work for professionals and activists ijw.org

Lindenmayer and Franklin *Conserving Forest Biodiversity – A Comprehensive Approach* Yes, this is the infamous Dr. Old Growth, alias Dr. Jerry Franklin

Langford, Cameron *The Winter of the Fisher* - a 1971 novel which beautifully portrays the boreal forest of central Canada

Wildlife Conservation Society   wcs.org/hoopafisher
WCS Hoopa Fisher Project, PO Box 368, Hoopa CA 95546
Wildlife Conservation is their magazine, New York based

Mowat, Farley *Never Cry Wolf* - Both the movie and the book, among many by this prolific and controversial, best selling Canadian author

Owl, Grey *The Men of the Last Frontier, Pilgrims of the Wild, The Adventures of Sajo and Her Beaver People, and Tales of an Empty Cabin,* hard to find but sometimes available from Piragis Northwoods Company in Ely, Minnesota www.piragis.com

GREY OWL, the movie, starring Pierce Brosnon, does a good job of bringing this conflicted character to life

McGuffin, Gary and Joanie *In The Footsteps Of Grey Owl – Journey Into The Ancient Forest* - also Canadian, but sometimes available from Piragis (above)

Colinvaux, Paul *Why Big Fierce Animals are Rare* The best quick explanation for the perceptive activist

Craighead, Frank and John *Hawks Owls and Wildlife* This is the book summarizing their joint PhD thesis. It's not light reading, but is one the best summaries of predation ecology.

Baron, David *The Beast in the Garden* - cougars and new age refugees in snow country weave the tragic tale of environmental sentiment gone astray - outstanding author

Kobalenko, Jerry *Forest Cats of North America – Cougars – Bobcats – Lynx* The most detailed discussion yet of the Lynx - Snowshoe Hare cycles, in what is primarily the best photography book of all three cats

Hornocker, Maurice and 12 other pros *Cougar Management Guidelines, First Edition 2005* - thorough but concise scientific reporting   www.opalcreekpress.com

Canadian Wildlife Federation *Canadian Wildlife* magazine, published 5 times a year   cwf-fcf.org

National Wildlife Federation *National Wildlife* (magazine) published bimonthly; this organization worked with Defenders of Wildlife to get Wolves into Yellowstone

Chrisler, Herb and Lois *The Olympic Elk* - Academy Award winning Disney "True Life Adventure" film

Conibear, Frank and Blundell, J.L. *The Wise One* – and one of the best true to life novels about one of the most important keystone species in North America – the Beaver

Fisher, Hank *Wolf Wars - The Remarkable inside Story of the Restoration of Wolves to Yellowstone* - 1995, the year it finally happened, by the guy who clinched the deal

Smith, Douglas W. and Ferguson, Gary *Decade of the Wolf - Returning the Wild to Yellowstone* 2005 by the locals who lived with the results

Mech, David L. and Boitani, Luigi *Wolves – Behavior, Ecology, and Conservation* - The definitive work on the keystone species that lets the Beavers get back to work

Dutcher, Jim and Jamie *Living with Wolves* Idaho based narrative, in a spectacular coffee table format photography collection which includes interaction with pups in addition to free roaming packs

Mason, Bill *Cry of the Wild* Similar to Dutcher's book (above) but in DVD format and covering a wide range of Canadian habitat – National Film Board of Canada nfb.ca

Evans, Nicholas *The Loop* - a novel about wolves and their sociology, post Yellowstone reintroduction (1995) also cited in the ranger chapter for it's perhaps overly melodramatic human story.

www.nationalgeographic.com *Wolves: A Legend Returns to Yellowstone* DVD (and/or video) with the clearest images and explanations of wolf behavior in snow, and a brief introduction to their ecological effects; National Geographic is also cited under the Wilderness chapter 9 for their earlier publication of the Craighead's work.

Maser, Chris *Mammals of the Pacific Northwest – From the Coast to the High Cascades* - Pocket Gophers and the rest of the supporting cast in fur coats; his other books such as *Forest Primeval* (a novel), *The Redesigned Forest*, and *Our Forest Legacy: Today's Decisions, Tomorrow's Consequences* (2005) - are also excellent

Chadwick, Douglas H. *A Beast the Color of Winter* - Mountain Goats and their ecology – classic natural history by one of Montana's most prolific writers; his *True Griz* takes us to new age bear country with Finnish bear dogs

Canning, Richard and Canning, Sydney *British Columbia – A Natural History* This 2004 edition, beautifully illustrated, gives the best overall picture and feel for the geographic area that contains both the most spectacular skiing and the most varied wildlife habitat.

Fenger, Manning, Cooper, Guy, and Bradford *Wildlife & Trees in British Columbia* – although western in setting most of this unique 2006 book applies to all boreal forests

Rezendes, Paul *Tracking and the Art of Seeing, 2 nd ed. How to Read Animal Tracks and Signs* One of the best illustrated track books, with references to the older classics

Elbroch, Mark *Mammal Tracks and Signs* With even more photos and diagrams than Rezendes (above) in a thick field guide size, and including references to work that can help establish and manage biological corridors

Lanner, Ron *Made For Each Other – A Symbiosis of Birds and Pines* - co-evolution of stone pines and nutcrackers, world wide

Allen, Durward L. *Our Wildlife Legacy* 1962 This was the text Starker Leopold chose for his basic wildlife management class at Berkeley in 1964

Leopold, Aldo *Game Management* 1933 – but still a classic treatment by the North American pioneer

Loo, Tina *States of Nature: Conserving Canada's Wildlife in the Twentieth Century* - another take on Grey Owl, Farley Mowat, Bill Mason, and others from a very northern viewpoint. The "balance of nature" as a concept with destructive effects for wildlife is concisely examined.

Bailey, James A. *Principles of Wildlife Management* 1984 – just one of many more modern texts for the serious student, but his explanation of the political process is very objective and illuminating on credibility

Society for Conservation Biology *Conservation Magazine* - A quarterly journal that includes brief reviews of the bewildering profusion of literature and periodicals out now - conservationmagazine.org

The Wildlife Society *The Wildlife Professional* - new (2007) quarterly magazine with references to the many publications and on-line sources specific to wildlife and wildlife habitat, including their increasing interaction with, and dependence on, the exploded human population

Morrison, Michael L. *Wildlife Restoration: Techniques for Habitat Analysis and Animal Monitoring* - 2002 first in a series sponsored by the Society for Ecological Restoration – see Fire chapter for the 2006 Pacific North- west book by this society

Craighead, Charles S. (author) with Lawrence Ormsby (illustrator) *Who Ate the Backyard: Living with Wildlife on Private Lands* - practical advice for snow country by Teton National Park second generation neighbors with outstanding illustrations and photography

www.wolverinefoundation.org – contains an extensive bibliography in addition to this NGO's many efforts to help correct popular misinformation and begin science based management

Biohabitats Incorporated - professional conservation, planning, ecological restoration, and regenerative design U.S. based - 800.220.0919   www.biohabitats.com

ALCES: An Integrated Landscape Management Tool
Alberta Research Council   www.foremtech.com

Pearson Ecological: aquatic consulting, management, inventory and Monitoring, habitat assessment, Design and Construction in BC Canada, mike@pearsonecological.com

Chapter 12: HURRICANE RIDGE

Twight, Ben W. *Organizational Values and Political Power - The Forest Service Versus the Olympic National Park* - the most objective scholarly work on the formation of a National Park, with a very thorough bibliographical reference by Chapter headings

Moorhead, Bruce B. *The Forest Elk – Roosevelt Elk in Olympic National Park* - for non-professionals, but with all the references needed to pursue this in depth, by the Park biologist who lived there for most of his career

Egan, Timothy *The Good Rain – Across Time and Terrain in the Pacific Northwest* - maybe the easiest reading account of the essential elements

Lien, Carsten *Olympic Battleground: The Power Politics of Timber Preservation* - the Mountaineers' version

Mathews, Daniel *Cascade-Olympic Natural History – A Trailside Reference* - the field guide with the most ecology

McNulty, Tim *Olympic National Park: A Natural History* By long time naturalist, poet, and former trail crew professional; *Pawtracks, In Blue Mountain Dusk, and Reflected Light* are some of his poetry books.

Sax, Joseph *Mountains Without Handrails* - National Park access development examined, especially tramways

Olympic National Park – 600 East Park Avenue
Port Angeles, WA 98362 www.nps.gov/olym
800-833-6388

Chapter 13: EARLY WINTERS

Portman, Sally *Smiling Country – a history of the Methow Valley – 2nd edition* - events up to 2002 by a cross-country ski instructor and former Wilderness ranger

Portman, Sally *Ski Touring Methow Style* The Methow Valley ski scene during the ski wars, as MVSTA (Methow Valley Ski Touring Association) was just getting started. The "S" and "T" in MVSTA now stand for "Sport Trails."

Devin, Doug *MAZAMA The Past 100 Years* - events up to 1997 and the Freestone Inn - look for a 2nd edition about 2008 - by the gentleman who was closest to the saga

Pigott, James C. *A View of the Methow: From Moccasin Lake Ranch* – a 2005 ranch owner's take on the early history, the ski wars, and cultural change including the Methow Conservancy and its relation to wildlife

Hurwitz, Laura; Lumry, Amanda; and Wengerd, Loren *The Methow Valley: Between Home and Heaven* (2007) – prose and photographic praise for the unique legacy of nordic skiing and rural life style that came out of the Early Winters ski wars controversy and resolution.

Roe, JoAnn *North Cascades Highway, The North Cascadians, Ghost Camps and Boom Towns* - just the three books closest to the North Cascades, by this prolific author who's books cover much of Pacific Northwest history, mostly on the American side – homing in on specific places or persons, like Donald McDonald

Stamper, Marcy *High Hopes and Deep Snows* - mining history of the Methow Valley

Nisbet, Jack *Tracking David Thompson* - the Canadian contemporary of Lewis and Clark ; This is one of the best history books on the fur trade and its influence on events in Canadian-American interactions, including the North Cascades, but with emphasis on Canada. Nisbet has many other books on Northwest history.

257

Miles, John C. (editor) *Impressions of the NORTH CASCADES – Essays about a Northwest Landscape* - many varied view points from those closely involved: rural residents, Park Naturalists, an NGO pioneer, a poet, and an archeologist, to name a few

Friedman, Mitch and Lindholdt (editors) *CASCADE WILD – Protecting an International Ecosystem* - views collected by the Northwest Ecosystem Alliance 1993 This advocacy organization now calls themselves Conservation Northwest, but still is enthusiastically ecosystem oriented

National Parks and Conservation Association *Nature Has No Borders – A Conference on the Protection and Management of the North Cascades Ecosystem* 1993 - writings from the failed 1990's attempt to create an international peace Park similar to Glacier-Waterton on the Alberta, British Columbia, Montana border

Manning, Harvey and the North Cascades Conservation Council *Wilderness Alps: Conservation & Conflict in Washington's North Cascades* – 2007 view by the original architects of preserves here   www.northcascades.org

Parish, Coup, and Lloyd (editors) with 7 other writers *Plants of Southern Interior British Columbia* - the field guide that works best for the North Cascades

Porsild, A.E. and Tande Lid, Dagny (illustrator) *Rocky Mountain Wild Flowers* Canadian Rockies but still including many North Cascades trees, rushes, sedges, and grasses - with the clearest illustrations, from Norway

North Cascades Institute - an apolitical nonprofit educational organization based at Diablo Lake Reservoir and Sedro-Woolley on the west side, but they run many courses on the east side too – ncascades.org

Methow Valley Sport Trails Association (MVSTA) *Trails* is their biannual newspaper   mvsta.com

Wiesel, Jonathan *Cross-Country Ski Vacations: A Guide to the Best Resorts, Lodges, and Groomed Trails in North America* - which features the Methow photographically

258

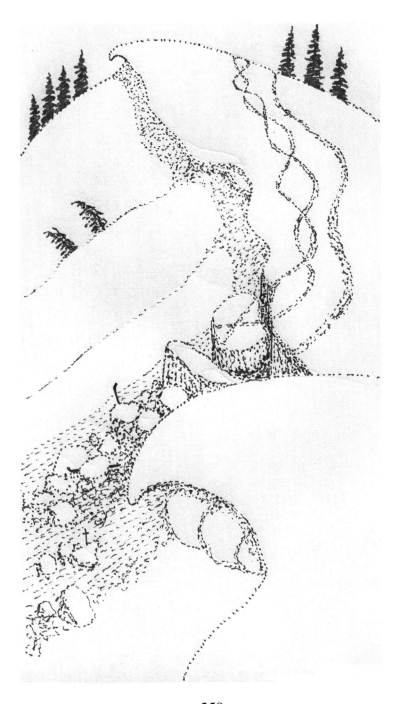